D[...]
Of 1[...]
New [...]ament

2nd Edition
Revised & Updated

J.M. Harden BD LLD

© 2007 Simon Wallenberg ISBN 1-84356-017-8
Second Edition

First Edition 1975
Simon Wallenberg

Published by The Simon Wallenberg Press
wallenberg.press@gmail.com

© Book Block & Cover design Simon Wallenberg Press
Printed in the United Kingdom

Published by The Simon Wallenberg Press

Dictionary
Of The Vulgate
New Testament

J.M. Harden BD LLD

Simon Wallenberg Press

INTRODUCTION

THIS Dictionary is based on the smaller Oxford edition of the Vulgate New Testament, which was published in 1911.[1] Founded as that edition is on the oldest and best manuscripts of the Vulgate, used in accordance with the methods and results of modern textual criticism, its text differs materially as to vocabulary and still more as to orthography from the received text of the Vulgate New Testament, which is that of the edition[2] published at the end of the sixteenth century by Pope Clement VIII.

It will therefore be necessary to say something by way of introduction about each of these : (1) Vocabulary, and (2) Orthography.

(1) VOCABULARY. Many words, over forty in all, are found in the text of the Oxford edition which have no place in the Clementine. The list of them is as follows :—

aegrotus (Mk.6,13 ; 16,18)
altarium (1 C.9,13 (bis); H.7,13)
amarico (Ap.10,9)
bithalassus (A.27,41)
carcedonius (Ap.21,19)
consul (A.19,38)
deformatio (1 T.1,16)
dein (Jas.1,15)
deludo (Mt.20,19)
deuerto (L.9,12)
deuinco (H.11,33)
effluo (H.2,1)
enauigo (L.8,26 ; A.20,13)
exin (1 C.12,28)

---

[1] Nouum Testamentum Latine secundum editionem sancti Hieronymi ad codicem manuscriptorum fidem recensuerunt ✠ Iohannes Wordsworth, S.T.P. episcopus Sarisburiensis et Henricus Iulianus White, A.M., S.T.P., Noui Testamenti interpretationis Professor apud Collegium Regium Londini (Editio Minor curante Henrico I. White).
[2] Or rather, editions, for there were three, published respectively in 1592, 1593, 1598.

exsuscito (J.11,11)   praegredior (Mk.2,23)
fusio (H.9,22)   pridem (G.4,13)
gallicula (A.12,8)   quantulus (H.10,37)
immolaticius (1 C.10,28)   quartanus (A.10,30)
inaniloquium (2 T.2,16)   quippini (L.11,28)
infreno (1 T.5,18)   ruo (H.11,30)
ingrauo (Mk.14,40)   secundoprimus (L.6,1)
inoperor (Mk.6,14)   senecta (L.1,36)
inquisitor (1 C.1,20)   sparsio (H.12,24)
lino (J.9,6)   subtilitas (Co.2,4)
magicus (A.8,11)   superexulto (Jas.2,13)
nouellus (Mk.2,22)   suprascriptio (Mt.22,30)
nudius (A.10,30)   timefactus (A.24,26)
paulo (H.2,7)   unoculus (Mt.18,9)
placitum (E.1,9)   ualide (A.27,18)
potiono (Ap.14,8)

The majority of these are, in form at least, quite
classical. All, with three exceptions, are to be found
duly registered in Lewis and Short's *Latin Dictionary*.
These three exceptions are *bithalassus* (Clem. *dithalassus*), *secundoprimus* (Clem. separates into two words),
suprascriptio (Clem. *superscriptio*). Of the others, *carcedonius*, i.e. καρχηδόνιος, Carthaginian (stone), is found
in Pliny; *gallicula* (Clem. *caliga*) is a diminutive form
of *gallica*, and is found elsewhere in the writings of
St. Jerome; *inaniloquium* (Clem. *uaniloquium*) is peculiar
to the Vulgate; *immolaticius* is found in the Epistles of
St. Augustine; *inoperor* is used by Tertullian; *superexulto*
is not found earlier than in the Vulgate; *unoculus*, which
has been introduced by conjecture in Mt.18,9, is found in
Plautus and elsewhere. The words *consul, nudius, paulo,
pridem*, can hardly perhaps be considered as new forms,
as they come into the list only in consequence of a different
division of words by the Oxford editor, *pro consule* for
proconsule : paulo minus for *paulominus : nudius quartana*
for *nudiusquarta*.

On the other hand some words found in the Clementine
edition form no part of the new text. These may be divided

into two classes : (1) Compound words which have been separated into these component parts, e.g. *amodo, lucrifacio* (but *lucrifio* remains), *malefacio, materfamilias, pater-familias, paulominus, quoadusque, usquequo, uerumtamen,*[1] etc. (2) Words which have dropped out owing to change of reading. The list of these is as follows :—

aliquantulus (1 C.16,7; H.10,37)   liberi (L.20,28)
bolis (A.27,28)   linio (J.9,6)
calcedonius (Ap.21,19)   luxuriosus (2 P.2,7)
caliga (A.12,8)   magia (A.8,11)
conquisitor (1 C.1,20)   motio (J.5,4)
demeto (Ap.14,16)   nudiusquartus (A.10,30)
dithalassus (A.27,41)   pereffluo (H.2,1)
exuro (2 P.3,10)   pertimeo (1 P.3,6)
illo, thither (Mt.2,22)   prosequor (Mk.1,36)
informatio (1 T.1,16)   senectus (L.1,36)
infremo (J.11,33)   sepono (1 C.16,2)
lacteo (Mt.21,16)   superexalto (Jas.2,13).

(2) ORTHOGRAPHY. One of the chief reasons for variation between the two editions is to be found in the different treatment of words whose first element is a prefix such as *ad, con, in,* etc. The Clementine, as a rule, assimilates when possible the last letter of such a prefix. The Oxford edition, following the manuscripts, has no fixed plan, but varies considerably even in the orthography of the same word.

The following details will show this :—

adf-, aff-, adfectio, adfigo, but affluo (der.),[2] afflictio. The following vary :[3] adficio (5), afficio (5) ; adfirmo (3) ; affirmo (2) ; adfligo (2), affligo (4) ; adfero (17), affero (9).

---

[1] The treatment of *manufactus, beneplaceo, satisfacio*, etc., varies.|
[2] When (der.) follows any word, it indicates that one or more derivatives are similarly spelled.
[3] The numbers after each form indicate the number of times the form in question is found.

adm-, amm-, assimilation does not occur except once
(L.11,14) in ammiror; admiror occurs thirteen times.

adp-, app-, adpono, adprehendo, adpretio, adprobo,
adpropinquo, adproprio, but appareo, appeto (der.).

adl-, all-, adlcuio, adleuo, but allido, alligo, alloquor.

ads-, ass- or as-, adsequor, adsideo, adsigno, adsimilo,
adsisto, adsuo (der.), adsumo (der.), adsto, adstringo,
but assiduus, aspergo (der.), aspicio (der.). Variable:
adspiro (1), aspiro (1).

adt-, att-, adtracto, but attendo, attineo.

conl-, conn-, all unassimilated except colligo (der.).

conm-, comm-, all assimilated, except conmanduco,
conmuto.

conp-, comp-, conparticeps, conpatior, conpingo, conplanto,
conpungo (der.), but complaceo, compleo, complexor,
comprehendo, comprobo, computo.

Variable conparo (2), comparo (2); conpello (1),
compello (2); conperio (2), comperio (1); conprimo
(1); comprimo (5); compono always, [in]conpositus (1).

conn-, con-, connumero, but conecto, conubium.

conr-, corr-, conregno, conresuscito, conroboro, but corrigo
(der.), corripio (der.), corrumpo (der.).

exs-, ex-, "s" dropped except in exsupero, exsurgo, exsuscito,
and exspiro (3) beside expiro (2).

inm-, imm-, the form inm- everywhere except in immolo
(der.).

inp-, imp-, generally inp-, but impedimentum, imperitus,
impius (der.), impleo (der.), imputo (der.). Variable:
inplico (1), implico (1).

inr-, irr-, inrationabilis, inreprehensibilis, inrideo, inruo,
but irrito, irritus.

Compounds of iacio make: -iicio in Clementine, -icio in
Oxford edition.

Initial "h" is another cause of variation, the Oxford edition
reading harena,[1] harundo, haue, holus, hordiaceus for
arena, etc., of the Clementine.

---

[1] Except in R.9,27.

ae, oe.[1] In the Oxford edition "oe" of the Clementine
becomes "ae" in caena, caeno (but cenaculum),
faenum, faeneror, paenitet, etc.; "ae" of the Clementine
becomes "oe" in proelium.

Several Greek words beginning with *ch* drop the *h* in
the Oxford edition, e.g. *caracter*, *clamys*, *crysolitus*,
crysoprassus, though it is retained in *chaos*, *charisma*,
chirographum, etc. Besides those instances of words found
spelled in two different ways which have already been
given under the head of assimilation, the following also
occur :—

claudus (10), clodus (3)	pedagogus (2), paedagogus (1)
clausi (2), clusi (2)	scabillum (1), scabellum (7)
idololatres (1), idolatres (1)	solacium (4), solatium (1)
intingo (4), intinguo (1)	transduco (1), traduco (2)
obtuli (5), optuli (10)	

[1] The treatment of *ae* in the Oxford edition varies much. Thus we have *eger*
for *aeger*, but *aegrotus*, *aegrotatio*; *heresis*, but *haereticus*; *coetaneus*, *longeuus*,
but *coaequalis*.

METHOD OF THE PRESENT DICTIONARY

Many words have been intentionally omitted. These may be grouped under two classes.[1]

(1) Pronouns, prepositions, numerals, etc., whose meaning is best learned from the Grammar.

(2) Words which have the same form and meaning in English and Latin, e.g. corruptio.

. Except in the case of words enclosed within square brackets the form given first is that of the Oxford edition. When the form found in the Clementine Vulgate differs, the variation is noted by giving in brackets the variant in whole or in part. The words enclosed within square brackets are those peculiar to the Clementine edition.

In order that the Dictionary may to some extent answer the purpose of a Concordance, the verses where a word is found are given, except in the case of the most frequently occurring words. An asterisk after the last reference indicates that all the passages have been mentioned where the word in question is found in the Oxford edition.

Other symbols that have been employed are as follows :—

° prefixed to a Greek word.

† prefixed to a word found but once in the Vulgate.

* prefixed to a word not found in the Vulgate Old Testament.

§ prefixed to a word peculiar to the Oxford edition. The same symbol prefixed to a reference indicates that the word is found in the passage referred to in the Oxford edition only.

---

1 Words belonging to these classes have sometimes been retained when they occur but seldom, in order to draw attention to the fact of such rare occurrence.

‖ before a reference to a passage in the Gospels indicates
that the word in question is found also in a parallel
passage in one or more Gospels.

[ ] when a reference is thus enclosed it indicates that the
word, though found in the passage in the Clementine
edition, has been dropped or changed by the Oxford
editor.

The chief parts of irregular verbs have not been given,
unless the stem in question is found in the New Testament.
Where it is possible the perfect participle passive has been
given instead of the supine.

LIST OF ABBREVIATIONS

In addition to the symbols already explained on pp. xiii
and xiv, the following abbreviations have been used in this
Dictionary :—

Books of the New Testament : Mt., Mk., L., J., A., R.,
1 C., 2 C., G., E., Ph., Co., 1 Th., 2 Th., 1 T., 2 T., Ti.,
Philem., H., Jas., 1 P., 2 P., 1 J., 2 J., 3 J., Jude, Ap.
f. after a reference to a verse indicates that the word is
found in it and the following verse.
ff. similarly used indicates that the word is found once or
oftener in the verses immediately following.
partic.=participle.
P.P.=perfect participle.
pers.=personal.
impers.=impersonal.
depon.=deponent.
pass.=passive.
compar.=comparative.
superl.=superlative.
met.=metaphorically.
bis=indicates that the word is found twice in the verse.
L. & S.=Lewis and Short's *Latin Dictionary*.
E.V.=English version.

DICTIONARY OF
THE VULGATE NEW TESTAMENT

A

*Abba (Aram.), *Father,* Mk. 14,36; R.8,15; G.4,6.*

[abbreuio], 1, *shorten,* R.9, 28.*

†abdico, 1, *renounce,* 2 C.4, 2.*

abduco, 3, *lead away,* A.20, 30; H.13,9.*

abeo, ii, 4, *go,* Mt.4,24; A. 1,25; Ap.9,12; *go away,* J.4,8; Jas.1,24; *depart,* Mt.19,15; Mk.6,1.

†aberro,1, *go astray,* 1 T.1,6.*

abicio (-iicio), 3, *put aside, cast away,* R.13,12; G. 2,21; Jas.1,21.*

abluo, utus, 3, *wash,* 1 C.6, 11; H.10,22; *wash away,* A.22,16; *disprove* (accusation), A.25,16.*

*abnego, 1, *deny,* ||Mt.16,24; L.22,34; 2 T.3,5; Ti. 2,12.*

aboleo, 2, *abolish, do away,* R.4,14.*

abominor, 1, *abhor,* R.2,22; P.P. *abhorred, accursed,* A.10,28; Ti.1,16.*

abortiuum, i, *n., abortion,* 1 C.15,8.*

abscido (-scindo), di, 3, *cut off,* ||Mt.5,30; J.18,10; A. 27,32; G.5,12.

abscondo, di, ditus, 3, *hide,* Mt.5,14; J.8,59; P.P., *hidden, secret,* R.2,29; Ap.2,17.

†absentia, ae, *f., absence,* Ph. 2,12.*

*absit, *far be it ! God forbid !* Mt.16,22; L.20,16; A. 10,14.

absoluo, 3, *decide, settle,* A. 19,39.*

absorbeo, bui, ortus (orptus), 2, *swallow up,* 1 C.15,54; 2 C.2,7; 5,4; Ap.12, 16.*

absque, *without,* J.16,2; R. 1,31; H.4,15.*

abstergo, 3, *wipe away,* Ap. 7,17; 21,4.*

B

adiutor, oris, *m., helper,* R. 16,3 ff.; H.13,6.

adiutorium, ii, *n., help,* A. 27,17.*

adiuuo, iuui, iutus, 1, *help, aid, assist,* Mk.9,22 ; L. 5,7 ; Ap.12,16.

adleuio (alle-), 1, (1) *lighten,* A.27,38 ; (2) *relieve,* Jas. 5,15.*

adleuo (alle-), 1, *raise up,* A.3,7.*

[†administratio], onis, *f., ministry,* 2 C.4,1.*

†administratorius, a, um, *ministering,* A.1,14.* Gk. λειτουργικός.

administro, 1, (1) *minister, serve,* A.13,36 ; 1 P.4,10 ; (2) *furnish,* 2 C.9,10 ; 1 P. 4,11.*

admirabilis, e, *marvellous,* 2 Th.1,10 ; 1 P.2,9.*

admiratio, onis, *f., wonder,* Ap.17,6.*

admiror, also **ammiror** (L. 11,14), 1, *wonder, marvel at,* Mk.6,2 ; A.4,13 ; Ap. 13,3.

admisceo, mixtus, 2, *mingle,* H.4,2.*

admitto, misi, 3, (1) *permit,* Mk.5,19 ; 5,37 ; (2) *commit,* A.25,25.*

admoneo, 2, *warn, admonish,* Mt.2,22 ; 2 T.1,6 ; Ti. 3,1.*

†adnauigo, 1, *sail to,* A.27,7.*

adnumero (annu-), 1, *count, reckon,* A.1,26 ; H.7, 6.*

*adnuntiatio (annu-), onis, *f., message,* 1 J.1,5 ; 3, 11.*

†adnuntiator (annu-), oris, *m., proclaimer, announcer,* A.17,18.*

adnuntio (annu-), 1, *announce, proclaim,* Mk. 5,19 ; J.4,25.

adplico (appl-), cui, 1, *put in to shore, touch at,* Mk. 6,53 ; A.20,15.*

adpono (appono), posui, positus, 3, (1) *set before,* Mk. 8,6 ; L.10,8 ; A.16,34 ; (2) *place beside,* A.18,10 ; (3) *add,* A.2,41 ; Ap. 22,18.

adprehendo (appr-), di, nsus, 3, *take, lay hold of,* Mt. 14,31 ; L.23,26.

adpretio (appr-), 1, *value, estimate,* Mt.27,9.*

adprobo (appr-), 1, *approve,* A.2,22.*

adpropinquo (appr-), 1, *draw nigh,* L.7,12 ; Jas.4,8.

adpropio (appr-), 1, *draw nigh,* L.10,34 ; 12,33 ; A.23,15.*

†adorator, oris, *m., worshipper.* Gk. προσκυνητής. J.4,23.*

adoro, 1, *worship, adore,* J. 4,20 ; H.1,6.

adquiesco (acq-), eui, 3, *acquiesce in, give assent to,* R.2,8 ; G.1,16 ; 1 T.6,3.*

adquiro (acq-), isiui, 3, *acquire, get by possession, obtain,* L.19,16 ; A.20, 28 ; 1 T.3,13.

adquisitio (acq-), onis, *f., acquiring, possession,* E. 1,14 ; 1 P.2,9 ; *wealth,* A.19,25.

*****adsequor (ass-), secutus, 3,** *follow, follow up,* L.1,3 ; 1 T.4,6 ; 2 T.3,10.*

adsideo (ass-), 2, *sit* or *be beside,* A.26,30.*

*****adsigno (ass-), 1,** (1) *hand over, present,* A.9,41 ; (2) *seal,* R.15,28.*

adsimilo (ass-), 1, *liken,* Mt. 6,8 ; H.7,3.

adsisto (ass-), 1, 3, *stand by,* J.18,22 ; *appear before,* A.27,24 ; *assist,* R.16,2.

adspiro, also **aspiro** (A.9,1), 1, *blow, breathe,* A.27,13.*

adsto (asto), stiti, 1, *stand,* A.4,10 ; *stand up,* A.4, 28 ; *stand by,* Mk.14,70 ; A.1,10.

adstringo (ast-), xi, 3, *bind,* A.22,25.*

adsum, adfui, esse, *be present,* L.13,1 ; *be come,* Mk.4,29 ; *stand by,* 2 T. 4,16.

adsumentum (ass-), i, *n., patch,* Mk.2,21.*

adsumo (ass-), sumsi, sumtus, 3, *take,* Mt.17,1 ; E.6,17 ; *take up,* A.1,2 ; 1 T.3,16.

adsumtio (assumptio), onis, *f.,* (1) *taking up,* L.9,51 ; (2) *receiving again,* R.11, 15.*

†**adsuo (assuo), 3,** *sew on,* Mk.2,21.*

adtracto (attrecto), 1, *feel after,* A.17,27.*

adulatio, onis, *f., flattery,* 1 Th.2,5.*

adulescens (ado-), entis, *m., young man,* Mt.19,20 ; L.7,14.

adulescentia (ado-), ae, *f., youth,* 1 T.4, 12.*

adulescentior (adol-), *younger,* L.15,12 f. ; 1 T.5, 11.*

adulescentula (adol-), ae, *f., young woman,* Ti.2,4.*

adulter, teri, *m., adulterer,* 1 C.6,9 ; Jas.4,4.

adulter, tera, terum, *adulterous,* Mt.12,39 ; 16,4 ; Mk.8,38.*

adultera, ae, *f., adulteress,* R.7,3.*

adulterium, ii, *n., adultery,* J.8,3.

adultero, 1, (1) *commit adultery,* Mt.5,32 ; (2) *adulterate,* 2 C.2,17 ; 4,2.

aduena, ae, *c., stranger, alien,* A.2,10 ; 1 P.1,1.

aduenio, ueni, 4, *come*, Mt.
[6,10; *arrive*, A.9,39;
come upon, Jas.5,1.
aduentus, us, *m.*, *coming*,
Mt.24,3; 2 C.7,6.
aduersarius, ii, *m.*, *adversary*,
Mt.5,25; 1 P.5.8.
aduersor, 1, *resist, be contrary to*, G.5,17; 1 Th.
2,15; 2 Th.2,4; 1 T.1,
10.*
aduesperasco, 3, *be evening*,
L.24,29.*
†aduocatus, i, *m.*, *advocate*.
Gk. παράκλητος. 1 J.2,1.*
aduoco, 1, *call*, Mt.18,2;
Mk.7,14; A.2,39.*
*aduoluo, ui, 3, *roll*, ‖Mt.
27,60.*
aedes, is, *f.*, *temple, shrine*,
L.11,51; A.19,24.*
aedificatio, onis, *f.*, *a building*, Mt. 24,1; 1 C.3,9;
edifying, R.14,19; E.
4,12.
aedifico, 1, *build*, Mk.12,1;
J.2,20; *edify*, 1 C.8,1;
1 Th.5,11.
aeger, v. eger.
aegrotatio, onis, *f.*, *sickness*,
Mt.8,17.*
§aegrotus, i, *m.*, *sick person*,
Mk.6,13; 16,18.*
aemulatio, onis, *f.*, *zeal*, R.
10,2; Ph.3,6; *emula-
tion, jealousy*, R.13,13;
G.5,20.
aemulator, oris, *m.*, *zealous*

observer or *imitator*, A.21,
20; 1 P.3,13.
aemulor, 1, *be zealous for, be
desirous of*, 2 C.11,2; G.
4,17; *be jealous*, A.7,9.
aenigma, v. en-.
aequalis, e, *equal*, Ph.2,6;
Ap.21,16.
aequalitas, tatis, *f.*, *equality*,
2 C.8,13 f.*
aequitas, tatis, *f.*, *righteousness, equity*, A.17,31;
R.9,28; H.1,8,*
aequus, a, um, *just, right*,
A.6,2; Co.4,1; *cheerful*,
Jas.5,13.*
°aer, aeris, acc. -rem, -ra,
m., *air*, A.22,23; 1 Th.
4,17.
aeramentum, i, *n.*, *a vessel
of copper or bronze*, Mk.
7.4; Ap.18,12.*
aerarius, ii, *m.*, *copper-smith*,
2 T.4,14.*
aereus, a, um, *made of copper
or bronze*, Ap. 9.20.*
aerug-, v. erug-.
aerumna, ae, *f.*, *trouble, toil*,
Mk.4,19; 2 C.11,27.*
aes, aeris, *n.*, (1) *bronze*, 1 C.
13,1; (2) *money*, Mk.
6,8; J.2,15.
aestas, tatis, *f.*, *summer*, ‖Mt.
24,32.*
aestimo, 1, *think, suppose*,
L.7,43; A.2,15; *con-
sider*, H.11,26; *account*,
A.26,2.

aestuo, 1, *be burnt, scorched,*
Mt.13,6 ; Ap.16,9.*
aestus, us, *m., heat,* Mt.20,
12 ; Ap.7,16.
aetas, tatis, *f., age,* L.2,52 ;
J.9,21.
aeternitas, tatis, *f., eternity,*
2 P.3, 18.*
aeternus, a, um, *eternal,* Mk.
3,29 ; in aeternum, *for
ever,* J.4,13.
aff-, v. adf-.
affero and adfero, attuli, alla-
tus, ferre, *bring,* 2 T.4,
13 ; *bring forth,* Mt.13,23 ;
J.12,24.
afflictio, onis, *f., affliction,*
A.7, 34.*
†affluenter, *abundantly,* Jas.
1,5.*
affluo, 3, *abound in,* 2P.2,13.*
Africus, i, *m., south-west
wind,* A.27,12.*
ager, agri, *m., field.*
agito, 1, *shake, agitate,* Mt.
11,7 ; [L.7,24.]*
agnitio, onis, *f., knowledge,*
1 T.2,4.
agnosco, nitus, 3, *know,* Mt.
12,33 ; J.10,15.
agnus, i, *m., lamb,* J.1,29 ;
A.8,32.
ago, egi, actus, 3, *do,* L.23,
15 ; A.5,35 ; *shew* (penitence), Mk.6,12; A.17,30 ;
live, A.24,2 ; 1 T.2,2 ;
give (thanks), Mt.15,36 ;
2 Th.1,3 ; *take* (care), L.

10,34 ; *hold* (assembly),
A.19,38 ; *lead,* L.4,1 ;
R.8.14.
°agon, onis, *m., contest,
games,* 1 C.9,25 ; 2 T.2,5.*
†°agonia, ae, *f., agony,* L.22,
43.*
agricola, ae, *m., husbandman,*
Mt.21,33 ; J.15,1.
agricultura, ae, *f., husbandry,*
1 C.3,9.*
aio, *defect. verb, say.*
ala, ae, *f., wing,* Mt.23,37 ;
Ap.4,8 ; 9,9 ; 12,14.*
alabaster, tri, *m., alabaster
box or phial,* ||Mt.26,7 ;
L.7,37.*
*alapa, ae, *f., blow with hand,*
Mk.14,65 ; J.18,22 ; 19,3.*
albus, a, um, *white,* Mt.5,36 ;
Ap.1,14.
alias, *in another place,* A.
13,35.*
alienigena, ae, *m., stranger,*
L.17,18 ; A.10,28.*
alieno, 1, *alienate, estrange,*
E.2,12 ; 4,18 ; Co.1,21.*
alienus, a, um, *belonging to
another, strange,* Mt.17,
25 f.; A.7,6 ; H.9,25.
alimenta, orum, *n., food,*
1 T.6,8.*
alloquin, *otherwise,* Mt.6,1 ;
H.9,17.
aliquando, *at any time, at
one time, once.*
[aliquantulum], *a little,* 1 C.
16,7 ; H.10,37.*

aliquantus, a, um, *some, considerable,* A.18,23 ; 28,3.*

aliquot, *some, a few.*

aliter, *otherwise,* Ph.3,15 ; 1 T.1,3 ; 5,25 ; 6,3.*

†aliunde, *from another side,* J.10,1.*

†°allegoria, ae, *f., allegory,* G.4,24.*

alleluia (Hebr.), *Hallelujah,* Ap.19,1 ff.*

allido, 3, *dash down,* Mk. 9,18.*

alligo, 1, *bind,* L.10,34 ; A.9, 14.

alloquor, locutus, 3, *speak,* A.20,11 ; 21,40 ; 28,20.*

alo, 3, *nourish,* A.12,20 ; Ap. 12,14.*

°aloe, es, *f., aloe,* J.19,39.*

altare, ris, *n., altar,* Mt.5,23 ; L.1,11.

§altarium, ii, *n., altar,* 1 C.9, 13 (*bis*) ; H.7,13.*

altercor, 1, *dispute,* Jude 9.*

alteruter, tra, trum, *one another,* Jas.4,11 ; 1 J. 3,11.

altilis, e, *fattened,* Mt.22,4.*

altitudo, dinis, *f., height,* R. 8,39 ; *depth, deepness,* ||Mt.13,5 ; Ap.2,24.

altus, a, um, *high,* Ap. 21,10 ; *deep,* L.6,48 ; J.4,11.

amabilis, e, *lovely,* Ph.4,8.*

amare, *bitterly,* ||Mt.26,75.*

§amarico, 1, *be bitter,* Ap. 10,9.*

amaricor, 1, *be bitter,* Ap. 10,10.*

amaritudo, dinis, *f., bitterness,* A.8,23 ; R.3,14 ; E.4,31 ; H.12,15.*

amarus, a, um, *bitter,* Co.3, 19 ; Jas.3,11 ff. ; Ap.8, 11.*

amator, oris, *m., lover,* 2 T. 3,4 ; 1 P.3,8.*

†ambigo, 3, *doubt,* A.5,24.*

ambitio, onis, *f., pomp, display,* A.25,23.*

†ambitiosus, a, um, *vainglorious,* 1 C.13,5.*

ambulo, 1, *walk,* J.1,36 ; (met.) R.6,4 ; E.2,2.

amen (Hebr.), *verily, so be it.*

°amethystus, i, *f., amethyst,* Ap.21,20.*

amica, ae, *f., friend,* L.15,9.*

amicio, ctus, 4, *clothe,* Mk. 14, 51 ; Ap.7,9.

amicitia, ae, *f., friendship,* Jas.4,4.*

amictus, us, *m., robe, vesture,* H.1,12.*

amicus, i, *m., friend,* Mt.20, 13 ; Jas.2,23.

amissio, onis, *f., loss,* A.,27, 22 ; R.11,15.*

amitto, 3, *lose,* H.10,35.*

amo, 1, *love,* Mt.6,5 ; 1 C. 16,22.

[amodo] a modo, *henceforth,* J.13,19; 14,7 ; Ap.14,13.

†§°**amomum, i,** *n., amomum, spice,* Ap.18,13.*

amor, oris, *m., love,* 1 P.1,22; 2 P.1,7.*

amoueo, moui, motus, 2, *put away, remove,* L.16,4 ; A.5,6 ; 13,22.* ·

amphora, ae, *f., jar, pitcher,* L.22,10.*

†**amplector,** 3, *embrace, hold fast,* Ti.1,9.*

amplior, ius, *greater, larger, longer,* A.18,20 ; H.3,3 ; 9,11.*

amplius, *more,* L.3,13 ; *further,* A.4,17 ; *longer,* R. 14,13.

amputo, 1, *cut off,* ||Mt.26,51; Mk.9,45 ; 2 C.11,12.*

°**anathema, atis,** *n., an accursed thing, a curse,* R. 9,3 ; 1 C.12,3 ; *anathema,* G.1,8 f.*

anathematizo, 1, *curse,* Mk. 14,71.* ·

anceps, cipitis, *two-edged,* H. 4,12.*

*anchora, ae,** *f., anchor,* A. 27, 29 ff. ; H.6,19.*

ancilla, ae, *f., female slave, handmaid,* ||Mt.26,69 ; A.2,18 ; G.4,22. '

†°**anethum, i,** *n., dill, anise,* Mt.23,23.*

*angario,** 1 (Persian), *exact service, compel,* Mt.5,41 ; ||27,32.*

angularis, e, *belonging to the corner, corner,* E.2,20 ; 1 P.2,6.*

angulus, i, *m., corner,* Mt.6,5.

angustia, ae, *f., anguish, tribulation,* R.2,9 ; 2 C.2,4.

angustio, 1, *straiten, distress,* 2 C.4,8 ; 6,12 ; H.11,37.*

angustus, a, um, *narrow,* ||Mt. 7.13 f.

†**anilis, e,** *old-womanish,* 1 T. 4,7.*

anima, ae, *f., soul,* L.1,46.·

animaequior, ius, *of good courage,* Mk.10,49 ; A. 27,36.*

animal, alis, *n., animal, beast,* H.13,11 ; · *living creature,* Ap.4,6.

*animalis, e,** *animal, natural, psychic.* Gk. ψυχικός, 1 C.2,14 ; Jas,3,15.

animositas, tatis, *f., enmity, wrath,* 2 C.12,20; H.11,27.*

animus, i, *m., mind,* 2 C.9,2 ; · Jas.4,8 ; *accord,* A.18, 12 ; 19,29. · ·

annulus, v. anu-.

annuo, ui, 3, *b:ckon,* L.5,7; A.12,17 ; 21,40 ; 24,10.*

antea, *formerly,* L.23,12.*

antecedo, 3, *go before,* Mt.2 9 ; L.22,47.*

antecessor, oris, *m., predecessor,* G.1,17.*

*°**antichristus, i,** *m., antichrist,* 1 J.2,18 ff.; 4,3 ; 2 J.7.*

†**antiquo,** 1, *make old,* H.8,13.*

antiquus, a, um, *old, ancient,*
　A.15,7 ; Ap.12,9 ; in pl.
　men of old, Mt.5,21 ff.
anulus (ann-), *m., ring,* L.
　15,22 ; Jas.2,2.*
anus, us, *f., old woman,* 1 T.
　5,2 ; Ti.2,3.*
aperio, erui, ertus, 4, *open,*
　A.5,19 ; 1 C.16,9.
apertio, onis, *f., opening,*
　E.6,19.*
apex, icis, *m., point* (of a
　letter), *tittle,* ||Mt.5,18.*
*°apocalypsis, is (acc. -sin),
　f., apocalypse, 1 C.14,26 ;
　Ap.1,1.*
°aporior, 1, *doubt,* 2 C.4,8.*
*apostolatus, us, *m., office of
　an apostle, apostleship,*
　A.1,25.
appareo, 2, *appear,* A.1,3.
appello, 1, *call,* A.1,19 ;
　appeal, A.25,11 ff.
†appetitor, oris, *m., one that
　strives or longs for,* 1 P.
　4,15.*
appeto, 3, *seek for, desire,*
　1 T.6,10 ; H.11,16.*
apto, 1, *fashion, frame,*
　§R.9,22 ; H.10,5 ; 11,3 ;
　11,7 ; 13,21.*
aptus, a, um, *fit, fitted,* L.9,
　62 ; A.27,12.*
aquila, ae, *f., eagle,* ||Mt.24,
　28 ; Ap.4,7.
aquilo, onis, *m., the North,*
　L.13,29 ; Ap.21,13.*
ara, ae, *f., altar,* A.17,23.*

aratrum, i, *n., plough,* L.9,
　62.*
arbitror, 1, *think,* L.7,7 ; H.
　11,19.
arbor, oris, *f., tree,* Mk.8,24 ;
　L.21,29.
arca, ae, *f.,* (1) *ark* (of Noah),
　||L.17,27 ; (2) *ark* (of
　covenant), H.9,4 ; Ap.
　11,19.
arcanus, a, um, *secret,* 2 C.
　12,4.*
arcarius, ii, *m., treasurer,* R.
　16,23.*
*°archangelus, i, *m., arch-
　angel,* 1 Th.4,16 ; Jude
　9.*
°archisynagogus, i, *m., ruler
　of a synagogue,* Mk.5,22
　ff ; L.13,14 ; A.18,8.*
°architectus, i, *m., master-
　builder,* 1 C.3,10.*
*°architriclinus, i, *n., master
　of a feast,* J.2,8 f.*
arctus, v. art-.
arcus, us, *m., bow,* Ap.6,2.*
ardeo, si, 2, *burn, be burning,*
　L.24,32 ; *be burnt,* J.15,
　6 ; 1 C.3,15 ; 13,3.
ardor, oris, *m., heat,* Jas. 1,
　11 ; 2 P.3,12.*
area, ae, *f., threshing-floor,*
　||Mt. 3,12.*
arefacio, feci, factus, 3,
　wither, dry up, Mt.21,19 ;
　Jas.1,11.*
arena, v. har-.
areo, 2, *be* or *become dry,*

withered, Mt.21,20 ; Ap.
14,15.
Areopagita, v. Ario-.
aresco, 3, *wither, pine away,
faint*, Mk.9,18 ; L.21,26.*
argentarius, ii, *m., silver-
smith*, A.19,24.*
argenteus, a, um, *made of
silver*, A.19,24 ; 2 T.2,
20 ; Ap.9,20.*
argenteus, i, *m., piece of
silver*, Mt.26,15 ; 27,3 ff.*
argentum, i, *n., silver*, A.3,6 ;
money, A.7,16.
argumentum, i, *n., proof,
proving*, A.1,3, ; H.11,
1.*
arguo, 3, *reprove, convict*, J.
8,46 ; A.19,40
arida, ae, *f., dry land, land*,
Mt.23,15.*
aridus, a, um, *dry, withered*,
||Mt.12,10; *waterless*, Mt.
12,43.
°**Ariopagita (Are-), ae**, *m.,
Areopagite, member of the
court of Areopagus*, A.
17,34.* .
arma, orum, *n., arms : in-
struments*, R.6,13.
†**armamenta, orum**, *n., tackle*
(of a ship), A.27,19.*
[**armatura**], **ae**, *f., armour,
panoply*, E.6,11 ff.*
armo, 1, *arm*, L.11,21 ; 1 P.
4,1.*
aro, 1, *plough*, L.17,7 ; 1 C.
9,10.*

°**aroma, atis**, *n.* (only in pl.),
spices, Mk.16,1 ; L.23,56 ;
24,1 ; J.19,40.*
arripio, reptus, 3, *seize, catch*,
L.8,29 ; A.27,15.*
ars, artis, *f., art, craft*, A.17,
29 ; 18,3 ; Ap.18,22.*
†°**artemon, onis**, *m., top-sail*,
A.27,40.*
artifex, ficis, *m., craftsman
builder : author*, A.19,
24 ; 19,38 ; H.11,10 ;
Ap.18,22.*
†**artificium, ii**, *n., craft, trade*,
A.19,25.*
artus (arct-), a, um, *narrow,
cramped*, Mt.7,14.*
arundo, etc., v. **har-**.
†**as, assis**, *m., as* (E.V. farthing), Mt.10,29.*
ascendo, di, sum, 3, *go up,
ascend*, L.2,4 ; R.10,6 ;
embark, L.8,22 ; A.27,2.
asellus, i, *m., young ass*,
J.12,14.*
asina, ae, *f., she-ass*, ||Mt.
21,2 ; J.12,15.*
*****asinarius, a, um**, *belonging
to an ass, turned by an
ass*, ||Mt.18,6.*
asinus, i, *m., ass*, L.13,15 ;
14,5.*
aspectus, us, *m.,* (1) *appearance*, Mt.28,3 ; 1 Th.2,
17 ; Ap.4,3 ; (2) *seeing*,
2 P.2,8.*
asper, era, erum, *rough,
rocky*, L.3,5 ; A.27,29.*

aspergo, rsi, rsus, 3, *sprinkle*,
H.9,13 ff.; 10,22 ; Ap.
19,13.*

aspersio, onis, *f.*, *sprinkling*,
1 P.1,2.*

†aspernor, 1, *despise*, L.18,9.*

aspicio, 3, *behold*, *look at*,
L.20,17 ; H.12,2 ; *look
up*, Mt.14,19 ; A.1,11.

aspiro, v. adspiro.

aspis, idis, *f.*, *viper*, *asp*, R.
3,13.*

ass-, v. ads-.

assiduus, a, um, *unceasing*,
constant, Jas.5,16.*

assus, a, um, *roasted*, L.24,
42.*

asto, v. adsto.

astutia, ae, *f.*, *craftiness*,
guile, 1 C.3,19 ; 2 C.4,2 ;
11,3 ; E.4,14.*

astutus, a um, *crafty*, 2 C.
12,16.*

atramentum, i, *n.*, *ink*, 2 C.
3,3 ; 2 J.13 ; 3 J.13.*

atrium, ii, *n.*, *court*, *court-
yard*, L.11,21 ; Ap.11,2.

attendo, 3, *give heed*, *beware*,
Mt.6,1 ; L.12,1.

attente (only in compar.), *in-
tently*, *earnestly*, 1 P.1,
22.*

†attineo, 2, *belong to*, *concern*,
A.24,26.*

attrecto, v. adtracto.

auctor, oris, *m.*, *author*,
originator, A.3,15 ; 24,5 ;
H.2,10 ; 12,2.*

audacter (compar. -cius),
boldly, Mk.15,43 ; R.15,
15.*

audax, acis, *bold*, *daring*,
2 P.2,10.*

†audenter, *boldly*, A.2,29.*

audeo, ausus, 2, *dare*, A.5,
13 ; *be bold*, R.10,20.

audio, 4, *hear*.

auditor, oris, *m.*, *hearer*, R.
2,13 ; Jas.1,22 ff.*

†auditorium, ii, *n.*, *place of
hearing*, A.25,23.*

auditus, us, *m.*, (1) *sense of
hearing*, *hearing*, Mt.13,
14 ; 2 P.2,8 ; (2) *report*,
J.12,38 ; R.10,16 ; (3)
ears (abstr. for concr.),
2 T.4,4.

aufero, abstuli, ablatus, ferre,
take away, Mk.2,20 ; J.
2,16.

augeo, 2, *add*, *increase*, A.
2,47 ; 5,14 ; 2 C.9,10.*

augmentum, i, *n.*, *increase*, E.
4,16 ; Co.2,19.*

aura, ae, *f.*, *breeze*, A.27,
40.*

aureus, a, um, *made of gold*,
H.9,4 ; Ap.1,12 ff.

aurich-, v. ori-.

auricula, ae, *f.*, *little ear*,
ear, ‖Mt.26,51 ; Mk.7,
33 ; J.18,26.

auris, is, *f.*, *ear*.

aurum, i, *n.*, *gold*, H.9,4 ;
Ap.3,18.

ausculto, 1, *hearken*, A.8,10.*

Auster, tri, *m., South wind,*
A.27,13 ; 28,13 ; *South,*
‖Mt.12,42 ; L.13,29 ; Ap.
21,13.

†**austeris, e (austerus),** *aus-*
tere, L.19,21 f.*

†**autumnalis, e,** *belonging to*
the autumn, autumn, Jude
12.*

auxilior, 1, *help,* H.2,18.*

auxilium, ii, *n., help,* A.26,
22 ; H.4,16.*

auaritia, ae, *f., avarice,*
covetousness, L.12,15 ;
Co.3,5.

auarus, a, um, *covetous,* L.
16,14 ; E.5,5.

aue, v. **have.**

auello, auulsus, 3, *remove,*
withdraw, L.22, 41.*

auersor, 1, *turn away* (trans.),
Ti.1,14.*

auerto, erti, ersus, 3, *turn*
away, Mt.5,42 ; R.11,
26 ; *lead astray,* L.23,14 ;
A.5,37.

†**aula, ae,** *f., grandmother,*
2 T.1,5.*

auiditas, tatis, *f., avidity,*
zeal, A.17,11.*

auis, is, *f., bird,* Mk.4,32 ;
L.13,34 ; Ap.19,17 ff.*

°**azyma, orum,** *n.,* (feast of)
unleavened bread, Mk.
14,1 ;   A.20,6 ;   *un-*
leavened bread, 1 C.5,8.

°**azymus, a, um,** *unleavened,*
1 C.5,7.*

B

***baiulo,** 1, *bear, carry,* Mk.
14,13 ;   L.14,27 ;   J.19,
17 ; A.3,2.*

*°**baptisma, atis,** *n., baptism,*
A.1,22 ; *washing, sprink-*
ling, Mk.7,4 ff.

°**baptismum (-mus), i,** *n.,*
baptism, Mk.1,4.

°***baptista, ae,** *m., baptist,*
Mt.3,1 ;· L.7,20.

°**barbarus, i,** *m., foreigner,*
non-Greek, barbarian, A.
28,2 ff.; R.1,14 ; 1 C.14,
11 ; Co.3,11.*

°**basis, is** and **eos,** *f., base :*
foot, A.3,7.*

beatifico, 1, *account happy,*
Jas.5,11.*

beatitudo, dinis, *f., blessed-*
ness, R.4,6 ff. ; G.4,15.*

beatus, a, um, *blessed,* Mt.
5,3 ff.

belligero, 1, *wage war,* Jas.
4,2.*

bellum, i, *n., war.*

bene, *well.*

benedico, xi, ctus, 3, *bless.*

benedictio, onis, *f., blessing,*
1 C.10,16 ; Jas.3,10.

[**benefacio**] **bene facio.**

benefactum, i, *n., good deed,*
A.4,9 ; 1 P.4,19.*

†**beneficentia, ae,** *f., kind-*
ness, beneficence, H.13,
16.*

†beneficus, a, um, *beneficent, kind*, L.22,25.*

beneficium, ii, *n.*, *benefit*, 1 T.6,2*.

beneplaceo, 2, *please, be pleasing*, 1 C.10,5. [In 1 C.16,2, as two words.]

beneplacitum, i, *n.*, *good pleasure*, E.[1,9] ; 5,10. [Perhaps, in E.5,10, an adj. = *well-pleasing*.]*

benigne, *kindly*, A.28,7.*

benignitas, tatis, *f.*, *kindness, benevolence*, R.2,4 ; G.5,22 ; Co.3,12 ; 2 T.3,3 ; Ti.3,4.*

benignus, a, um, *kind*, L.6,35 ; 1 C.13,4 ; E.4,32 ; Ti.1,8 ; 2,5.*

°beryllus, i, *m.*, *beryl*, Ap.21,20.*

bestia, ae, *f.*, *beast; wild beast.* (In Ap. *the beast.*)

bibo, bi, bitus, 3, *drink.*

biduum, i, *n.*, *space of two days*, ‖Mt.26,2.*

biennium, ii, *n.*, *space of two years*, A.19,10 ; 24,28 ; 28,30.*

†bilibris, e, *weighing two pounds.* (In Ap.6,6 as subst. = *two pounds' weight.*)*

bilinguis, e, *double-tongued*, 1 T.3,8.*

†bimatus, us, *m.*, *age of two years*, Mt.2,16.*

bini, ae, a, *two by two, two apiece*, ‖Mk.6,7 ; J.2,6.*

†§bithalassus, a, um, *between two seas*, A.27,41.*

bivium, ii, *n.*, *place where two ways meet*, Mk.11,4.*

°blasphemia, ae, *f.*, *blasphemy; reviling*, E.4,31 ; Co.3,8.

°blasphemo, 1, *blaspheme, revile, speak evil of.*

°blasphemus, a, um, as subst. *blasphemer*, 1 T.1,13 ; 2 T.3,2.*

[†°bolis], idis, *f.*, *sounding-line*, A.27,28.*

bonitas, tatis, *f.*, *goodness, kindness*, R.2,4 ; 11,22 ; G.5,22 ; E.2,7 ; 5,9 ; 2 Th.1,11.*

bonum, i, *n.*, *good deed or thing*; in pl., *goods, possessions.*

bonus, a, um, *good.*

bos, bouis, *c.* [gen. pl., boum ; dat. pl., §bubus] *ox*, 1 C.9,9 ; 1 T.5,18.

°botrus, i, *f.*, *grape*, Ap.14,18.*

brachium, ii, *n.*, *arm*, L.1,51 ; J.12,38 ; A.13,17.*

*°brauium, ii, *n.*, *prize*, 1 C.9,24 ; Ph.3,14.*

breuio, 1, *shorten*, ‖Mt.24,22 ; R.9,28.*

breuis, e, *short, brief*, A.5,34 ; 1 C.7,29 ; E.3,3 ; Ap.17,10.*

*breuiter, *shortly, briefly,*
A.24,4 ; 1 P.5,12.*
buccella, ae, *f., morsel, sop,*
J.13,27 ff.*
°byssinum, i, *n., garment of
byssus,* Ap.§18,16 ; 19,
8 ; 19,14.*
°byssus, i, *f., fine linen,* L.
16,19 ; Ap.18,12.*

C

cadauer, eris, *n., corpse,*
H.3,17.*
cado, cecidi, casum, 3, *fall,
fall down.*
°cadus, i, *m., cask ; measure*
(liquid), L.16,6.*
caecitas, tatis, *f., blindness,*
Mk.3,5 ; R.11,25 ; E.
4,18.*
†caeco, 1, *blind, make blind,*
Mk.8,17.*
caecus, a, um, *blind.*
caedes, is, *f., slaughter,* A.
9,1 ; H.7,1.*
caedo, cecidi, caesum, 3, (1)
beat, strike, L.20,10 ; (2)
cut down, ||Mt.21,8.
caelestis (coe-), e, *heavenly,*
J.3,12 ; A.26,19.
caelum (coe-), i, *n., sky,
heaven* ; in pl., caeli,
orum, *heaven.*
caena (coe-), ae, *f., dinner,
supper ; feast.*

caeno (coe-), 1, *dine, sup.*
caet-, v. cet-.
°calamus, i, *m.,* (1) *reed,* Mk.
15,36 ; Ap.11,1 ; (2) *pen,*
3 J.13.*
calcaneus, i, *m., heel,* J.
13,18.*
[†°calcedonius], i, *m., chal-
cedony,* Ap.21,19.*
calciamentum (calce-), i, *n.,
shoe,* ||Mt.3,11 ; A.7,33.
calcio (calceo), 1, *put on
shoes, shoe,* Mk.6,9 ; A.
12,8 ; E.6,15.*
calcitro, 1, *kick,* A.[9,5] ; 26,
14.*
calco, 1, *tread,* L.10,19 ;
tread down, L.21,24.
calculus, i, *m., small stone,
pebble,* Ap.2,17.*
calefacio, 3, *warm :* pass.
imperat., calefacimini,
Jas.2,16.
calidus, a, um, *hot,* Ap.3,
15 f.*
[caliga], ae, *f., shoe,* A.12,8.*
caliginosus, a, um, *dark,*
2 P.1,19.*
caligo, inis, *f., mist ; darkness,* A.13,11 ; H.12,18 ;
2.P.2,17 ; Jude 6.*
calix, icis, *m., cup,* ||Mt.26,
27 ; 1 C.11,25.
calor, oris, *m., heat,* A.28,3 ;
2 P.3,10.*
calumnia, ae, *f., calumny,
false accusation,* L.3,14 ;
[A.23,25.]*

calumnior, 1, *accuse falsely, calumniate*, ‖Mt.5,44 ; 1 P.3,16.*

°**camelus**, 1, *m., camel*, ‖Mt. 3,4 ; ‖19, 24 ; 23,24.*

°**caminus**, 1, *m., furnace*, Mt.13,42 ; Ap.1,15.*

campester, tris, tre, *level*, L.6,17.*

†**cancer**, cri, *m., cancer, gangrene*, 2 T.2,17.* ·

candelabrum, 1, *n., candlestick*, ‖Mt.5,15 ; Ap.1,12.

candidus, a, um, *white*, Mk. 9,3 ; A.10,30.

canis, is, *c., dog.*

cano, cecini (fut. part., **caniturus**), 3, *play, sound* (an instrument), Mt.6,2 ; 1 C.14,7. (Not used for " sing.")

canticum, 1, *n., song*, E.5,19 ; Co.3,16 ; Ap.5,9 ; 14,3 ; 15,3.*·

canto, 1, (1) *sing, play* ; (2) *crow* (of cock), ‖Mt.26, 34 ff.

cantus, us, *m., crowing* (of cock), Mk.13,35.*

·†**capillatura**, ae, *f., dressing of hair*, 1 P.3,3.*

capillus, 1, *m.,* Mt.5,36 ; 1 C. 11,15.

capio, cepi, 3, (1) *take, catch*, L.5,5 ; 2 C.12,16 ; (2) *receive*, 2 C.7,2 ; (3) *contain*, J.2,6 ; 21,25 ; (4) impers., *is possible, fit-*

ting, L.13,33 ; (5) for Gk. χωρεῖν, *progress, succeed*, J.8,37.

†**capitulum**, 1, *n., chief or prominent part.* Gk. κεφάλαιον, H.8,1.*

†**caprinus**, a, um, *pertaining to goats*, H.11,37.*

captio, onis, *f., catching, seizing : trap, snare*, R. 11,9 ; 2 P.2,12.*

captiuitas, tatis, *f., captivity*, 2 C.10,5 ; Ap.13,10 ; *body of captives*, E.4,8.*

captiuo, 1, *lead captive*, R. 7,23.*

captiuus, a, um, *captive*, L.21,24 ; as subst., *a captive*, L.4,18.

captura, ae, *f., taking, draught* (of fish), L.5, 4 ff.*

caput, itis, *n.,* (1) *head :* (2) *chapter* (of book). Gk. κεφαλίς, H.10,7.

carbo, onis, *m., coal*, R.12, 20.*

†°**carcedonius**, ii, *m., Carthaginian* (stone), *carbuncle*, Ap.21,19.*

carcer, eris, *m., prison*, J. 3,24 ; Ap.2,10.

caritas (cha-), tatis, *f., love*, 1 C.13,1 ff.

caro, carnis, *f., flesh.*

carus (cha-), a, um (only in superl., **carissimu**), *beloved.*

castellum, i, *n., town, village.*

†castifico, 1, *purify, make pure,* 1 P.1,22.*

castigo, 1, *chasten, discipline,* 1 C.9,27 ; 2 C.6,9 ; H. 12,6 ; Ap.3,19.*

castitas, tatis, *f., chastity, purity.*

castra, orum, *n., castle, fortress; camp,* H.13,11 ff. ; *host,* H.11,34.

†castro, 1, *castrate,* Mt.19, 12.*

castus, a, um, *chaste, pure,* 2 C.11,2 ; 1 T.5,22 ; Ti. 2,5 ; 1 P.3,2.

casula, ae, *f., small hut or house,* H.11,9.*

catechizo, v. cathecizo.

*catellus, i, *m., little dog,* ||Mt.15,27.*

catena, ae, *f., chain.*

†°cathecizo (catech-), 1, *catechize, instruct,* G.6,6.*

°cathedra, ae, *f., seat,* ||Mt. 21,12.

*catinus, i, *m., dish, platter,* Mk.14,20 ; L.11,39.*

cauda, ae, *f., tail,* Ap.9,10 ; 9,19 ; 12,4.*

causa, ae, *f.,* (1) *cause, reason, occasion,* Mt.15,9 ; A.10,21 ; *case :* (2) *reason for punishment, fault,* A. 25,7 ff. (Abl., causā, *for the sake of.*)

causor, 1, *plead, lay to the charge of anyone,* R.3,9.*

caute, *safely, cautiously,* Mk. 14, 44 ; E.5,15.*

†cauterio, 1, *mark with brand, brand,* 1 T.4,2.*

†cautio, onis, *f., security, bond,* L.16,6.*

caueo, 2, *take heed, beware,* Mt.10,17 ; L.12,15.

cauerna, ae, *f., cavern,* H. 11,38.*

cedo, cessi, 3, *yield, give place,* G.2,5.*

celebro, 1, *keep, celebrate,* H. 11,28.*

celer, eris, ere, *swift,* 2 P.2,1.*

celeriter (compar. -erius), *speedily,* A.17,15 ; H. 13,19 ff.*

cellarium, ii, *n., storehouse,* L.12,24.*

cenaculum (coe-), i, *n., dining-room, upper room.* Gk. ἀνάγαιον and ὑπερῷον.

census, us, *m., tribute,* Mt. 17,25 ; 22 ff.*

centeni, ae, a, *by hundreds,* Mk.6,40.*

centesimus, a, um, *hundredth, hundred-fold,* Mt. 13,8 ; [13,23].*

centies, *a hundred times,* Mk.10,30.*

centuplus, a, um, *a hundred-fold,* Mt.19,29 ; L.8,8.*

certamen, minis, *n., contest, fight,* Ph.1,30 ; 1 T.6,12 ; 2 T.4,7 ; H.10,32 ; ·12, 1.*

c

certe (only superl.), *most*
  certainly, A.2,36 ;   24,
  23.*
certo, 1, *strive*, Co.1,29 ;
  1 T.6,12 ; 2 T.2,5.*
certus, a, um, (1) *certain,
  sure ;* (2) *strict*, A.26,5.
ceruical, alis, *n., pillow,
  cushion*, Mk.4,38.*
ceruix, icis, *f., neck*, A.7,51 ;
  15,10 ; R.16,4.*
cesso, 1, *cease*, Mt.14,32 ; L.
  5,4 ; *delay*, 2 P.2,3.
ceteri (cae-), ae, a, *the others,
  the rest*, L.8,10 ; A.15,
  17.
ceterum (cae-), i, *n., the rest*
  (only in phrase **de cetero**),
  finally, E.6,10 ; Ph.3,1.
ceterum (cae-), (1) *otherwise*,
  1 C.14,16 ; (2) *further*,
  1 C.1,16.*
°cetus, i, *m., sea-monster,
  whale*, Mt.12,40.*
†°chaos, *n., dark gulf*, L.
  16,26.*
eharacter, v. car-.
†°charisma, atis, *n., spiritual
  gift*, 1 C.12,31.*
°charta, ae, *f., paper*, 2 J.
  13.*
charus, v. car-.
cherubin (-bim) (Hebr. with
  Aram. termination), *cher-
  ubim*, H.9,5.*
°chirographum, i, *n., bond*,
  Co.2,14.*
chlamys, v. cla-.

°chorus, i, *m., dance, dancing*,
  L.15,25.*
chorus (co-), i, *m., north-
  west wind*, A.27,12.*
Christianus, i, *m., Christian*,
  A.11,26 ;   26,28 ;   1 P.
  4,16.*
chry-, v. cry-.
cibo, 1, *feed*, R.12,20.*
cibus, i, *m., food.*
cilicinus, a, um, *made of
  hair-cloth*, Ap.6,12.*
cilicium, ii, *n., hair-cloth*,
  ||Mt.11,21.*
cingo, 3, *gird*, J.21,18 (bis).*
cinis, eris, *m., ashes*, ||Mt.
  11,21 ; H.9,13 ; 2 P.2,6.*
°cinnamomum, i, *n., cinna-
  mon*, Ap.18,13.*
circiter, *about*, A.2,41 ;   5,
  36.*
circuitus, us, *m.*, (1) *going
  round, encircling*, H.11,
  30 ; (2) *space around,
  environment ;* **in circuitu,**
  round about, Mk.3,34 ;
  Ap. 4,3 ff.
circum, *around, about*, Mt.
  8,18.*
circumamicio, ictus, 4, *clothe*,
  Ap.4,4.*
circumcido, cisus, 3, *circum-
  cise.*
†circumdatio, onis, *f., putting around* or *on*, 1 P.
  3,3.*
circumdo, dedi, datus, 1,
  surround,   put   around,

Mk.9,42 ; A.28,20 ; *clothe,*
A.12,8.

circumduco, 3, *lead round,*
1 C.9,5 ; Jas.3,2.*

circumeo, ii, 4, *go round.*

circumfero, ferre, *bear* or
carry round, Mk.6,55 ;
Jas.1,6.

*****circumfulgeo, si,** 2, *shine
round,* L.2,9 ; A.9,3 ; 22,
6 ; 26,13.*

†**circumlego,** 3, *sail* or *coast
round,* A.28,13.*

circumpono, 3, *place* or *wrap
round,* Mk.15,36 ; J.19,
29.*

circumsedeo, 2, *sit round,*
L.22,55.*

circumspicio, spectus, 3, *look
round, look round on,*
Mk.3,5 ; L.6,10.

circumsto, steti, 1, *stand
round,* J.11,42 ; *surround,*
H.12,1.

†**circumtego, tectus,** 3, *cover
round about,* H.9,4.*

circumuenio, ueni, 4, *cir-
cumvent, deceive,* A.7,19 ;
2 C.2,11 ; 1 Th.4,6.

†**circumuentio, onis,** *f., cir-
cumventing, defrauding,
deceit,* E.4,14.*

°**cithara, ae,** *f., cithara, lute,*
1 C.14,7 ; Ap.5,8 ; 14,2 ;
15,2.*

*°**citharizo,** 1, *play the
cithara,* 1 C.14,7 ; Ap.
14,2.*

*°**citharoedus, i,** *m., one who
plays the cithara,* Ap.14,
2 ; 18,22.*

cito, 1, *cite, summon,* A.
24,2.*

cito (compar. **citius**), *quickly,
speedily, soon.*

[†**ciuilitas], tatis,** *f., citizenship,* A.22,28.*

ciuis, is, *c., citizen.*

ciuitas, tatis, *f.,* (1) *city :* (2)
citizenship, §A.22,28.

clam, *secretly, privily,* Mt.
2,7.*

clamo, 1, *call, cry, cry out.*

clamor, oris, *m., cry,* Mt.25
6 ; *crying,* H.5,7 ; *clam-
our,* E.4,31.

°**clamys (chl-), ydis,** *f., cloak,*
Mt.27,28 ; 27,31.*

clare, *clearly,* Mk.8,25.*

†**claresco, ui,** 3, *become glorious,* 2 C.3,10.*

*****clarifico,** 1, *glorify.* Gk.
δοξάζω, J.12,28 (and fre-
quently) ; H.5,5.

claritas, tatis, *f., brightness,
honour, glory,* L.2,9 ; 1 C.
15,41.

claudico, 1, *limp, halt, be
lame,* H.12,13.*

claudo, clausi or **clusi, clau-
sus,** 3, *shut.*

claudus or **clodus** (Mt.15,
30 f.; 18,8), **a, um,**
lame.

clauis, is, *f., key,* Mt.16,19 ;
Ap.1,18.

clauus, i, *m.*, *nail*, J.20,25 (bis).*

clementia, ae, *f.*, *clemency*, A.24,4.*

°clerus, i, *m.*, pl. *lots, estates, curé* (of presbyters), 1 P. 5,3.*

°clibanus, i, *m.*, *oven*, ‖Mt. 6,30.*

clodus, v. claudus.

coaceruo, 1, *heap together*, 2 T.4,3.*

[†coacte], *constrainedly, by compulsion*, 1 P.5,2.*

†coaedifico, 1, *build together*, E.2,22.*

coaequalis, e, *equal, like*, 2 P.1,1 ; as subst., *comrade*, Mt.11,16.*

coaetaneus, v. coet-.

†coagito, 1, *shake together*, L.6,38.*

coangusto, 1, *confine, hem in*, L.19,43.*

coarto (-arcto), 1, *confine, straiten*, L.12,50 ; Ph. 1,23.*

coccineus, a, um, *scarlet-coloured*, Mt.27,28 ; H. 9,19 ; Ap.17,3.*

coccinum, i, *n.*, *scarlet*, Ap. 17,4.*

°coccum, i, *n.*, *scarlet*, Ap.18, 12 ; 18,16.*

coelectus, v. conel-.

coelestis, coelum, v. cael-.

coena, coeno, v. caen-.

coenaculum, v. cen-.

coepi, isse, *begin*.

coerceo, 2, *restrain*, 1 P.3, 10.*

coetaneus (coaet-), i, *m.*, *contemporary, an equal in age*, G.1,14.*

cogitatio, onis, *f.*, *thought*.

cogito, 1, *think, take thought, ponder*.

cognata, ae, *f.*, *kinswoman, female relation*, L.1,36.*

cognatio, onis, *f.*, *kindred*, Mk.6,4 ; L.1,61 ; A.7,3 ; 7,14.*

cognatus, i, *m.*, *kinsman*, J.18,26.

*cognitio, onis, *f.*, (1) *knowledge*, R.3,20 ; 2 P.1,3 ; (2) *examination, trial*, A.25,21.

cognomino, 1, *call, name*, J.5,2 ; *surname*, L.6,14 ; A.1,23.

cognosco, noui, nitus, 3, *know*.

cogo, coegi, coactus, 3, *constrain, compel*.

†cohabito, 1, *dwell together* [A.22,12], 1 P.3,7.*

coheres (-haeres), edis, *c.*, *co-heir*, R.8,17 ; E.3,6 ; H.11,9 ;. 1 P.3,7.

cohors, ortis, *f.*, *cohort*. Gk. σπεῖρα.

coinquinatio, onis, *f.*, *pollution, defilement*, 2 P.2,13 ; 2,20.*

coinquino, 1, *defile*, ‖Mt. 15,11 ; Ap.14,4.

*°colaphizo, 1, *buffet*, 2 C.
12,7 ; 1 P.2,20.*
*°colaphus, i, *m.*, *cuff, blow*,
‖Mt.26,67 ; 1 C.4,11.*
coll-, v. conl- in many cases.
collecta, ae *f.*, *contribution*,
1 C.16,1 f.*
collectio, onis, *f.*, *gathering
together, assembling*, H.
10,25.*
colligo, legi, lectus, 3, (1)
gather, gather together ;
(2) *entertain, take in* (as
guest), Mt.25,35 ff.
collis, is, *m.*, *hill*, L.3,5 ; 23,
30.*
collum, i, *n.*, *neck*, ‖Mt.18,6 ;
L.15,20.
†°collyrium, ii, *n.*, *eye-salve*,
Ap.3,18.*
colo, lui, 3, (1) *worship*, Mk.
7,7 ; R.1,25 ; (2) · *till*,
H.6,7.
colonia, ae, *f.*, *colony*, A.16,
12.*
colonus, i, *m.*, *husbandman*,
Mk.12,7 ff. ; L.20,9 ff.*
columba, ae, *f.*, *dove*, ‖Mk.
1,10 ; L.2,24.
columna, ae, *f.*, *pillar*, G.2,9;
1 T.3,15 ; Ap.3,12 ; 10, 1.*
coma, ae, *f.*, *hair*, 1 C.11,
14 f.*
comburo, ussi, ustus, 3, *burn,
burn up*, Mt.3,12 ; A.19,
19.
combustio, onis, *f.*, *burning*,
H.6,8.*

comedo, edi, estus (Jas.5,2),
3, *eat, devour*.
comes, itis, *c.*, *companion*,
A.19,29 ; 22,11 ; 2 C.8,
19.*
comisatio (comess-), onis, *f.*,
revelling, R.13,13 ; G.
5,21 ; 1 P.4,3.*
comitatus, us, *m.*, *company*,
L.2,44.*
comitor, 1, *accompany*, A.9,
7 ; 10,23 ; 20,4.*
commanduco, v. conm-.
commemoratio, onis, *f.*, *remembrance*, L.22,19 ; 1
C.11,24 f. ; H.10,3.* Gk.
ἀνάμνησις.
commemoro, 1, *recall, remember*, A.10,31.*
†commendaticius (-itius), a,
um, *commendatory*, 2 C.
3,1.*
commendo, 1, *commend*, R.
3,5 ; 1 C.8,8 ; *entrust*,
L.12,48 ; 1 T.1,18.
*commilito, onis, *m.*, *fellow-
soldier*, Ph.2,25 ; Philem.
2.*
comminor, 1, *charge, rebuke,
threaten* (ἐπιτιμᾶν in Mk.).
comminuo, nui, 3, *break* or
crush in pieces, Mk.5,4 ;
L.20,18 ; J.19,36.*
commisceo, 2, *mingle, inter-
mingle*, 1 C.5,9 ff.; 2 Th.
3.14.*
commissura, ae, *f.*, *patch*,
‖Mt.9,16.*

committo, 3, (1) *entrust* [Mt. 25,27] ; A.27,40 ; (2) *commit* (adultery), Mk. 10,11 ; (3) *engage in* (war), L.14,31.*

commodo, 1, *lend*, L.11,5.*

†commonefacio, 3, *put in mind*, 1 C.4,17.*

commoneo, 2, *remind*, 2 P. 1,12 ; Jude 5 ; *call to mind*, 2 T.2,14 ; 3 J.10 ; *admonish*, Co.3,16.*

commonitio, onis, *f.*, *reminding, admonition*, 2 P.1,13 ; 3,1.*

†commoratio, onis, *f.*, *habitation*, A.1,20.*

commoror, 1, *abide*, A.12,19.*

commoueo, moui, motus, 2, *move, stir up, excite*, Mt. 21,10 ; L.23,5.

communicatio, onis, *f.*, (1) *joint-partaking*, 1 C.10, 16 ; (2) *communion, fellowship*, 2 C.13,13. Gk. κοινωνία.

†communicator, oris, *m.*, *partaker*, 1 P.5,1.*

communico, 1, (1) *participate in*, R.12,13 ; 1 T.5,22 ; (2) *defile*, Mk.7,15 ff.

communio, onis, *f.*, *communion, mutual participation*, H.13,16.*

communis, e, (1) *common, held in common*, A.2,44 ; Ti.1,4 ; (2) *unclean*, Mk. 7,2 ff.; A.10,14.

commutatio, onis, *f.*, *exchange*, ||Mt.16,26.*

commuto, v. conm-.

compages, is, *f.*, *joining together, joint*, H.4,12.*

compar, aris, as subst. *comrade, colleague*, Ph.4,3.*

comp-, v. conp- in many cases.

compello, also conpello (A. 26,11), puli, pulsus, 3, *compel*, [Mt.14,22] ; L. 14,23 ; G.2,3.*

compes, edis, *f.*, *fetter*, ||Mk. 5,4.*

complaceo, 2, (1) *be well pleased*, ||Mt.3,17 ; (2) *be pleasing*, L.12,32.

complector, plexus, 3, *embrace*, Mk.9,36 ; A.20, 10.*

compleo, eui, etus, 2, (1) *fill*, L.8,23 ; (2) *fulfil*, A.2,1 ; *fill up*, 1 Th.3,10 ; *accomplish*, A.14,25.

†complexor, 1, *embrace*, Mk. 10,16.*

†complures, ra, *very many*, Mk.5,26.*

compono, positus, 3, (1) *mend*, Mk.1,19 ; (2) *arrange, settle*, H.9,6.*

comprehendo, di, sus, 3, (1) *take, take hold of*, Mt. 4,24 ; A.1,16 ; (2) *overtake*, 1 Th.5,4 ; (3) *attain*, Ph.3,12 f.; (4) *understand*, E.3,18.

comprimo, also conprimo
(A.28,27), pressi, 3, (1)
hem in, throng, Mk.3,9 ;
(2) shut (eyes), A.28,27.
comprobo, 1, prove, verify,
2 C.8,8.*
computo, 1, reckon, count up,
L.14,28 ; A.19,19 ; Ap.
13,18.*
concaptiuus, i, m., fellow-
prisoner, R.16,7 ; Co.
4,10 ; Philem.23.*
concedo, cessi, 3, grant, give
leave, Mk.5,13.*
conceptio, onis, f., concep-
tion, H.11,11.*
concido, 3, cut, Mk.5,5.*
concilium, ii, n., council.
concionor, v. cont-.
concipio, cepi, 3, conceive,
L.1,24 ; Jas.1,15.
concisio, onis, f., concision,
mutilation, Ph.3,2.*
concito, 1, stir up, excite,
Mk.15,11 ; A.17,5 ff.
concludo, clusi, clusus, 3,
shut up, enclose, L.5,6 ;
G.3,22 f.
†concordo, 1, agree, A.15,
15.*
†concorporalis, e, belonging
to the same body (Gk.
σύνσωμος), E.3,6.*
concremo, 1, burn up, consume, Ap.[8,7] ; 17,16.*
concubitor, oris, m., bed-
fellow, 1 C.6,9; 1 T.1,
10.*

concubitus, us, m., lying-
together, coition, R.9,10.*
conculco, 1, tread, tread
underfoot, Mt.5,13 ; 7,6 ;
H.10,29.
concupiscentia, ae, f., eager
desire, longing, lust, Mk.
4.19 ; coveting, R.7,7.
concupisco, iui, 3, desire,
1 P.2,2 ; lust after, covet,
Mt.5,28 ; A.20,33.
concurro, concurri, 3, run
together.
†concursio, onis, f., running
together, attack (Gk.
συνδρομή), A.21,30.*
*concursus, us, m., (1) con-
course, A.19,40 ; (2) up-
roar, tumult, A.24,12.*
concutio, 3, terrify, alarm,
trouble, L.3,14.*
†condelector, 1, be delighted
with, R.7,22.*
condemnatio, onis, f., condemnation, R.5,16 ; 2 C.
7,3.*
condemno, 1, condemn.
condignus, a, um, worthy,
R.8,18.*
condio, 4, season, ||Mk.9,50 ;
Co.4,6.*
†condiscipulus, i, m., fellow-
disciple, J.11,16.*
conditor, oris, m., founder,
author, H.11,10.*
condo, ditus, 3, make, create,
found, Mk.13,19 ; E.2,
15 ; Co.1,16.*

condoleo, 2, *suffer with, sympathize*, H.5,2.*
conduco, xi, 3, *hire*, Mt.20,1 ; 20,7.*
†**conductum, i**, *n.*, *hired house*, A.28,30.*
conecto (conn-), nexus, 3, *join together*, E.4,16.*
conelectus (coel-), a, um, *elect together*, 1 P.5,13.*
confercio, fertus, 4, *crowd or press together*, L.6,38.*
confero, tuli, ferre, (1) *bring together*, A.19,19 ; (2) *be of use to*, A.18,27 ; (3) *consider, confer*, L.2,19 ; (4) *contribute, bestow on*, G.2,6 ; (5) *abide*, A.16, 12.
confestim, *immediately*.
confidenter, *boldly*, Co.2,15 ; H.13,6.*
confido, 3, *be of good cheer*, Mt.9,2 ; *trust, be confident*, R.2,19 ; Ph.1,6.
configo, fixus, 3, *transfix, fix*, G.2,19.*
configuro, i, fashion according ing (to something), *conform*, Ph.3,10 ; 3,21 ; 1 P.1,14.
confirmatio, onis, *f.*, *confirmation*, Ph.1,7 ; H.6, 16.*
confirmo, 1, *strengthen, confirm, establish*.
confiteor, fessus, 2, (1) *confess, acknowledge* : (2)

give thanks, L.2,38 ; (3) in A.7,17 *answers to swear*. Gk. ὁμολογεῖν.
†**conflictatio, onis**, *f.*, *dispute*, 1 T.6,5.*
†**conformo**, 1, *conform*, R. 12,2.*
conforto, 1, *strengthen, make strong*.
†**confrico**, 1, *rub together*, L.6,1.*
confringo, fractus, 3, *break*, Mt.12,20 ; 21,44 ; L.4, 18 ; Ap.2,27.*
confugio, fugi, 3, *flee for refuge*, A.14,6 ; H.6,18.*
confundo, fusus, 3, *confuse, confound*, A.19,32 ; *make ashamed*, 1 C.1,27 ; 1 P. 2,6.
confusio, onis, *f.*, (1) *confusion*, A.19,29 ; (2) *shame*, H.12,2 ; Ap.3,18.
*congaudeo**, 2, *rejoice together with*, 1 C.12,26 ; 13,6.*
congero, 3, *heap together*, R.12,20.*
†**conglorifico**, 1, *glorify together with*, R.8,17.*
congratulor, 1, *congratulate, rejoice with*, L.1,58 ; 15, 6 ff.; Ph.2,17 f.*
congregatio, onis, *f.*, *assembling together*, 2 Th.2,1.*
congrego, 1, *gather together*.
coniunctio, onis, *f.*, *union, fastening*, Co.2,19.*

coniungo, iunxi, iunctus, 3,
join together, join, ||Mt,
19,6 ; A.5,13.

coniuratio, onis, f., conspir-
acy, A.23,13.*

coniux, ugis, c., wife, Mt.1,
20 ; 1,24.*

*conlaboro (coll-), 1, work
together, Ph.1,27 ; 2 T.
1,8.*

conlactaneus (coll-), i, m.,
foster-brother, A.13,1.*

conlatio (coll-), onis, f., col-
lection, contribution, R.
15,26.*

conlaudo (coll-), 1, praise,
A.2,47.*

conloquium (coll-), ii, n.,
conversation, speech, 1 C.
15,33.*

conloquor (coll-), 3, converse.

†conluctatio (coll-), onis, f.,
wrestling with, struggle,
E.6,12.*

†conmanduco (comm-), 1,
gnaw, Ap.16,10.*

conmuto (comm-), 1, change,
R.1,25.*

connecto, v. conecto.

connubium, v. conubium.

†connumero, 1, number with,
reckon among, A.1,17.*

conor, 1, try, attempt, struggle,
L.1,1 ; A.24,6 ; 27,15.*

conparo, also comparo (1 C.
2,13 ; 2 C.10,12), 1, com-
pare, Mk.4,30 ; Jas.1,
23.*

†conparticeps (comp-), cipis,
partaking together, E.3,
6.*

conpatior (comp-), passus, 3,
suffer along with, have
compassion, R.8,17 ; 1 C.
12,26 ; H.4,15 ; 10.34 ;
1 P.3,8.*

conpello, v. compello.

conperio, also comperio (A.
25,25), peri, pertus, 4,
learn, find out.. A.4,13 ;
10,34 ; 25,25.*

conpingo (comp-), pactus,
3, unite together, E.4,
16.*

†conplanto (comp-), 1, plant
together with, R.6,5.*

conprimo, v. comprimo.

conpunctio (comp-), onis, f.,
penitence, remorse, R.11,
8.*

conpungo (comp-), punctus,
3, prick ; make to feel
remorse, A.2,37.*

conquasso, 1, break in pieces,
L.20,18.*

conquiro, 3, enquire (συζητεῖν,
Mk.).

†conquisitio, onis, f., search-
ing ; enquiry, dispute,
A.15,7.*

[conquisitor], oris, m., dis-
puter, 1 C.1,20.*

conregno, 1, reign together
with, 2 T.2,12.*

conresuscito, 1, raise up
together with, E.2,6.*

conroboro (corr-), 1, strengthen, E.3,16.*

conscientia, ae, f., (1) consciousness, knowledge, H. 10,2 ; (2) conscience, A. 24,16 ; H.9,9.

conscindo, scissus, 3, rend, A.14,14.*

conscius, a, um, (1) privy, A.5,2 ; (2) conscious of, 1 C.4,4.*

conscribo, scriptus, 3, write, H.12,23.*

consedeo, sedi, 2, sit down, E.2,6 ; H.8,1.*

†consenior, oris, m., fellow-elder, 1 P.5,1.*

consensus, us, m., consent, agreement, 1 C.7,5 ; 2 C. 6,16.*

consentio, sensi, 4, agree, 1 C.7,12 f.; agree together, Mt.18,19 ; take part with, A.5,36 f.

consepelio, sepultus, 4, bury together with, R.6,4 ; Co. 2,12.

consequor, secutus, 3, (1) follow after, 1 C.10,4 ; (2) obtain, attain, A.22,28 ; H.11,2 ff.

conseruo, 1, keep, preserve, ||Mt.9,17.

conseruus, i, m., fellow-servant, Mt.18,28 ff. ; Co. 1,7 ; Ap.6,11.

considero, 1, (1) look at closely, examine, A.7,31 ;

11,6 ; (2) consider, reflect on, R.4,19 ; (3) perceive, A.27,39.

consiliarius, ii, m., counsellor, R.11,34.*

consilium, ii, n., counsel, advice ; plan.

consisto, 3, subsist, exist, 2 P.3,5.*

consobrinus, i, m., cousin, Co.4,10.*

consolido, 1, make firm or strong, A.3,7.*

consolor, 1, (1) comfort, A. 27,9 ; 1 Th.5,14 ; (2) be comforted, Mt.2,18 ; L. 16,25.

consors, sortis, c., partaker, sharer, 2 P.1,4.*

consparsio (-spersio), onis, f., paste, dough ; lump, 1 C. 5,7.*

conspectus, us, m., sight, presence (always with one of the prepositions ; a, ante or in).

conspicio, 3, see clearly, R. 1,20.*

†conspiro, 1, agree together, J.9,22.*

conspuo, 3, spit on, Mk.10, 34 ; 14,65 ; 15,19 ; L. 18,32.*

constanter, (1) boldly, A.13, 46 ; 26,26 ; (2) vehemently, L.23,10.*

constantia, ae, f., boldness, A.4,13.*

consterno, 1, *alarm, dismay,* L.24,4.*

constituo, ui, utus, 3, *set,* L.7,8; *make,* G.2,18; *appoint,* A.28,23; Ti. 1,5.

constitutio, onis, *f., making, creation* (only in phrase cons. mundi.), L.11,50; Ap.17,8.

consto, 1, (1) *consist,* Co.1,17; (2) (in partic.) *steadfast, bold,* A.23,11.*

construo, structus, 3, *make, construct,* E.2,21; Co.2, 19.*

consuesco, eui, 3, *be wont,* Mt.27,15; Mk.10,1.*

consuetudo, dinis, *f., custom, wont.*

§consul, ulis, *m., consul,* A. 19,38.*

consummatio, onis, *f., accomplishing, perfection; end,* Mt.13,39 ff.; H.6,8.

†consummator, oris, *m., finisher,* H.12,2.*

consummo, 1, *end,* Mt.7,28; *complete,* J.17,4; *perfect,* H.2,10; *fulfil,* 1 P.4,3.

consumo, sumtus, 3, (fut. part., -sumpturus, II.10, 27), *consume,* L.9,54; *devour,* A.12,23.

consurgo, surrexi, 3, *rise, arise.*

contaminatio, onis, *f., pollution, defilement,* A.15,20.*

contamino, 1, *defile,* J.18,28; 1 T.1,9.*

contemno, mptus, 3, *despise.*

contemplor, 1, *look at, observe, give heed,* 2 C.4,18; H.12,15.*

contemptibilis, e, *comtemptible, of slight account,* 1 C. 1,28; 6,4; 2 C.10,10.*

contemtor (-temptor), oris, *m., despiser,* A.13,41.*

contendo, 3, *contend, strive.*

contenebro, 1, *darken, make dark,* Mk.13,24.*

contentiosus, a, um, *contentious,* 1 C.11,16.*

contentus, a, um, *content,* L.3,14; 1 T.6,8; H.13, 5.*

contero, tritus, 3, *break, crush, bruise,* Mt.21,44; [L.4,18]; R.16,20.*

conterreo, 2, *terrify,* L.24, 37.*

contestor, 1, (1) *call to witness,* A.20,26; (2) *bear witness, testify,* H. 2,4; 7,8.

contexo, textus, 3, *weave,* J.19,23.*

continens, entis, *temperate, continent,* Ti.1,8.*

continentia, ae, *f., temperance, continence,* G.5,23.*

contineo, 2, (1) *hold, keep, hold fast,* G.5,1; (2) *contain,* A.23,26; (3) *stop* (ears), A.7,57.

contingo, tigi, 3, *happen, befall, fall to one's lot,* R.11,25 ; 2 P.2,22.

continuo, *forthwith.*

continuus, a, um, *continuous, uninterrupted,* R.9,2 ; 1 P.4,8.*

†**contionor (conc-),** 1, *make a speech,* A.12,21.*

contradico (in Ti.1,9, **contra dico**), 3, *speak against, contradict,* A.13,45 ; *gainsay,* R.10,21.

contradictio, onis, *f., contradiction, gainsaying,* H. 7,7 ; 12,3 ; Jude 11.*

contrarius, v. e contrario.

contrecto, 1, *handle,* Co.2,21 ; 1 J.1,1.*

contremesco (-isco), 3, *tremble,* Jas.2,19.*

contribulis, is, *m., man of same tribe,* 1 Th.2,14.*

contristo, 1, *sadden, make sad,* 2 C.2,2 ; E.4,30.

contritio, onis, *f., calamity, grief,* R.3,16.*

controuersia, ae, *f., controversy,* H.6,16.*

contubernium, ii, *n., company,* Mk.6,39.*

contumelia, ae, *f., insult, abuse, reproach,* A.5,41 ; H.10,29 ; *dishonour,* R. 9,21 ; 2 T.2,20.

contumeliosus, a, um, *insolent, abusive,* R.1,30 ; 1 T. 1,13.*

conturbo, 1, *trouble,* G.1,7 ; 1 P.3,14.

conubium (conn-), ii, *n., marriage,* H.13,4.*

conualesco, iui, 3, *grow strong,* A.9,22 ; H.11, 34.*

conuenio, ueni, 4, (1) *come together,* Mt.1,18 ; *assemble,* Mk.1,45 ; (2) *go along with* (others), J. 18,2 ; (3) *agree,* L.5,36 ; *be agreed,* Mk.14,56 ; (4) *be convenient, fitting,* R.1,28.

conuentio, onis, *f., agreement,* Mt.20,2 ; 2 C.6, 15.*

conuentus, us, *m., assembly,* A.19,38 ; Jas.2,2.*

conuersatio, onis, *f., manner of life.* Gk. ἀναστροφή, G.1,13 and often ; in E.2,12 = *commonwealth* (πολιτεία) ; in Ph.3,20 = *citizenship* (πολίτευμα).

conuersio, onis, *f., conversion,* A.15,3.*

conuersor, 1, *live, pass one's life,* A.11,26.

conuerto, uerti, uersus, 3, *turn,* Mt.7,6 ; *return, turn again,* L.22,32 ; *convert,* J.12,40 ; *turn into,* A.2, 20 ; Ap.11,6 ; *pervert,* G.1,7.

conuescor, 3, *eat together with,* A.1,4.*

conuicior, 1, *revile, taunt,*
Mk.15,32.*

conuinco, 3, *convince,* 1 C.
14,24.*

*conuiuifico, 1, *quicken to-
gether,* E.2,5 ; Co.2,13.*

conuiuium, ii, *n., feast,* L.5,
29 ; 2 P.2,13.

conuiuo, 3, *live together with,*
2 C.7,3 ; 2 T.2,11.*

conuiuor, 1, *feast together,*
Jude 12.*

conuoco, 1, *call together,* Mt.
15,10 ; *assemble,* A.5,21.

*cooperator, oris, *m., fellow-
worker,* Ph.2,25 ; 3 J.8.*

cooperio, erui, ertus, 4, *cover,
clothe,* Mt.6,29 ; Mk.16,5 ;
Ap.19,8.

*cooperor, 1, *work together,*
Mk.16,20 ; R.8,28 ; 1 C.
16,16 ; Jas.2,22.*

°cophinus, i, *m., basket,* ||Mt.
14,20 ; ||16,9.*

copiosus, a, um, *great, abun-
dant,* L.5,6.

cor, cordis, *n., heart.*

†corban (Hebr.), *gift,* Mk.
7,11.*

†corbana (-bona), (acc. -an),
(Aram.) *treasury,* Mt.27,
6.*

coriarius, ii, *m., tanner,*A.9,
43 ; 10,6 ; 10,32.*

cornu, us, *n., horn.*

corona, ae,*f., crown, garland.*

corono, 1, *crown,* 2 T.2,5 ;
H.2,7 ff.*

corporalis, e, *bodily,* L.3,22 ;
1 T.4,8.*

†corporaliter, *bodily, in a
bodily form,* Co.2,9.*

corpus, oris, *n., body.*

correctio, onis, *f., correction,
amendment,* H.9,10.*

correptio, onis, *f., admonition, reproof,* 1 C.10,11 ;
E.6,4 ; Ti.3,10; 2 P.2,16.*

corrigia (cori-), ae, *f., shoe-
latchet,* ||Mk.1,7.*

corrigo, 3, *correct, set right,*
A.24,2 ; §2 T.3,16 ; Ti.
1,5.*

corripio, reptus, 3, (1) *reprove,* L.3,19 ; *correct,* H.
12,7 ; *chasten, chastise ;*
(2) *seize,* A.10,4.

corroboro, v. conr-.

corrumpo, rupi, ruptus, 3,
corrupt, G.5,9 ; Ap.11,
18.

corus, v. cho-.

°corus, i, *m., cor, measure*
(dry), L.16,7.*

corusco, 1, *flash,* L.17,24.*

coruus, i, *m., raven,* L.12,
24.*

cotidianus (quo-), a, um,
daily, L.11,3 ; A.6,1 ; 2
C.11,28 ; Jas.2,15.*

cotidie (quo-), *daily, day by
day.*

†coutor, 3, *have dealings
with,* J.4,9.*

crapula, ae, *f., surfeiting, intoxication,* L.21,34.*

cras, *to-morrow.*

crastinus, a, um, *of to-morrow,* *to-morrow's,* Mt.6,34; Jas. 4,13 f.

†creatio, onis, *f., creation,* H.9,11.*

creator, oris, *m., creator,* R. 1,25; 1 P.4,19.*

creatura, ae, *f.,* (1) *creation,* R.1,20; 2 P.3,4; (2) *creature;* H.4,13.

crebro, *frequently, often,* Mt. 17,15; Mk.7,3.*

credo, didi, ditus, 3, (1) *believe,* J.1,7. (2) *entrust, commit,* J.2,24; R.3,2.

cremo, 1, *burn, consume,* H. 13,11.*

creo, 1, *create.*

crepo, ui, 1, *crack; be rent* or *torn with a noise,* A.1,18.*

cresco, eui, 3, *grow, increase.*

cribro, 1, *sift,* L.22, 31.*

crimen, inis, *n., charge, accu-, sation,* Ti.1,6 f.; *crime, guilt,* Mt.12,5; A.25,5.

criminator, oris, *m., accuser, calumniator,* 2 T.3,3.*

†criminatrix, icis, *f., female accuser, calumniator,* Ti. 2,3.*

crinis, is, *m., hair,* 1 T.2,9.*

cruciatus, us, *m., torment, torture,* Ap.9,5.*

crucifigo, fixi, fixus, 3, *crucify.*

crucio, 1, *torture, torment,* L. 16,24; 2 P.2,4 ff.

crus, uris, *n., leg,* J.19,31 ff.*

crux, ucis, *f., cross.*

°crysolitus (chrysolithus), i, *m.* or *f., chrysolite,* Ap. 21,20.*

°crysoprassus (chrysoprasus), i, *m., chrysoprasus,* Ap. 21,20.*

°crystallum, i, *n., crystal,* Ap.4,6; 21,11; 22,1.*

cubiculum, i, *n., bedchamber,* Mt.6,6; L.12,3; A.12, 20.*

cubile, is, *n., bed,* L.11,7; (in pl.) *chambering, fornication,* R.13,13.*

cubitus, i, *m., cubit,* ||Mt.6,27; J.21,8; Ap.21,17.*

†culex, icis, *m., gnat,* Mt.23, 24.*

culpa, ae, *f., fault,* H.8,7.*

cultor, oris, *m.,* (1) *cultivator,* L.13,7; 20,10; (2) *worshipper,* J.9,31; H.10, 2.*

†cultrix, icis, *f., worshipper,* A.19,35.*

cultura, ae, *f., worship, worshipping,* 1 C.10,14; H. 9,1.*

cultus, us, *m.,* (1) *worship, adoration,* 1 P.4,3; (2) *adornment,* 1 P.3,3.*

cumi, (Aram.) *arise!* Mk.5, 41.*

cuncti, ae, a, *all,* A.8,40; R. 16,4; 16,26; Ph.1,4.*

†cupide, *earnestly,* 1 Th. 2,8.*

cupiditas, tatis, *f., desire ; covetousness,* R.15,23 ; 1 T.6,10.*

cupidus, a, um, *desirous,* G.5,26 ; 1 T.3,3 ; 2 T.3,2 ; Ti.1,7.

cura, ae, *f., care, anxiety,* Mt.22,16 ; A.18,17 ; *healing,* L.9,11.

curatio, onis, *f., healing,* 1 C.12,28 ff.*

curiose, *curiously, inquisitively,* 2 Th.3,11.*

curiosus, a, um, *curious, inquisitive,* A.19,19 ; 1 T.5,13.*

curo, 1, (1) *heal, cure,* Mt. 12,10 ; (2) *care for,* A.8,2 ; (3) *be careful, take heed,* 2 T.2,15 ; Ti.3,8 ; (4) *care about,* Mk.12,14.

curro, cucurri, 3, *run.*

currus, us, *m., chariot,* A.8, 28 ff ; Ap.9,9.*

cursus, us, *m., course,* A.13, 25 ; 16,11 ; 2 T.4,7.

curuo, 1, *bend, bow,* R.11, 4.*

custodia, ae, *f.,* (1) *watch, guard,* Mt.27,65 ; (2) *prison, custody,* A.4,3 ; Ap. 18,2 ; (3) In A.27,1 ; 27,42 = Gk. δεσμώτης, *prisoner.*

custodio, 4, (1) *guard,* Mk.6, 20 ; 2 C.11,32 ; (2) *keep, observe,* J.9,16 ; 1 J.2,4 ; Ap.12,17.

custos, odis, *c., keeper, guard.*

°**cymbalum, i,** *n., cymbal,* 1 C.13,1.*

°**cyminum, i,** *n., cumin,* Mt. 23,23.*

D

°**daemon, onis,** *m., evil spirit.*

°**daemonium, ii,** *n., evil spirit.*

***damnatio, onis,** *f., judgment,* A.25,15 ; *condemnation,* L.23,40 ; R.3,8.

damno, 1, *judge, condemn.*

damnum, i, *n., loss,* A.27, 10.*

dator, oris, *m., giver,* 2 C.9, 7.*

datum, i, *n., giving, gift,* L.11,13 ; Ph.4,15 ff.; Jas. 1,17.*

dea, ae, *f., goddess,* A.19,37.*

dealbo, 1, *whiten, make white,* Mt. 23,27 ; A.23,3 ; Ap. 7,14.*

deauro, 1, *gild, cover with gold,* Ap.18,16.*

debeo, 2, (1) *ought* ; (2) *owe.*

debilis, e, *weak, infirm,* Mt. 15,30 ; Mk.9,43 ; L.14, 13.

debitor, oris, *m., debtor,* L. 7,41 ; R.1,14.

debitum, i, *n., debt,* R.4,4 ; 1 C.7,3.

decaluo, 1, *make bald, cut the hair,* 1 C.11,5 f.*

deceptio, onis, *f.,* *deceit,*
deceitfulness, Mk.4,19 ; 2
P.3,3.*

decerno, creui, cretus, 3,
decree, A.4,28 ; 16,4 ;
Co.2,20.*

†**decerto,** 1, *fight to the end,*
J.18,36.*

decet, 2, (impers.) *it is fitting,*
seemly, it becomes ; in
[Ti.2,1] used in 3rd per.
plur.

decido, cidi, 3, *fall,* A.15,16 ;
Jas.1,11.

decima, ae, *f., tithe,* L.18,12 ;
H.7,2 ff.*

*****decimo,** 1, (1) *pay tithes,*
||Mt.23,23 ; (2) *make to*
pay tithes, H.7,9.*

decipio, 3, *deceive,* Co.2,4 ;
2,8.*

declaro, 1, *make manifest,*
1 C.3,13 ; H.12,27.*

declino, 1, (1) *turn aside*
(trans.), L.24,5 ; (2) *turn*
aside (intrans.), J.5,13;
R.3,12 ; (3) (of the day)
decline, wear away, L.9,
12.

decollo, 1, *behead,* ||Mt.14,10;
Ap.20,4.

decor, oris, *m., grace, beauty.*
Jas.1,11.*

decretum, i, *n., decree,* A.17,
7 ; E.2,15 ; Co.2, 14.*

†**decumbo,** 3, *lie down, lie*
sick, Mk.1,30.*

decurio, onis, *m., decurion ;*

in ||Mk.15,43, *counsellor*
(of Joseph of Arima-
thæa).*

decurro, decucurri, 3, *run*
down, L.22,44 ; A.21,32 ;
27,16.*

dedecus, oris, *n., shame, dis-*
grace, 2 C.4,2.*

dedico, 1, *dedicate,* H.9,18.*

dedo, ditus, 3 (only in P.P.),
given over to, A.17,16 ;
1 T.3,8.*   .

deduco, xi, ctus, 3, *bring* or
lead down, R.10,6 ; Ap.
7,17 ; *escort,* A.20,38 ;
2 C.1,16.

defendo, fensus, 3, *defence,*
A.25,16 ; 26,2 ; R.2,15 ;
12,19.*

defensio, onis, *f., defence.*
Gk. ἀπολογία, 1 C.9,3 ; 2
C.7,11 ; Ph.1,7 ; 1,16 ;
2 T.4,16.*

defero, tuli, ferre, *bring,* A.
19,12 ; 25,18 ; with **sen-**
tentiam = *vote,* A.26,10.*

deficio, feci, 3, *fail,* L.16,9 ;
J.2,3 ; *be wanting,* Jas.
1,4 ; *faint,* ||Mt.15,32.

definio, 4, *define, determine,*
L.22,22 ; A.2,23 ; 17,
26.*

deforis, *outside,* ||Mt.23,25 f.*

†§**deformatio, onis,** *f., rough*
draft, pattern (Gk.
ὑποτύπωσις), 1 T.1,16.*

deformo, 1, *delineate,* 2 C.
3,7.*

defraudo, 1, *defraud*, L.19,8.*
defungor, functus, 3, *die*,
   Mk.12,22 ;   A.2,29 ;   H.
   11,13.
deglutio, 4, *swallow down*,
   1 P.3,22.*
deicio (deii-), 3, *cast down*,
   2 C.4,9.*
. †§dein, *then*, Jas.1,15.*
deinceps, *afterwards*, L.7,11 ;
   8,1 ; A.3,24 ; Jas.4,14.
[*deintus], de intus, *from
   within*, L.11,7 ; *within*,
   L.11,40.*
†delabor, lapsus, 3, *come
   down, descend*, 2 P.1,17.*
deleo, 2, *blot out*, A.3,19 ;
   Co.2,14 ; Ap. 3,5.*
†delibatio, onis, *f., first fruits,
   representative part*, R.11,
   16.*
†delibo, 1, (in pass.) *be
   plucked, ripe for pluck-
   ing, about to die*, 2 T.4,6.*
deliciae, arum, *f., delight,
   pleasure, luxury*, 2 P.2,
   13.
delictum, i, *n., fault, offence,
   sin*, Mk.3,29 ; R.3,25 ;
   defect, 1 C.6,7.
delinquo, 3, *offend, sin*, Ti.
   3,11.*
†deliramentum, i, *n., folly,
   nonsense*, L.24,11.*
§deludo, 3, *mock*, Mt.20,
   19.* .
†demento, 1, *drive mad ;
   bewitch, delude*, A.8,11.*

   D

demergo, 3, *plunge down,
   sink* (tr.), Mt.18,6 ; L.
   10,15.*
[demeto], messus, 3, *reap*,
   Ap.14,16.*
†§deminutio, onis, *f., diminu-
   tion, lessening*, R.11,12.*
demolior, 4, *demolish, lay
   waste*, Mt.§6,16 ; 6,19 f.*
demonstro, 1, *show*, Mk.14,
   15 ; J.5,20 ; 1 C.12,31 ;
   teach, Mt.3,7.*
demoror, 1, *abide, dwell*, J.
   3,22 ; A.14,3.
*denarius, ii, *m., denarius,
   penny*.
denego, 1, *deny*, Mk.8,34 ;
   §L.12,9.*
dens, ntis, *m., tooth*.
denuntio, 1, (1) *announce,
   declare*, 2 Th.3,6 ; *order*,
   A.23,30 ;   (2) *menace,
   threaten, warn*, 1 T.1,3.
denuo, *again*, Mk.14,40 ;
   J.3,3 ff ; G.4,9.*
deorsum, *down, downwards*,
   Mt.27,51 ff ; *beneath*, Mk.
   14,66 ; A.2,19.
depereo, ii, 4, *perish*, Jas.1,
   11.*
depono, posui, positus, 3,
   take down, Mk.15,36 ; *put
   or lay down*, L.1,52 ; A.
   7,58 ; *lay aside*, H.12,1 ;
   1 P.2,1.
.*depositio, onis, *f., laying
   down, putting aside*, 1 P.
   3,21 ; 2 P.1,14.*

depositum, i, *n.*, *deposit*, 1 T.
6,20 ; 2 T.1,12 ff.* Gk.
παραθήκη.

deprauo, 1, *pervert, distort*,
2 P.3,16.*

deprecatio, onis, *f.*, *prayer*,
L.1,13 ; Ph.1,4 ; Jas.
5,16.*

deprecor, 1, *pray*, A.10,2 ;
beseech, Ph.4,2.

deprehendo, hensus, 3, *take*,
J.8,3 f.*

deputo, 1, *account, reckon*,
L.22,37.*

derelinquo, liqui, lictus, 3,
leave, A.2,27 ff.; *forsake*,
H.13,5.

derideo, 2, *mock, deride*, Mt.
9,24 ; L.8,53 ; 16,14 ;
23,35.*

descendo, di, 3, *come* or *go
down, descend*.

descensus, us, *m.*, *descent*,
L.19,37.*

describo, 3, *enrol*, L.2,1.*

descriptio, onis, *f.*, *enrolment*,
L.2,2.*

desero, sertus, 3, *desert, forsake*, H.10,25 ; 13,5.*

desertum, i, *n.*, *desert*, 1 C.
10,5 ; H.3,8.

desertus, a, um, *deserted,
desert*.

deseruio, 4, *serve*, H.8,5 ;
13,10 ; *wait on*, Mk.3,9.

[†**desideratus], a, um** (only
superl.), *wished for, longed
for*, Ph.4,1.*

desiderium, ii, *n.*, *longing,
desire*, 2 C.7,7 ff.; *lust*,
2 P.2,18.

desidero, 1, (1) *desire*, 1 Ti.
3,1 ; (2) *have need of,
need*, ||Mk.14,63 ; 1 Th.
4,12. (The superl. of the
partic. §**desiderantissimus**
= *best beloved* in Ph.4,1.)

designo, 1, *appoint*, L.10,1.*

desino, sii, 3, *cease*, A.13,10 ;
1 P.4,1.*

desolatio, onis, *f.*, *desolation*,
||Mt.24,15 ; L.21,20.*

desolo, 1, *forsake, desert*, 1
Th.2,17 ; 1 T.5,5 ; *make
desolate*, ||Mt.12,25.

despero, 1, *despair, be hope-
less*, E.4,19.*

despicio, 3, *neglect, overlook*,
A.6,1 ; 17,30.*

†**despolio,** 1, *strip, spoil*, L.
10,30.*

despondeo, di, 2, *espouse*,
2 C.11,2.*

desponso, 1, *betroth*, Mt.1,18 ;
L.1,27 ; 2,5.*

†**despumo,** 1, *foam out*, Jude
13.*

destino, 1, *doom, determine,
appoint*, 1 C.4,9 ; 2 C.8,
19 ; 9,7 ; Ph.3,14.*

destituo, tutus, 3, *forsake,
desert ; make desolate*, 2
C.4,8 ; Ap.18,17.*

†**destitutio, onis,** *f.*, *putting
away, abandoning*, H.9,
26.*

*destructio, onis, f., *destruction*, 2 C.10,4 ff.; 13,10.
destruo, struxi, 3, *destroy*, R.3,31 ; H.2,14.
desum, fui, esse, *be wanting*, Co.1,24 ; 1 Th.3,10 ; *fail*, H.12,15.
desuper (Mt.21,7), also de super (J.19,11), *from above, above.*
[desursum], de sursum, *from above*, J.3,31 ; Jas.1,17 ; 3,15 ff.*
deterior, ius, *worse.*
detestor, 1, *curse*, Mt.26,74.*
detineo, 2, *hold* [J.5,4] ; *hold back*, R.1,18 ; *retain, constrain*, L.4,42.
detractio, onis, f., *slander, back-biting*, 2 C.12,20 ; 1 P.2,1.*
†detracto (-trecto), 1, *depreciate, speak evil of*, 1 P.2,12.*
detractor, oris, m., *slanderer, back-biter*, R.1,30.*
detraho, traxi, tractus, 3, (1) *pull down*, A.19,33 ; 2 P.2,4 ; (2) *detract from, disparage*, 1 T.3,11 ; Jas. 4,11 ; 1 P.3,16.*
detrimentum, i, n., *loss*, 1 C.3,15 ; Ph.3,7 f.
†deturpo, 1, *defile, dishonour*, 1 C.11,4 f.*
Deus, i, m., *God ;* pl. dii, *false Gods*, A.14,11.
deuasto, 1, *lay waste*, A.8,3.*

deuenio, ueni, 4, *come*, A.26, 7 ; *come down*, A.9,32 ; *arrive*, A.27,3 ff.
†§deuerto, 3, *put up, lodge*, L.9,12.*
†§deuinco, uici, 3, *subdue*, H.11,33.*
deuito, 1, *avoid*, 1 T.4,7 ; Ti.3,9.
deuorator, oris, m., *glutton*, L.7,34.*
deuoro, 1, *eat up*, Ap.10,9 f.; *devour*, L.15,30 ; *engulf* (of sea), H.11,29.
†deuotio, onis, f., *cursing, curse*, A.23,14.*
deuoueo, uoui, 2, *devote one's self, take a curse on one's self*, A.23,12 ff.*
dexter, era, erum (acc. sing. dextrum, dat. and abl. plur. dextris), *of the right hand, right.*
dextera, ae, f., *right hand.*
°diabolicus, a, um, *devilish*, Jas.3,15.*
°diabolus, i, m., *devil.*
*°†diaconus, i, m., (only in pl. nom. diacones (-coni), acc. diaconos, abl. diaconibus), *deacon*, Ph.1,1 ; 1 T.3,8 ff.*
°diadema, atis, n., *crown*, Ap.12,3 ; 13,1 ; 19,12.*
dico, xi, ctus, 3, *say.*
dictum, i, n., *saying, command*, Ti.3,1.*
°didragma (-drachma), atis,

n., *didrachma*, *half-shekel*, Mt.17,24 (bis).*

dies, ei, *m.* and *f.*, *day.*

diffamo, 1, (1) *spread abroad, publish,* Mt.9,31 ; Mk. 1,45 ; 1 Th.1,8 ; (2) *slander, accuse,* L.16,1.*

†**differens,** **entis** (compar. **-entior**), *superior, excellent,* H.1,4.*

differo, distuli, ferre, (1) *put off,* A.24,23 ; (2) *differ,* R. 12,6 ; 1 C.15,41 ; G.4,1.*

difficile, *with difficulty, hardly,* ‖Mt.19,23.*

difficilis, e, *difficult,* Mk.10, 34 ; 2 P.3,16.*

***diffidentia, ae,** *f.*, *want of faith ; disobedience,* R.4, 20 ; E.2,2 ; 5,6.*

diffundo, fusus, 3, *shed abroad,* A.1,18 ; R.5,5.*

digitus, i, *m.*, *finger,* Mk.7, 33 ; J.8,6.

digne, *worthily,* R.16,2 ; 3 J.6.

dignor, 1, *deem worthy,* 2 Th. 1,11.*

dignus, a, um, *worthy,* ‖Mt. 3,8 ; L.7,4.

diiudico, 1, *judge,* 1 C.14,24 ; *discern,* 1 C.11,29.

†**dilanio,** 1, *tear,* L.9,39.*

dilatio, onis, *f.*, *delay,* A. 25,17.*

dilato, 1, *make wide, enlarge,* Mt.23,5 ; 2 C.6,11 ff.*

dilectio, onis, *f.*, *love.*

diligenter, *well, diligently.*

diligentia, ae, *f.*,(1) *diligence,* A.5,23 ; (2) **diligentiam habere,** *take care of,* 1 T. 3,5.*

diligo, lexi, lectus, 3, *love.*

diluculo, *early in the morning, at daybreak,* Mk.1,35 ; L. 24,1.; J.8,2.*

diluuium, ii, *n.*, *flood,* Mt.24, 38 f.; L.17,27 ; 2 P.2,5.*

dimidium, ii, *n.*, *half,* Mk.6, 23 ; L.19,8 ; Ap.12,14.*

dimidius, a, um, *half,* Ap. 11,9 ; 11,11.*

diminuo, ui, 3, *diminish, take away,* Ap.22,19.*

[**diminutio**], **onis,** *f.*, *diminishing,* R.11,12.*

dimitto, misi, missus, 3, (1) *send away, dismiss,* L.1, 53 ; *put away, divorce,* Mt.1,19 ; *forgive,* Mt.6, 12 ; (2) *leave, leave behind* Mk.10,28 ; *let alone,* L.13, 8 ; (3) ? *let down,* 2 C.11, 33 ; (4) *permit, suffer,* Mt.3,15.

dinumero, 1, *number,* Ap.7, 9.*

†**dipondius, ii,** *m.*, *the sum of two asses,* L.12,6.*

directus, a, um, *straight,* L.3 5.*

dirigo, 3, *make straight,* J.1, 23 ; *direct,* L.1,79 ; 1 Th.3,11 ; 2 Th.3,5 ; Jas. 3,4.*

diripio, 3, *spoil, despoil, rob,*
‖Mt.12,29.*
dirumpo, v. **disr-.**
diruo, rutus, 3, *demolish,
destroy,* A.15,16.*
discedo, cessi, 3, *depart.*
disceptatio, onis, *f., disputa-
tion, discussion,* R.14,1 ;
1 T.2,8.*
discepto, 1, *dispute,* A.11,2.*
discerno, creui, 3, *make a
difference, discern,* A.15,
9 ; R.14,23 ; *make to
differ,* 1 C.4,7.*
discerpo, 3, *tear asunder,
tear in pieces,* Mk.1,26 ;
9,26 ; A.23,10.*
***discessio, onis,** f. ; (1) *going
away, departure,* A.20,29;
21,21 ; (2) *apostasy,* 2
Th.2,3.*
disciplina, ae, *f., instruc-
tion, knowledge,* E.6,4 ;
chastening, H.12,5 ff.
disciplinatus, a, um, *in-
structed, disciplined,* Jas.
3,13.*
†**discipula, ae,** *f., female disciple,* A.9,36.*
·**discipulus, i,** *m., disciple.*
disco, didici, 3, *learn.*
†°**discolus (dys-), a, um,**
peevish, irritable, 1 P.2,
18.*
***discretio, onis,** *f., discern-
ing,* 1 C.12,10 ; H.5,14.*
†**discretor, oris,** *m., dis-
cerner,* H.4,12.*

discubitus, us, *m., place at
table,* ‖Mk.12,39.*
discumbo, cubui, 3, *sit down,
recline,* J.6,10 f.; *sit at
table,* Mt.9,10 ; J.12,2.
°**discus, i,** *m., dish,* ‖Mt.14,
8.*
***dispensatio, onis,** *f., man-
agement, stewardship,* 1
C.9,17 ; *economy, dis-
pensation,* E.1,10 ; 3,2 ff.;
Co.1,25.*
dispensator, oris, *m., steward,*
L.12,42 ; 1 C.4,1 f.; Ti.
1,7 ; 1 P.4,10.*
disperdo, 3, *destroy,* A.13,41;
1 C.3,17.*
dispergo, ersi, ersus, 3, *scatter, disperse,* J.10,12 ; 2
C.9,9.
dispersio, onis, *f., scattering
abroad ;* dispersion, J.7,
35 ; Jas.1,1 ; 1 P.1,1.*
Gk. διασπορά.
dispertio, 4, *divide, distribute,*
Mk.3,25 f.; A.2,3.*
dispono, posui, 3, *arrange,
set in order,* 1 C.11,34 ;
appoint, L.22,29 ; *make
(covenant),* A.3,25 ; H.
8,10.
dispositio, onis, *f., disposi-
tion, appointment,* A.7,
53.*
disputo, 1, *dispute, contend.*
disrumpo, rupi, 3, *rend,
burst,* Mt.7,6 ; Mk.2,22 ;
5,4.*

disseco, 1, *cut asunder ;* in pass., *be cut* (to the heart), A.5,33 ; 7,54.*

dissemino, 1, *spread abroad,* A.13,49.*

dissero, 3, (1) *dispute, discuss,* A.17,2 ; 17,18 ; (2) *explain, expound,* §Mt.13, 37 ; Mk.4,34.*

dissipo, 1, (1) *scatter abroad,* A.5,36 ; (2) *waste, squander,* L.15,13 ; 16,1 ; (3) *rend,* L.9,39 ff.

dissoluo, 3, *unloose, dissolve,* Ph.1,23 ; *destroy,* Mk. 14,58 ; 1 J.3,8.

distendo, tentus, 3, *stretch asunder, torture,* H.11, 35.*

*distinctio, onis, *f.*, *distinction, difference,* R.3,22 ; 10,12 ; 1 C.14,7.*

distribuo, ui, 3, *distribute, divide,* J.6,11 ; 1 C.13,3.

distributio, onis, *f.*, *division, distribution,* H.2,4.*

[†°dithalassus], a, um, *between two seas,* A.27,41.*

diu (compar. diutius, A.24,4), *for a long while,* A.20,9 ; 28,6.*

†diurnus, a, um, *daily, day by day,* Mt.20,2.*

diuersorium, ii, *n.*, *lodging-place, inn ; guest chamber,* L.2,7 ; 22,11.*

diuerto, uerti, 3, *turn aside, lodge,* [L.9,12] ; 19,7 *

(same Greek word in both verses).

diues, itis, *rich.*

diuido, uisi, uisus, 3, *divide.*

*diuinitas, tatis, *f.*, *divinity, godhead,* R.1,20 ; Co.2,9; Ap.5,12.*

diuinitus, *divinely,* 2 T.3,16.*

diuino, 1, *prophesy, predict,* A.16,16.*

diuinum, i, *n.*, *the Deity,* A.17,29.*

diuinus, a, um, *divine,* R.11, 4 ; 2 P.1,3 f.*

diuisio, onis, *f.*, (1) *dividing,* H.4,12 ; (2) *diversity,* 1 C.12,4 ff.*

†diuisor, oris, *m.*, *divider,* L.12,14.*

diuitiae, arum, *f.*, *riches.*

diuulgo, 1, *spread abroad,* L. 1,65 ; 4,37 ; A.4,17 ; R. 16,19.*

do, dedi, datus, 1, *give.*

doceo, cui, doctus, 2, *teach.*

*docibilis, e, *teachable, easily taught,* J.6,45 ; 2 T.2,24.*

doctor, oris, *m.*, *teacher,* A. 13,1 ; 1 C.12,28 ; *doctor* (of the law), Mt.22,35.

doctrina, ae, *f.*, *teaching, doctrine,* J.7,16 f.; H. 6,1.

dogma, atis, *n.*, *decree,* A. 16,4.*

doleo, 2, (only in partic. dolens), *grieve, sorrow,* L.2,48 ; A.4,2.

dolor, oris, *m.*, *grief, sorrow,*
Mt.24,8 ; *pain,* A.2,24 ;
Ap.16,10 f.
dolose, *deceitfully,* R.3,13.*
dolus, i, *m.*, *guile,* 2 Co.12,16;
craft, deceit, 1 P.2,1 ff.
domesticus, a, um, *belonging
to a house, household,*
Mt.10,25 ; E.2,19.
domicilium, ii, *n.*, *dwelling,
abode,* Mk.5,3 ; Judc 6.*
domina, ae, *f.*, *lady,* 2 J.
1 ff.*
dominatio, onis, *f.*, *dominion,
power,* 2 P.2,10 ; Jude 8 ;
in pl. (Co.1,16) *of angelic
powers, dominations.*
dominator, oris, *m.*, *ruler,
master,* Jude 4.*
dominicus, a, um, *belonging
to the Lord, the Lord's,*
1 C.11,20 ; Ap.1,10.*
dominor, 1, *have* or *exercise
dominion, rule,* R.7,1 ;
Ap.19,16 ; *prevail over,*
A.19,16.
dominus, i, *m.*, *lord.*
domo, mitus, 1, *tame,* Mk.
5,4 ; Jas.3,7 f.*
domus, us, *f.*, *house.*
donatio, onis, *f.*, *giving, gift,*
R.5,17 ; 12,6 ; 2 C.1,11 ;
E.4,7.*
dono, 1, *give, grant.*
donum, i, *n.*, *gift.*
dormio, 4, *sleep,* Mk.4,27 ;
J.11,11 f.; *fall asleep,*
1 C.15,6 ; 2 P.3,4.

dormitio, onis, *f.*, *sleeping,*
J.11,13.*
dormito, 1, *slumber,* Mt.25,
5 ; 2 P.2,3.*
dorsum, i, *n.*, *back,* R.11,10.*
draco, onis, *m.*, *dragon,* Ap.
12,3 ff.; 13,2 ff.; 16,13 ;
20,2.*
°dragma (drach-), ae, *f.*,
drachma, L.15,8 f.*
dubitatio, onis, *f.*, *hesitation,*
A.10,29.*
dubito, 1, *doubt,* Mt.14,31 ;
28,17 ; A.10,20.*
dubius, a, um, *doubtful,* 1 T.
6,7 ; sine dubio, *doubt-
less,* 1 C.15,27.*
ducatus, us, *m.*, *leading,
guidance,* Mt.15,14.*
duco, xi, ctus, 3, (1) *lead,
lead away,* 1 C.12,2 ; 2
T.3,6 ; (2) *marry,* Mt.
22,24 f.; (3) *think, consider,* H.10,29.
dulcis, e, *sweet.*
dummodo, *if only, provided
that,* A.20,24.*
duplex, icis, *double,* 1 T.5,17 ;
Jas.1,8 ; 4,8 ; Ap.18,6.*
duplico, 1, *double,* Ap.18,
6.*
†duplo, *doubly,* Mt.23,15.*
duplus, a, um, *double,* Ap.
18,6.*
dure (compar. -rius), *hardly,
harshly,* 2 C.13,10 ; Ti.
1,13.*
duritia, ae, *f.*, *hardness,* Mt.

19,8 ; Mk.10,5 ; 16,14 ;
R.2,5.*

durus, a, um, *hard.*

dux, cis, *c., leader, chief ;
guide.*

dyscolus, v. **disc-.**

°**dysenteria, ae,** *f., dysentery,*
A.28,8.*

E

ebrietas, tatis, *f., drunken-
ness,* L.21,34 ; R.13,13 ;
G.5,21.*

ebriosus, a, um, *drunken*
[Mt.24,50] ; 1 C.5,11 ; 6,
10.*

ebrius, a, um, *drunken,* A.2,
15 ; 1 C.11,21.

ebur, oris, *n., ivory,* Ap.18,
12.*

°**ecclesia, ae,** *f., assembly*
(A.19,32 ff.) ; (Jewish)
Church, A.7,38 ; *the
Christian Church.*

[**econtra**], **e contra,** *on the
contrary,* G.2,7.*

[**econtrario**], **e contrario,** *con-
trariwise, on the contrary,*
2 C.2,7 ; 1 P.3,9.*

edictum, i, *n., edict, decree,*
L.2,1 ; H.11,23.*

edissero, 3, *declare, explain,*
Mt.[13,36] ; 15,15.*

ĕdo, 3,'*eat.*

edoceo, doctus, 2, *teach,*

· *instruct* [Mt.28,15] ; A.
18,25 ; E.4,21.*

edūco, 1, *bring up, train,
educate,* E.6,4 ; 1 T.5,
10.*

edūco, xi, 3, *lead out* or *forth,*
J.10,3 ; *pull out,* L.6,
42.

effero, extuli, elatus, ferre,
(1) *bring forth* (for burial),
L.7,12 ; A.5,6 ff.; (2)
puff up, 1 T.3,6.*

†**effetha (ephph-),** (Aram.),
be opened, Mk.7,34.*

†**efficax, cacis,** *efficient,
powerful,* H.4,12.*

efficio, fectus, 3, *make,* H.1,
4 ; *perform,* R.15,18 ;
(in pass.) *become,* Mt.13,
22 ; 1 P.3,22.

effigies, ei, *f., form,* Mk.16,
12.*

§**effluo,** 3, *flow* or *slip away,*
H.2,1.*

effodio, 3, *dig, dig out,* Mt.
6,19 f.*

effugio, fugi, 3, *escape,* A.19,
16 ; R.2,3.

effundo, fudi, fusus, 3, (1)
pour out, J.2,15 ; Ap.16,
1 ff.; *shed,* L.11,50 ; R.
3,15 ; (2) (in pass.) *rush
on thoughtlessly,* Jude 11.

effusio, onis, *f., shedding* (of
blood), H.[9,22] ; 11,28.*

egenus, a, um, *poor, needy* ;
J.12,5 f.; 13,29 ; 2 C.
8,9 ; *beggarly,* G.4,9.*

egeo, 2, *need, be in want,* A. 4,34 ; Ap.3,17.

*****eger (aeg-), gra, grum,** *sick,* [Mk.6,13 ; 16,18], A.5, 16.*****

egredior, gressus, 3, *go* or *come out,* L.1,22 ; *depart,* A.12,17.

eicio (elicio), ieci, iectus, 3, *cast out,* Mk.1,34 ; J.9, 34 f.; *drive out,* J.2,15.

eiulo, v. **helu-.**

*****eiusmodi,** *of such a kind, such,* R.2,14 ; 1 C.5,11 ; Ph.2,29.

elatus, v. **effero.**

elegans, antis, *proper, fine,* H.11,23.*****

elementa, orum, *n., elements,* 2 P.3,10 ff.; *first beginnings,* H.5,12.

°elemosyna (eleemo-), ae, *f., alms,* Mt.6,2 ff.; A. 3,2 ff.

eleuo, 1, *raise, lift* or *take up,* Mk.1,31 ; L.6,20 ; A.1,9.

Eli, v. **Heli.**

elido, si, sus, 3, *dash down,* ‖Mk.9,20.*****

eligo, legi, lectus, 3, *gather out,* Mt.13,48 ; *choose, elect,* L.6,13 ; J.15,16 ff.; 1 C.1,27 f.

Eloi, v. **Heloi.**

eloquens, entis, *eloquent,* A. 18,24.*****

eloquium, ii, *n., word, saying,* R.3,2.*****

†**eloquor,** 3, *speak,* A.2,4 ; §26, 25.*****

elucesco, 3, *become light ; break* (of day), 2 P.1,19.*****

emano, 1, *pour forth,* Jas. 3,11.*****

emendo, 1, *correct, chastise,* L.23,16.*****

emineo, 2 (only in partic. **eminens**), *conspicuous, prominent,* 2 C.9,14 ; Ph. 3,8.*****

emitto, misi, missus, 3, *send, put* or *cast forth,* Mt.15, 17 ; *cast off* [Ap.6,13].

emo, emi, emptus, 3, *buy.*

emortuus, a, um, *dead,* R. 4,19 ; H.11,12 ; §Jas.2, 26.*****

emundatio, onis, *f., cleansing,* ‖Mk.1,44 ; H.9.13.*****

emundo, 1, *cleanse,* 2 T.2, 21 ; H.9,14 ; Jas.4,8 ; 1 J.1,9.*****

enarro, 1, *declare,* J.1,18 ; A.8,33 ; *narrate, tell of,* H.11,32.

†**enato,** 1, *swim out,* A.27, 42.*****

†§**enauigo,** 1, *sail out* or *away,* L.8,26 ; A.20,13.*****

†°**encenia, orum,** *n., feast of dedication* (of Temple), J.10,22.*****

°enigma (aen-), atis, *n., enigma, riddle,* 1 C.13,12*****

enutrio, 4, *nourish, rear,* §A. 7,21 ; 1 T.4,6 ; Jas.5,5.*****

eo, ii, fut. part. iturus (J.7, 35), 4, go.

eo quod, for the reason that, because.

Epicurous, a, um, of Epicurus, Epicurean, A.17, 18.*

episcopatus, us, m., office, A.1,20 ; office of bishop, 1 T.3,1.*

°episcopus, i, m., bishop, overseer.

°epistula (-tola), ae, f., letter, epistle.

epulum, i, n., feast, Jude 12.*

epulor, 1, keep feast, 1 C.5, 8 ; be merry, L.12,19 ; 15,23 ff.; 16,19 ; Jas., 5,5.*

eques, itis, m., horseman, horse-soldier, A.23,23 ; 23 32.*

equester, tris, tre, of horsemen, cavalry, Ap.9,16.*

equus, i, m., horse.

eradico, 1, root up, Mt.13, 29; 15,13; L.17,6; Jude, 12.*

erga, towards, concerning, in respect to [L.10,41] ; Ph. 2,30.*

ergo, therefore.

erigo, rexi, rectus, 3, raise or lift up, L.1,69 ; A.9,41 ; 15,16.

eripio, pui, 3, snatch away, rescue, save, deliver, A.7,

10 ; 2 C.1,10 ; 1 Th.1, 10 ; 2 T.3,11.

erogo, 1, spend money, ||Mk. 5,26.*

erro, 1, go astray, ||Mt.18, 12 f.; err, make a mistake, H.3,10 ; Jas.1,16.

erubesco, bui, 3, be ashamed, L.13,17 ; 2 C.9,4 ; be ashamed of, L.9,26 ; R. 1,16.

eructo, 1, bring forth, declare, Mt.13,35.*

erudio, 4, teach, instruct, A.7,22.

eruditor, oris, m., teacher, instructor, R.2,20 ; H. 12,9.*

erugino (aer-), 1, become rusty, cankered, Jas.5,3.*

erugo (aer-), ginis, f., rust, Mt.6,19 f.; Jas.5,3.*

erumpo, 3, break forth, G.4, 27.*

eruo, ui, 3, pluck out, deliver, Mt.5,29 ; 18,9 ; 2 C.1, 10 ; G.4,15.*

esca, ae, f., food, meat, Mt. 3,4 ; 1 C.3,2 ; piece of food, H.12,16 ; eating, R.14,17.

esurio, 4, be hungry, Mk.2, 25 ; J.6,35 ; 1 C.4,11.

°ethnicus, i, m., heathen, gentile, Mt.5,47 ; 6,7 ; 18,17.*

euge, well done / ||Mt.25, 21 ff.*

°**eunuchus, i,** *m., eunuch,* Mt.
19,12 ; A.8,27 ff.*

†**euroaquilo, onis,** *m., north
east wind,* A.27,14.*

euacuo, 1, *make void, empty,*
R.3,3; *lay aside,* 1 C.13,11.

euado, si, 3, *escape,* A.27,
43 f.; 28,1 ff.*

euagino, 1; *unsheath,* A.16,
27.*

euanesco, nui, 3 ; (1) *vanish,*
L.24,31 ; (2) *become vapid,
saltless,* ||Mt. 5,13 ; (3)
become foolish, R.1,21.*

°**euangelista, ae,** *m., evan-
gelist,* A.21,8 ; E.4,11 ;
2 T.4,5.*

°**euangelium, ii,** *n., gospel.*

°**euangelizo,** 1, *preach,* E.2,
17 ; *preach the gospel,*
R.1,15.

euenio, uentum, 4, *come,
come upon,* Mk.10,32 ;
[11,24.]*

†**euerro,** 3, *sweep, sweep out,*
L.15,8 (where nearly all
MSS. read " euertit ").*

euersio, onis, *f., overthrow,
destruction,* 2 P.2,6.*

euerto, ti, 3, *overthrow,* ||Mt.
21,12 ; *disturb, agitate,*
A.15,24.*

euidens, entis, *evident,* 1 C.
16,9 ; Philem.6.*

euigilo, 1, *awake,* L.9,32 ;
1 C.15,34.*

euomo, 3, *spew out, vomit,*
Ap.3,16.*

exacerbatio, onis, *f., provo-
cation,* H.3,8 ff. (bis).*

exacerbo, 1, *provoke,* H.3,
16.*

exactor, oris, *m., officer,
minister* (of justice), L.
12,58.*

exaestuo, 1, *be scorched,* Mk.
4,6.*

exagito, 1, *drive,* 2 P.2,17.*

exaltatio, onis, *f., lifting up
exaltation,* Jas.1,9.*

exalto, 1, *lift up, exalt,* L.1,
52 ; 1 P.5,6.

examino, 1, *try, examine,
test,* 1 C.2,14.*

exardeo, arsi, 2, *burn, be in-
flamed,* R.1,27.*

exaresco, rui, 3, *dry up,
wither,* Mk.4,6 ; 1 P.1,
24.*

exaudio, 4, *hear.*

excaeco, 1, *blind, make blind,*
J.12,40 ; R.11,7 ; 2 C.
4,4.*

excedo, 3, *go beyond, pass
out of,* 2 C.5,13.*

excellens, entis, *excellent,* 1 C.
12,31 ; 2 C.3,10.*

excelsus, a, um, *high, lofty,*
||Mt.17,1 ; A.13,17 ; *the
Most High,* A.7,48.

excessus, us, *m.* ; (1)
decease, death, L.9,31 ;
(2) *ecstasy, trance,* A.10,
10 ; 11,5.*

excido, di, sus, 3, *cut down,*
Mt.3,10 ; *cut off,* R.11,

22 ff.; *hew out*, ||Mt.27, 60.

excido, di, 3, *fall, fall away ; fail*, A.27,32 ; G.5,4.

excipio, cepi, ceptus, 3 ; (1) *receive*, J.4,45 ; (2) *meet*, L.8,40 ; (3) *except*, Mt. 5,32 ; A.26,29.

excito, 1, *raise*, J.2,19 f.; *wake up*, Mk.4,38 ; *stir up*, A.13,50.

exclamo, 1, *call, cry out*.

excludo, clusus, 3, *shut out, exclude*, R.3,27 ; G.4,17.*

†**excolo**, 1, *strain out*, Mt.23, 24.*

excusatio, onis, *f*., *excuse*, J. 15,22.*

excuso, 1, *excuse ; make excuse*, L.14,18 f.; 2 C. 12,19 ; H.12,19.*

excutio, cussus, 3, *shake off*, ||Mt.10,14 ; *shake out*, A.18,6.

execrabilis, e, *accursed, detestable*, 2 P.2,11.*

execro, 1,. *curse ;* P.P. **execratus**, *accursed, detestable*, Ap.21,8.*

exemplar, aris, *n*., *pattern, copy*, H.8,5 ; 9,23 f.*

exemplum, i, *n*., *example*.

exeo, iui or **ii**, 4, *go out, come out, depart*.

exerceo, 2, *exercise*, Mt.20, 25 ; 1 T.4,7.*

exercitatio, onis, *f*., *exercise*, 1 T.4,8.*

exercito, 1, only in P.P. **exercitatus**, *exercised*, H. 5,14 ; 12,11 ; 2 P.2,14.*

exercitus, us, *m*., *army ; body of soldiers*, A.23,27.

†**exfornicatus, a, um**, *having committed fornication*, Jude 7.*

exhaurio, 4, *take away, remove*, H.9,28.*

exhibeo, 2, *deliver, present*, R.6,13 ff. ; 2 C.11,2 ; *shew, display*, 2 C.6,4 ; 7,11 ; *entertain*, A.28,7.

exhonoro, 1, *dishonour*, Jas. 2,6.*

exhortor, 1, *exhort*.

exigo, igi (**exigissem**, L.19, 23), 3, *exact, receive*, L.19,23.*

exiguus, a, um, *small*, A.27, 20.*

exilio, iui or **ii**, 4, *leap up*, Mk.10,50 ; A.3,8 ; 14, 10 ff.*

†**eximo, emi**, 3, *draw out* (sword), Mt.26,51.*

†§**exin**, *then, next*, 1 C.12,28.

exinanio, 4, *empty, make void*, R.4,14 ; Ph.2,7.*

exinde, *thenceforth, then*.

existimo, 1, *think, suppose*.

existo, 3, *exist, be*, G.1,14.*

exitus, us, *m*., *egress, outlet ; issue*, Mt.22,9 ; H.13,7 ; [Jas.5,10].*

†°**exorcista, ae**, *m*., *exorcist*, A.19,13.*

exordium, ii, *n., beginning,* H.5,12.*

exorior, ortus, 4, *rise, spring up.*

expando, di, 3, *spread forth,* R.10,21.*

expauesco, paui, 3, *be greatly terrified,* Mk.9,15 ; 16, 6.*

expecto, 1, *expect, look for,* ||Mt.11,3 ; *await, wait for,* J.5,3 ; A.1,4.

expedio, 4, *be expedient,* H. 13,17.

expello, puli, 3, *drive out* or *forth,* Mk.1,12 ; 5,10 ; L.13,28 ; A.7,45.*

expergefacio, factus, 3, *awaken,* A.16,27.*

experimentum, i, *n., proof, test, proving,* 2 C.2,9 ; 8, 2 ; 13,3 ; Ph.2,22.*

experior, pertus, 4, *try, make trial of,* H.11,29 ; 11,36.*

†**expers, ertis,** *having no part in, without share in,* H. 5,13.*

expeto, iui, 3, *seek after, desire,* L.22,31.*

*****expiro,** also **exspiro,** 1, *expire, give up the ghost,* ||Mk.15,37 ; A.5,5 ; 5, 10.*

expleo, pletus, 2, *fulfil,* A.7, 30 ; [21,5 ff.] ; 24,28.

expletio, onis, *f., fulfilment, accomplishment,* A.21,26 ; H.6,11.*

explico, plicitus, 1, *end,* §A. 21,5 ff. (bis).*

explorator, oris, *m., spy,* H.11,31.*

exploro, 1, *search out, examine,* G.2,4.*

†**expoliatio, onis,** *f., spoiling,* Co.2,11.*

expolio, 1, *rob, spoil, strip,* 2 C.5,4 ; 11,8 ; Co.2,15 ; 3,9.*

expono, posui, positus, 3, (1) *expound,* A.11,4 ; (2) *unlade, disembark,* A.21, 3 ; (3) *expose* (infant), A.7,19 ff.

exprobro, 1, *accuse, upbraid,* Mt.11,20 ; Mk.16,14 ; L. 6,22 ; 1 P.4,14.*

expugno, 1, *attack ; ?destroy, lay waste,* A.9,21 ; G.1, 13 ; 1,23.* Gk. πορθῶ.

expuo, ui, 3, *spit, spit upon,* Mk.7,33 ; J.9,6.

†**expurgo,** 1, *purge out,* 1 C.5, 7.*

exquiro, isii, 3, *enquire,* Mt. 2,16 ; 1 P.1,10.*

exspiro, v. expiro.

†**exsupero (exu-),** 1, *surpass,* Ph.4,7.*

exsurgo, surrexi, 3, *rise, arise.*

§**exsuscito,** 1, *arouse, awake,* J.11,11.*

°**extasis** (abl. i), *f., amazement,* A.3,10.*

extendo, di, tus, 3, *stretch out,*

J.21,18; A.4,30; Ph.3, 13.

extergo, ersi, 3, *wipe, wipe off.* L.10,11 ; J.11,2 ; 12, 3 ; 13,5.

exterior, oris, *outer* (always with **tenebrae**), Mt.8,12 ; 22,13 ; 25,30.*

exterminator, oris, *m.*, *destroyer,* 1 C.10,10.*

extermino, 1, *remove out of sight* [Mt.6,16] ; (2) *destroy,* A.3,23 ; Jas.4,15 ; Ap.9,11 ; 11,18.* (In Ap.9,11, **Exterminans** translates *Apollyon.*)

exterreo, 2, *terrify greatly,* Mt.28,4 ; Mk.9,6 ; H. 12,21.*

exterus, a, um, *foreign, alien,* A.26,11 ; H.11,34.*

extinguo, xi, 3, *quench, extinguish,* Mk.9,44 ff.; E. 6,16 ; 1 Th.5,19 ; H. 11,34.*

exto, titi, 1, *be conspicuous, rise up,* A.5,36 f.*

extollo, 3, *raise or lift up,* L.11,27 ; 2 C.10,5 ; 11, 20 ; 12,7 ; 2 Th.2,4.*

extraho, 3, *draw or pull out,* L.14,5.*

extremus, a, um, *outermost, utmost, extreme* ; hence **extremum, i,** *n., end, tip,* L.16,24 ; A.13,47 ; **in extremis,** *at the point of death, dying,* Mk.5,23.*

extrinsecus, *outside, without,* Mk.7,18 ; 2 C.11,28 ; 1 P.3,3.*

exultatio, onis, *f., rejoicing, gladness,* L.1,14 ; A.2,46 ; H.1,9 ; Jas.4,16 ; Jude 24.*

exulto, 1, *leap for joy, rejoice, be glad, exult.*

exuo, ui, 3, *strip,* ‖Mt.27, 28 f.*

exupero, exurgo, v. exsu-.

[exuro], 3, *burn up,* 2 P.3, 10.*

F

faber, bri, *m., carpenter,* ‖Mt.13,55.*

fabrico, 1, *build, make,* H.3, 3 f.; 1 P.3,20.*

fabula, ae, *f., story, fable,* 1 T.1,4 ; 4,7 ; 2 P.1,16.

†**fabulor,** 1, *talk, converse,* L.24,15.*

facies, ei, *f., face, appearance.*

facile, *easily, readily,* 1 T.6, 18.*

facilis, e (only in compar. **facilius**), *easy,* ‖Mt.9,5 ; ‖19,24 ; L.16,17.*

facinus, oris, *n., crime,* A.18, 14.*

facio, feci, factus, 3, *do, make ;* passive **fio, factus, fieri,** *be made, be done, become, happen.*

factor, oris, *m., doer,* R.2,13 ; Jas.1,22 ff.; 4,11.*

factum, i, *n., deed.*

factura, ae, *f., making, workmanship,* E.2,10.*

facula, ae, *f., torch,* Ap.8,10.*

facultas, tatis, *f.,* (1) *opportunity,* 1 C.7,35 ; (2) (in pl.) *goods, resources,* L.8, 3 ; 1 C.13,3.*

faenerator, (foe-), oris, *m., lender, creditor,* L.7,41.*

faeneror (foe-), 1, *lend on interest,* ·L.6,34.*

faenum (foe-), i, *n., grass, hay.*

fallacia, ae, *f., deceit, deceitfulness,* Mt.13,22 ; A.13, 10 ; Co.2,8 ; H.3,13.*

fallo, 3, *deceive,* Jas.1,22.*

falsus, a, um *false, lying.*

falx, cis, *f., sickle,* Mk.4,29 ; Ap.14,14 ff.*

fama, ae, *f., fame, report,* Mt.9,26 ; 2 C.6,8 ; Ph. 4,8.

fames, is, *f., hunger, famine.*

familia, ae and as, *f., family, household,* Mt.24,44 ; A. 3,25.

famulus, i, *m., servant, slave,* H.3,5.*

farina, ae, *f., meal,* ‖Mt.13, 33.*

fas (indecl.), *n., right, lawful,* A.22,22.*

fasciculus, i, *m., bundle,* Mt. 13,30.*

†**fascino,** 1, *bewitch* (Gk. βασκαίνω), G.3,1.*

fastigium, ii, *n., top, extremity,* H.11,21.*

*****fatigatio, onis,** *f., weariness,* 1 Th.2,9 ; 2 Th.3,8.*

fatigo, 1, *tire, make weary,* J.4,6 ; H.12,3 ff.*

fatuus, a, um, *foolish,* Mt. 5,22 ; 25,2 ff.*

fauus, i, *m., honey-comb,* L. 24,42.*

fax, cis, *f., torch,* J.18,3.*

*****febricito,** 1, *be ill of a fever,* ‖Mt.8,14.*

febris, is, *f., fever,* ‖Mt.8,15 ; J.4,52.

fel, fellis, *n., gall,* Mt.27,34 ; A.8,23.*

femina (foe-), ae, *f., woman.*

femur, (foe-), oris or inis, *n., thigh,* Ap.19,16.*

fenestra, ae, *f., window,* A. 20,9 ; 2 C.11,33.*

fere, *about* (with numbers), A.1,15 ; R.4,19.

fermento, 1, *cause to ferment,* ‖Mt.13,33.*

fermentum, i, *n., leaven.*

fero, tuli, ferre, *bear, carry, take up, take away.*

ferreus, a, um, *made of iron, iron,* A.12,10 ; Ap.2,27 ; 9,9.

ferrum, i, *n., iron.*

ferus, a, um, *fierce, raging,* Jude 13.*

ferueo, 2 (only in partic.

feruens), *be fervent*, A.18, 25 ; R.12,11.*

feruor, oris, *m., burning, heat,* 1 P.4,12.*

festinanter (only in compar. -tius), *speedily,* Ph.2, 28.*

festinatio, onis, *f., haste,* Mk. 6,25 ; L.1,39.*

festino, 1, *haste, make haste,* A.20,16 ; 2 T.4,9.

festiuitas, tatis, *f., festivity, feast,* J.7,37.*

*****festuca, ae,** *f., mote,* ||Mt.7,3 ff.*

festus, a, um, *festal, belonging to the feast,* Mk.14,2 ; J. 2,23 (always joined with **dies**).

°**fiala (phi-), ae,** *f., bowl, vial,* Ap.5,8 ; 15,7 ; 16,1 ff.; 17,1 ; 21,9.*

fictilis, e, *made of earthenware,* 2 C.4,7 ; 2 T.2,20.*

ficulnea, ae, *f., fig-tree,* Mt. 21,19 ff.; L.13,7 ; 21, 29.*

ficus, i and **us,** *f., fig-tree,* ||Mk.11,13 ; *fig,* L.6,44.

fidelis, e, *faithful, believing.*

fideliter, *faithfully,* 3 J.5.*

fidens, entis, *bold, confident,* 2 C.1,9 ; H.2;13.*

fides, ei, *f., faith, the faith, faithfulness.*

fiducia, ae, *f., boldness, confidence.*

fiducialiter, *boldly,* A.9.27 ;

14,3 ; 18,26* (always used with **ago**).

figmentum, i, *n., anything made* or *formed,* R.9, 20.*

figo, xi, xus, 3, *fix,* A.27,41 ; *pitch* (of tabernacle), H. 8,2.*

figulus, i, *m., potter,* Mt.27, 7 ff.; R.9,21 ; Ap.2,27.*

figura, ae, *f., figure* (idol), A.7,43 ; *figure* (type) ; 1 C.10,6 ; *fashion,* 1 C.7, 31.

filia, ae, *f., daughter.*

*****filiolus, i,** *m.,* (only in voc. plur.) *little children,* 1 J. 2,1 ff.; 3,7.

filius, i, *m., son.*

fimbria, ae, *f., edge, border,* ||Mt.9,20 ; ||14,36 ; 23, 5.*

fingo, xi, fictus, 3, (1) *make, fashion,* R.9,20 ; (2) *feign,* L.24,28, 1 T.1,5.

finio, 4, *finish, complete,* Ap.11,7.*

finis, is, *m.,* (1) *end,* Ap.1,8 ; (2) in pl. *territories, borders,* A.13,50.

finitimus, a, um, *neighbouring,* Jude 7.*

fio, v. facio.

firmamentum, i, *n., support, stay,* Co.2,5 ; 1 T.3,15.*

firmitas, tatis, *f., firmness, constancy, firm position,* 2 P.3,17.*

firmo, 1, *set fast, fix,* L.9,51 ;
16,26.*
firmus, a, um, *firm, strong,
sure.*
†fixura, ae, *f., print, imprint,*
J.20,25.*
flagello, 1, *beat, scourge,* J.
19,1 ; H.12,6.
flagellum, i, *n., scourge,* Mk.
15,15 ; J.2,15 ; A.22,
24.*
flamma, ae, *f., flame,* L.16,
24 ; H.1,7.
flatus, us, *m., blast, breeze,*
A.27,15 ; 27,40.*
flecto, flexus, 3 (only with
genu), *bend, bow,* Mk.1,
40; E.3,14.
fleo, eui, 2, *weep.*
fletus, us, *m., weeping.*
flo, 1, *blow* (of wind), L.12,
55 ; J.6,18.
flos, oris, *m., flower,* Jas.1,
10 f.; 1 P.1,24 (bis).*
fluctuo, 1, *waver, vacillate,*
E.4,14.*
fluctus, us, *m., wave.*
flumen, minis, *n., river ;
stream.*
fluo, 3, *flow,* J.7,38.*
fluuius, ii, *m., river,* Ap.22,1;
stream, flood, L.6,49.*
fluxus, us, *m., flow, flux,*
‖Mt.9,20.*
fodio, di, 3, *dig,* ‖Mt.21,33 ;
25,18 ; L.6,48.
foedus, eris, *n., covenant,*
R.1,31.*

foemina, v. femina.
foen-, v. faen-.
folium, ii, *n., leaf.*
fons, tis, *m., fountain, spring,*
Mk.5,29 ; *well,* J.4,6.
foramen, inis, *n.,* (1) *eye of
needle,* ‖Mt.19,24 ; (2)
opening, hole, Jas.3,11.*
foras, *out, outside,* J.6,37 ;
1 J.4,18.
†forensis, e, *belonging to the
forum* or *law-courts,* A.
19,38.*
fores, um, *f., doors,* J.20,19.*
foris, *without, outside,* Co.4,
5 ; Ap.5,1.
forma, ae, *f., fashion, form,*
R.2,20 ; Ph.2,6 ; 2 T.1,
13 ; *pattern,* A.7,44 ;
example, 2 Th.3,9.
formido, 1, *be afraid,* J.14,
27.*
formo, 1, *form,* G.4,19 ; 1 T.
2,13.*
fornax, acis, *f., furnace,* Ap.
9,2.*
fornicaria, ae, *f., harlot,* Ap.
17,16.*
fornicarius, ii, *m., fornicator,*
1 C.5,9 f.; 6.9 ; 1 T.1,
10.*
fornicor, 1, *commit fornication,* 1 C.6,18 ; Ap.2,14.
forsitan, *perchance, perhaps.*
forte, *haply, perhaps* (always
preceded except Mt.11,23
by ne, si or nisi).
fortis, e, *strong, steadfast.*

E

fortiter, *mightily, strongly,* A.19,20.*

fortitudo, dinis, *f., strength, power.*

forum, i, *n., market, market-place,* ||Mt.11,16 ; A.16, 19 ; 28,15.

fouea, ae, *f., pit, lair, hole,* ||Mt.8,20 ; 12,11 ; ||15, 14.*

foueo, 2, *cherish,* E.5,29 ; 1 Th.2,7.*

***fractio, onis,** f., breaking* (of bread), L..24,35 ; A.2, 42.*

fragmentum, i, *n., fragment,* ||Mt.14,20 ; ||15,37.*

frango, fregi, fractus, 3, *break,* J.19,31 ff.; 1 C.10, 16 ; *break off,* R.11,17 ff.

frater, tris, *m., brother.*

fraternitas, tatis, *f., brotherhood,* R.12,10 ; 1 P.2, 17.

fraudo, 1, *defraud,* 1 C.6,8 ; 7,5 ; Ti.2,10 ; *keep back,* A.5,2 ff.; Jas. 5,4.*

fraus, fraudis, *f.,* (1) *deceit, fraud,* Mk.10,19 ; (2) *wrong, injury,* 1 C.6,7.*

fremo, ui, 3, *murmur, rage,* Mk.14,5 ; A.4,25.

frenum, i, *n.* (acc. plur. **frenos** or [**frena**]), *bridle,* Jas.3,2 f.; Ap.14,20.*

frequens, entis, *constant, frequent,* L.10,40 ; 1 T. 5,23.*

frequenter, *often,* Mk.9,22 ; H.9,26.

frequentia, ae, *f., concourse, multitude,* H.12,22.*

fretum, i, *n., sea.* (Always with prep. **trans.**)

frigidus, a, um, *cold,* Mt.10, 42 ; Ap.3,15 f.*

frigus, oris, *n., cold,* J.18,18 ; A.28,2 ; 2 C.11,27.*

frondeo, 2, *put forth leaves,* H.9,4.*

frons, dis, *f., branch, leafy bough,* Mk.11,8.*

frons, tis, *f., forehead* (Ap. only).

fructifico, 1, *bring forth fruit, be fruitful,* Mk.4,20 ; Co. 1,6 ff.

fructus, us, *m., fruit,* Mk.4, 7 ; G.5,22 ; *offspring,* A.2,30.

fruges, um, *f., produce, fruits,* 2 C.9,10.*

frumentum, i, *n., corn, wheat,* Mk.4,28 ; J.12,24 ; A. 7,12.*

fruor, fruitus, 3, *enjoy,* R. 15,24 ; 1 T.6,17 ; Philem. 20.*

frustra, *in vain, vainly,* 1 C. 15,2 ; Co.2,18.*

fuga, ae, *f., flight,* Mt.24,20.*

fugio, gi, 3, *flee, flee away,* Mt.2,13 ; J.10,5 ff.; *flee from,* 1 T.6,11 ; 2 T.2,22.

fulgeo, 2, *shine,* Mt.13,43 ; L.17,24 ; 24,4 ; 2 C.4,4.*

fulgor, oris, *m.*, *brightness*, L.11,36.*

fulgur, uris, *n.*, *lightning*, L. 10,18 ; Ap.4,5.

fullo, onis, *m.*, *fuller*, Mk. 9,3.*

fumigo, 1, *smoke*, Mt.12,20.*

fumus, i, *m.*, *smoke*, A.2,19 ; Ap.8,4 ; 9,2 ff.

fundamentum, i, *n.*, *foundation*, 1 C.3,10 ff.; H.6,1.

fundo, 1, *found*, *lay foundation*, ||Mt.7,25 ; E.3,17 ; Co.1,23 ; H.1,10.*

fundo, 3, *shed*, L.22,20 ; A. 22,20.*

fungor, 3, *perform*, *execute*, L.1,8 ; 2 C.5,20 ; E.6, 20.*

funiculus, i, *m.*, *small cord*, J.2,15.*

funis, is, *m.*, *rope*, A.27, 32.*

fur, furis, *m.*, *thief*, J.10,1 ff.; 1 Th.5,2 ff.

furor, 1, *steal*, R.2,21 ; *steal away*, Mt.28,13.

furor, oris, *m.*, (1) *madness*, Mk.3,21 ; (2) *anger*, Ap. 19,15.*

furtum, i, *n.*, *theft*, ||Mt.15, 19 ; ||19,18 ; Ap.9,21.*

§fusio, onis, *f.*, *effusion*, *shedding*, H.9,22.*

fustis, is, *m.*, *staff*, *cudgel*, Mt.26,47 ; ||26,55.*

futurus, a, um, *about to be*, *future*.

G

galea, ae, *f.*, *helmet*, E.6,17 ; 1 Th.5,8.*

†§gallicula, ae, *f.*, *small shoe*, A.12,8.*

†gallina, ae, *f.*, *hen*, Mt.23, 37.*

gallus, i, *m.*, *cock*.

†garrio, 4, *prate*, *chatter*, 3 J. 10.*

gaudeo, gauisus, 2, *rejoice*.

gaudium, ii, *n.*, *joy*, *rejoicing*.

gaza, ae, *f.* (Pers.), *treasure*, A.8,27.*

°gazophylacium, ii, *n.*, *treasury*, Mk.12,41 ff.; L. 21,1 ; J.8,20.*

*gehenna, ae, *f.* (Hebr.), *hell*, *place of torment*.

gemitus, us, *m.*, *groaning*. A.7,34 ; R.8,26.*

gemo, 3, *groan*, *bemoan*, R. 8,23 ; H.13,17.*

°genealogia, ae, *f.*, *genealogy*, 1 T.1,4 ; Ti.3,9 ; H.7, 3.*

generatio, onis, *f.*, (1) *birth*, Mt.1,1 ; *bearing* (of children), 1 T.2,15 ; (2) *generation*, Mt.11,16 ; A. 2,40.

genero, 1, *beget*, A.7,29 ; *bring forth*, G.4,24 ; 2 T. 2,23 ; H.6,7 ; Jas.1,15.*

genimen, inis, *n.*, *offspring,
fruit*, Mt.23,33 ; ||26,29 ;
L.3,7.*

gentilis, e, *heathen, Gentile,
non-Jew*, Mk.7,26 ; (as
subst.) *Gentile*, 1 C.12,13.

†gentiliter, *in heathen fashion,
like the Gentiles*, G.2,14.*

gens, ntis, *f.*, (1) *race, nation*,
L.21,10 ; (2) *Gentile*, Mt.
4,15 ; A.4,25.

genu, us, *n., knee.*

genus, eris, *n., race*, A.4,6 ;
13,26 ; *kind*, Mt.13,47 ;
1 C.12,10.

germanus, a, um, *genuine,
real*, Ph.4,3.*

germino, 1, *shoot forth, spring
up*, Mk.4,27 ; H.12,15.*

gero, gessi, gestus, 3, *do*, L.
23,41 ; A.26,26 ; *have,
bear a part*, 3 J.9.

gigno, genui, genitus, 3,
beget, Mt.1,2 ff.; A.7,8 ;
bring forth, L.23,29 ; 1
P.2,2.

gladius, ii, *m., sword.*

gloria, ae, *f., glory*, R.1,23 ;
glorying, R.4,2 ; 2 C.1,
12 ; *boasting*, Ph.2,3.

gloriatio, onis, *f., glorying*,
R.3,27 ; *boasting*, 1 C.5,6 ;
2 C.7,4 ; 7,14 ; [11,10].*

glorifico, 1, *glorify.*

glorior, 1, *glory*, 1 C.1,29 ;
boast, R.2,17 ; G.6,13 f.

gloriose, *gloriously, with
glory*, L.13,17.*

gloriosus, a, um, *glorious*, E.
5,27.*

glutio, 4, *swallow*, Mt.23,24.*

°grabattus (-atum), i, *m.*
(Macedonian), *couch,
pallet*, Mk.2,4 ff.; 6,55 ;
J.5,8 ff.; A.5,15 ; 9,33.*

gradus, us, *m.*, (1) *step*, A.21,
35 ; 21,40 ; (2) *degree*,
1 T.3,13.* .

*graece, *in the Greek lan-
guage*, J.19,20 ; A.21,
37 ; Ap.9,11.*

graecus, a, um, *Greek*
(characters), L.23,38.*

grandis, e, *great, large,
lengthy*, Mk.14,15 ; H.
5,11 ; 11,24.*   .

grando, inis, *f., hail*, Ap.8,
7 ; 11,19 ; 16,21.*

granum, i, *n., grain*, ||Mt.
13,31 ; ||17,20 ; J.12,24 ;
1 C.15,37.*

gratia, ae, *f.*, (1) *favour, grace;*
(2) (in pl.) *thanksgiving.*

†gratifico, 1, *do a favour to,
gratify*, E.1,6.*

gratis, *for nothing*, Mt.10,8 ;
Ap.21,6.

gratulatio, onis, *f., rejoicing*,
Ph.1,26.*

gratus, a, um, (1) *pleasing*,
A.7,20 ; (2) *thankful*, Co.
3,15.*

grauis, e, *heavy*, Mt.23,4 ;
weighty, 2 C.10,10 ; *burdensome*, 2 C.12,14 ; 1
J.5,3 ; *grievous*, §A.20,29.

†grauitas, tatis, f., serious-
ness, gravity, Ti.2,7.*
grauiter, (1) vehemently, L.
11,53; (2) (with audire)
with chagrin, vexation,
Mt.13,15; A.28,27.*
grauo, 1, burden, 1 T.5,16;
make heavy, L.9,32.
gressus, us, m., path, H.12,
13.*
grex, gis, m., flock.
grossus, i, m. (also f.), un-
ripe fig, Ap.6,13.*
gubernaculum, i, n., helm,
rudder, A.27,40; Jas.3,
4.*
†gubernatio, onis, f., govern-
ment, direction (Gk.
κυβέρνησις), 1 C.12,28.*
gubernator, oris, m., helms-
man, pilot, A.27,11; Ap.
18,17.*
gusto, 1, taste, Co.2,21; eat
a little, A.10,10.
gutta, ae, f., drop, L.22,44.*
guttur, uris, n., throat, R.
3,13.*

H

habeo, 2, have.
habitaculum, i, n., (1) habitation, E.2,22; (2) room,
cell, A.12,7.*
habitatio, onis, f., habitation,
A.17,26; 2 C.5,1 f.; Ap.
18,2.*

habito, 1, dwell, inhabit.
habitus, us, m., appearance,
deportment, attire, Ph.2,
7; 1 T.2,9; Ti.2,3; Jas.
2,2.*
haedus (hoe-), i, m., kid,
Mt.25,32 f.; L.15,29.*
haer-, v. her-.
†°haereticus, a, um, heretic,
heretical, Ti.3,10.*
†haesitatio, onis, f., hesitation, embarrassment, Ph.
2,14.*
haesito, 1, doubt, A.11,12;
25,20; be at a loss, L.
9,7.
hamus, i, m., hook, Mt.17,
27.*
harena °(are-), ae, f., sand,
Mt.7,26; in R.9,27, arena.
harundo (ar-), dinis, f., reed,
‖Mt.11,7; Ap.21,16.
haut (haud), not, 1 T.6,7.*
haurio, 4, draw water, J.2,
8 f.; 4,7 ff.*
*haue (aue), (pl. hauete,
Mt.28,9), hail! 2 J.10,
11.
hebraice, in Hebrew, J.5,2;
19,13 ff.; Ap.9,11; 16,16.*
hebraicus, a, um, Hebrew,
L.23,38; A.26,14.*
heiulo (eiu-), 1, wail, lament,
Mk.5,38.*
Heli (Eli) (Hebr.), my God,
Mt.27,46.*
Heloi (Eloi) (Aram.), my
God, Mk.15,34.*

herba, ae, *f., grass, blade of grass,* etc., Mt.13,26 ; Mk.4,28 ; H.6,7.*

hereditas (hae-), tatis, *f., inheritance,* Mk.12,7 ; A. 7,5 ; 1 P.1,4.

heredito (hae-), 1, *inherit,* H.1,4 ; 6,12 ; 12,17.*

heres (hae-), edis, *c., heir,* H. 1,2 ; 1 P.3,22.

***°heresis (hae-), is** or **eos,** *f., sect,* A.5,17 ; 15,5 ; 24, 14 ; *heresy,* 1 C.11,19.

hiemo, 1, *pass the winter,* A. 27,12 ; 28,11 ; 1 C.16,6 ; Ti.3,12.*

hiems, mis, *f., winter.*

hilaris, e, *cheerful,* 2 C.9,7.*

hilaritas, tatis, *f., cheerfulness,* R.12,8.*

hinc, *hence ;* **hinc et hinc** (J.19,18), *on this side and on that.*

hircus, i, *m., he-goat,* H.9, 12 ff.; 10,4.*

hodie, *to-day.*

°holocaustoma (-cautoma), atis, *n., whole burntoffering,* Mk.12,33 ; H. 10,6 ff.*

holus (ol-), eris, *n., herb,* ||Mt.13,32 ; L.11,42 ; R. 14,2.*

homicida, ae, *c., murderer,* J.8,44 ; 1 T.1,9 ; Ap.21, 8.

homicidium, ii, *n., murder,* ||Mt.15,19 ; G.5,21.

homo, inis, *c., man, mankind.*

honestas, tatis, *f., honour,* 1 C.12,23.*

***honeste,** *decently, becomingly,* R.13,13 ; 1 C.14, 40 ; 1 Th.4,12.*

honestus, a, um, *honourable,* A.13,50 ; 17,12 ; 1 C.7, 35 ; 12,24.*

honorabilis, e, *honourable,* A.5,34 ; H.13,4.*

honoratus, a, um (only compar. **-tior),** *honourable,* L.14,8.*

honorifico, 1, *honour,* Mt.6, 2 ; *do honour to,* J.12, 26.

honoro, 1, *honour,* A.28,10 ; R.15,9.

hora, ae, *f., hour.*

hordeum, i, *n., barley,* Ap. 6,6.*

hordiaceus (ordea-), a, um, *of barley, barley-,* J.6,9 ff.*

horreo, 2 (only **horrendus),** *dreadful, terrible,* H.10, 31.*

hortor, 1, *exhort,* A.11,23 ; Ti.2,6.*

†hortulanus, i, *m., gardener,* J.20,15.*

hortus, i, *m., garden.*

hosanna (os-), v. **osanna.**

hospes, pitis, *m.,* (1) *stranger ;* (2) *host,* R.16,23.

hospitalis, e, *hospitable,* 1 T. 3,2 ; Ti.1,8 ; 1 P.4,9.*

*hospitalitas, tatis, *f.*, *hospitality*, R.12,13 ; H.13, 2.*

hospitium, ii, *n.*, *hospitality*, 1 T.5,10 ; H.13,2 ; *place of entertainment, lodging*, Philem.22.

hospitor, 1, *lodge*, A.10,6 ; 10,32 ; 21,16 ; [1 C.16, 19].*

hostia, ae, *f.*, *offering, sacrifice*, L.2,24 ; H.7,27 ; 10, 1 ff.; 1 P.2,5.

huiusmodi, *of this kind, such*, J.8,5 ; 2 C.12,3.

humane, *kindly, courteously*, A.27,3.*

humanitas, tatis,*f.*, *kindness, humanity*, A.28,2 ; Ti. 3,4.*

humanus, a, um, *belonging to man, of man, human*, R.6,19 ; Jas.3,7 ; 2 P. 1,21.

humerus, v. um-.

humilio, 1, *humble*, ||Mt.18,4; Ph.2,8 ; *make low*, L.3,5.

humilis, e, *humble, lowly*.

humilitas, tatis, *f.*, *humility, lowliness*, E.4,2 ; Jas.1, 10.

°hyacintinus (-thinus), a, um, *of* or *belonging to the hyacinth* (a precious stone), Ap.9,17.*

[°hyacinthus], i, *f.*, *hyacinth* (a precious stone), Ap. 21,20.*

°hydria, ae, *f.*, *water-pot*, J.2, 6 f.; 4,28.*

†°hydropicus, a, um, *dropsical*, L.14,2.*

°hymnus, i, *m.*, *hymn*, ||Mt. 26,30 ; E.5,19 ; Co.3, 16.*

*°hypocrisis, is,*f.*, *hypocrisy*, Mt.23,28 ; L.12,1 ; 1 T. 4,2.*

°hypocrita, or -tes, ae, *m.*, *hypocrite*, Mt.6,2 ff.; 23, 15 ff.

°hysopum · (hyss-), i, *n.*, *hyssop*, J.19,29 ; H.9, 19.*

I (vowel)

°iacinthus, i, *f.* = hyacinthus, *hyacinth* (precious stone), Ap.21,20.*

iaspis, idis,*f.*, *jasper*, Ap.4,3; 21,11 ff.*

ictus, us, *m.*, lit. *stroke, beat ; twinkling* (of eye), 1 C. 15,52.*

idcirco, *for this reason*, H.7, 23.*

*°idiota, ae, *m.*, *ignorant, unlearned person*, A.4,13; 1 C.14,16 ff.*

°idolatria (idolola-), ae, *f.*, *idolatry*, A.17,16.*

†°idolium, ii, *n.*, *idol-temple*, 1 C.8,10.*

*°idololatres, ae, *m.*, in Ap.
21,8, idolatres, *idolater*,
1 C.10,7.*

*°idolothytus, a, um, *per-
taining to sacrifices offered
to idols*, 1 C.8,7 ff.; Ap.
2,20.*

¬idolum, i, *n.*, *idol*, A.21,25 ;
2 C.6,16.

*idoneus, a, um, *capable,
sufficient*, 2 C.2,16 ; 3,6 ;
2 T.2,2.*

igneus, a, um, *fiery, like to
fire*, E.6,16 ; Ap.9,17.*

ignio, 4, only P.P. ignitus,
tried by fire, Ap.3,18.*

ignis, is, *m.*, *fire*.

ignobilis, e, *obscure, ignoble*,
1 C.1,28 ; 4,10 ; 12,23.*

ignobilitas, tatis, *f.*, *obscurity,
dishonour*, 1 C.15,43 ; 2
C.6,8 ; 11,21.*

ignominia, ae, *f.*, *shame*, R.
1,26 ; 1 C.11,14.*

ignoro, 1, *be ignorant of, not
to know*, J.3,10 ; Ph.1,
22 ; 1 J.2,21.

ignotus, a, um, *unknown*, A.
17,23 ; 21,39 ; 2 C.6,8 ;
G.1,22.*

ilico (illi-), *on the spot, in-
stantly*, L.1,64.*

ill-, v. inl- in many cases.

[†illo], *thither*, Mt.2,22.*

imago, ginis, *f.*, *image*.

imbec-, v. inbec-.

imber, bris, *m.*, *rain*, A.28,2 ;
H.6,7.*

imitor, 1, *imitate*, 2 Th.3,
7 ff.; II.13,7 ; 3 J.11.*

imm-, v. inm-, in many cases.

immo, *nay rather*, R.3,29 ; 8,
34 ; G.4,9.*

†§immolaticius, a, um, *of or
for a sacrifice*, 1 C.10,
28.*

immolo, 1, *sacrifice*, Mk.
14,12 ; 1 C.5,7 ; *do sacrifice to*, A.14,18.

imp-, v. inp- in many cases.

impedimentum, i, *n.*, *hindrance*, 1 C.7,35.*

imperitus, a, um, *unskilled*,
2 C.11,6.*

imperium, ii, *n.*, (1) *reign,
rule*, L.3,1 ; (2) *com-
mand*, 1 C.7,6 ; *authority*,
Ti.2,15 ; *power*, Ap.1,6.

impero, 1, (1) *command, give
command*, ||Mt.8,32 ; (2)
rebuke, Jude 9.

impetus, us, *m.*, *rush, attack*,
A.7,57 ; *violence*, H.11,
34.

impie, *impiously*, 2 P.2,6 ;
Jude 15.*

impietas, tatis, *f.*, *ungodli-
ness, impiety*, R.1,18 ;
11,26 ; Ti.2,12.

impius, a, um, *ungodly,
wicked*.

impleo, eui, etus, 2, *fill*, Ap.
8,5 ; *fulfil*, A.1,16 ; G.
5,14 ; *fill up*, J.2,7.

imputo, 1, *account, reckon ;
lay to the charge of*, R.4,

4 ff.; 5,13; [2 T.4,16];
Philem.18.*

†inaccessibilis, e, *unap-
proachable*, 1 T.6,16.*

inambulo, 1, *walk up and
down* (Gr. ἐνπεριπατῶ),
2 C.6,16.*

†§inaniloquium, ii, *n.*, *vain
talking*, 2 T.2,16.*

inanis, e, *empty*, L.1,53; 20,
10 f.; *vain*, 1 C.15,58;
Co.2,8; Jas.2,20.

†inaniter, *in vain*, Jas.4,
5.*

inaquosus, a, um, *waterless*,
L.11,24.* (Gk. ἄνυδρος.)

inauro, 1, *gild, cover with
gold*, Ap.17,4.*

inbecillis (imb-), e, *weak,
infirm*, 1 C.11,30; H.5,
11.*

inbecillitas (imb-), tatis, *f.*,
infirmity, R.15,1.*

incedo, 3, (1) *walk*, L.1,6;
(2) *approach, enter in*,
H.6,19.*

incendium, ii, *n.*, *burning*,
Ap.18,9; 18,18.*

incendo, 3, *set on fire*, Jas.
3,5.*

incensum, i, *n.*, *incense*,
L.1,9 ff.; in plural, Ap.8,
3 f.*

incertus, a, um, *uncertain*,
1 C.9,26; 14,8; 1 T.6,
17.*

†incessabilis, e, *unable to
cease*, 2 P.2,14.*

†inchoatio, onis, *f.*, *beginning*, H.6,1.*

incido, di, 3, *fall*, H.4,11;
Jas.1,2.

incipio, 3, *begin*.

incircumcisus, a, um, *un-
circumcised*, A.7,51.*

incito, 1, *move, stir*, A.17,16.*

inclino, 1, *stoop, bend, bow*,
L.13,11; J.8,6 ff.; 19,
30; 20,5 ff.; in pass.
decline (of the day), L.24,
29.*

includo, 3, *shut up, imprison*,
L.3,20; A.26,10.*

incola, ae, *c.*, *stranger*, A.13,
17.*

incolatus, us, *m.*, *dwelling
in a strange place, so-
journing*, 1 P.1,17.*

incomprehensibilis, e, *in-
comprehensible*, R.11,33.*

†inconfusibilis, e, *that cannot
be made ashamed*, 2 T.2,
15.*

†inconpositus (incomp-), a,
um, *disorderly, irregular*,
R.1,31.*

†inconstans, antis, *unstable*,
Jas.1,8.*

inconstantia, ae, *f.*, *fickleness,
instability*, Jas.3,16.*

†inconsutilis, e, *not sewed
together, without seam*,
J.19,23.*

incontaminatus, a, um, *undefiled, pure*, 2 C.7,11;
1 P.1,4; 1,19.*

†**Incontinens, entis,** *inconti-*
nent, 2 T.3,3.*
†**Incontinentia, ae,** *f., in-*
continence, 1 C.7,5.*
incorruptela, ae, *f., incorrup-*
tion, 1 C.15,50 ff.*
incorruptibilis, e, incorrup-
tible, R.1,23 ; 1 P.1,4 ;
1,23.*
†**incorruptibilitas, tatis,** *f.,*
imperishableness, 1 P.3,
4.*
incorruptus, a, um, *uncor-*
rupted, 1 C.9,25 ; 15,52.*
incrasso, 1, only in P.P.
incrassatus, *hardened,*
Mt.13,15 ; A.28,27.*
incredibilis, e, (1) *incredible,*
A.26,8 ; (2) *unbelieving,*
§L.1,17 ; Ti.1,16.*
incredulitas, tatis, f., un-
belief, R.3,3 ; 11,20 ff.;
H.4,6 ff.
incredulus, a, um, *faithless,*
unbelieving, H.3,18 ; Ap.
21,8.
incrementum, i, *n., increase,*
1 C.3,6 f.; 2 C.9,10.*
increpo, aui, 1, *chide, rebuke,*
Mk.8,32; L.4,35 ; 1 T.5,1.
incresco, 3, *grow,* Mk.4,27.*
incubo, ui, 1, *lie upon,* A.20,
10.* In this verse **incubui**
may be from the follow-
ing verb.
incumbo, 3, (1) *press upon,*
burden, 1 C.9,16 ; (2) ? *lie*
upon, A.20,10.*

incuruo, 1, *bow down,* R.11,
10.*
†**indeclinabilis, e,** *inflexible,*
unchangeable, H.10,23.*
indemnatus, a, um, un-
condemned, A.16,37 ; 22,
25.*.
†**indesinenter,** *without ceas-*
ing, H.10,1.*
indico, 1, *tell, declare,* J.11,
57 ; A.23,17 ff.; 1 C.10,28.
indico, 3, *proclaim, impose,*
A.13,16.*
indigeo, 2, *need,* L.9,11 ; 1
C.12,21 ; *lack,* Jas.1,5.
indignatio, onis, *f., indig-*
nation, 2 C.7,11 ; *wrath,*
R.2,8 ; Co.3,8.
indigne, (1) *unworthily,* 1 C.
11,27 ff.; (2) (with **ferre**),
be indignant, Mk.10,14 ;
14,4.*
indignor, 1, *be indignant.*
indignus, a, um, *unworthy,*
A.13,46 ; 1 C.6,2.*
indoctus, a, um, *unlearned,*
2 P.3,16.*
induco, xi, 3, *bring,* A.5,28 ;
bring or *lead in* or *into,*
‖Mt.6,13.
indulgentia, ae, *f., indul-*
gence, remission (Gk.
συνγνώμη), 1 C.7,6.*
indumentum, i, *n., clothing,*
putting on, 1 P.3,3.*
induo, ui, utus, 3, *clothe.*
induro, 1, *harden,* J.12,40 ;
A.19,9 ; R.9,18.*

inebrio, 1, *make drunken*,
L.12,45 ; J.2,10 ; E.5,
18 ; Ap.17,2.*
inenarrabilis, e, *unspeakable*,
R.8,26 ; 2 C.9,15 ; 1 P.
1,8.*
ineo, ii, itus, 4 (always with
consilium), *take counsel*,
Mt.22,15 ; 27,1 ff.*
†ineptus, a, um, *silly*, 1 T.
4,7.*
*inexcusabilis, e, *without ex-
cuse, inexcusable*, R.1,20;
2,1.*
inextinguibilis, e, *unquench-
able*, ‖Mt.3,12 ; Mk.9,
43 ff.*
†infamia, ae, *f.*, *ill report*,
2 C.6,8.*
infans, antis, *c.*, *babe, child.*
infantia, ae, *f.*, *childhood*,
Mk.9,21 ; 2 T.3,15.*
infelicitas, tatis, *f.*, *unhappi-
ness*, R.3,16.*
infelix, icis,   *unhappy,
wretched*, R.7,24.*
†infensus, a, um, *hostile,
angry*, H.3,10 ; 3,17.*
inferior, oris, *lower*, E.4,9.*
infernus, i, *m.*, *hell, Hades.*
infero, tuli, ferre, (1) *bring,
bring in*, J.20,27 ; A.17,
20 ; (2) *occasion, cause,
? inflict*, R.3,5.
inferus, i, *m.*, *hell, Hades*,
Mt.16,18 ; §6,8 ; §20,13 f.*
infidelis, e, *faithless, unbelieving.*

infirmo, 1, (only in pass.),
be weak, weakened, R.4,
19 ; 8,3 ; *be sick*, J.4,46;
Ph.2,26 f.
infirmus, a, um, *weak, infirm,
sick.*
inflammo, 1, *set on fire*, Jas.
3,6 (bis).*
†inflatio, onis, *f.*, *pride, puff-
ing up*, 2 C.12,20.*
inflo, 1, *puff up*, 1 C.4,6 ff.;
5,2 ; Co.2,18.
[†informatio], onis, *f.*, *pattern*, 1 T.1,16.*
infra, *below*, Mt.2,16.*
[infremo], ui, 3, *groan*, J.11,
33.*
§infreno, 1, *put bridle on*,
1 T.5,18.*
infringo, 3, *destroy, make
void*, 2 C.11,10.*
infructuosus, a, um, *un-
fruitful*, E.5,11 ; Ti.3,14 ;
Jude 12.*
infundo, 3, *pour in* or *into*,
L.10,34.*
ingemesco (-isco), mui, 3,
groan, Mk.7,34 ; R.8,22 ;
2 C.5,2 ff. ; *murmur*, Jas.
5,9.
†ingenium, ii, *n.*, *quality,
nature*, 2 C.8,8.*
ingratus, a, um, *thankless,
ungrateful*, L.6,35 ; 2 T.
3,2.*
§ingrauo, 1, *make heavy*, Mk.
14,40.*
ingredior, gressus, 3, *enter*,

go or *come into*, Mk.1,21 ;
J.10,9 ; *go along, advance*,
A.14,16 ; 3 J.2.

inhabito, 1, *dwell in, inhabit.*

inhonestus, a, um, *shameful,
unseemly*, 1 C.12,23.*

inhonoro, 1, *dishonour*, J.8,
49 ; R.2,23.*

inicio (-iicio), ieci, 3, *lay* or
place on, 1 C.7,35 ; (elsewhere only with **manus**),
‖Mt.26,50 ; A.4,3.

inimica, ae, *f.*, *enemy*, 1 C.
15,26; Jas:4,4.*

inimicitia, ae, *f.*, *enmity*, §R.
8,7 ; G.5,20 ; E.2,14 ff.*

inimicus, i, *m.*, *enemy.*

inimicus, a, um, *hostile,
unfriendly*, L.23,12 ; Co.
1.21 ; Jas.4,4.

†**ininterpretabilis, e**, *in-
explicable, hard to interpret*, H.5,11.*

inique, *unrighteously*, Co.3,
25.*

iniquus, a, um, *unjust, un-
righteous.*

initio, 1, *consecrate, dedicate,*
H.10,20.*

initium, ii, *n.*, *beginning.*

iniicio, v. **inicio.**

iniuria, ae, *f.*, (1) *wrong*, A.7,
24; 1 C.6,7 ; (2) *damage,
harm*, A.27,10 ; 27,21.

iniuste, *unjustly*, 1 P.2,19 ff.*

iniustitia, ae, *f.*, *unrighteous-
ness*, J.7,18 ; R.1,18 ;
2 P.2,13.*

iniustus, a, um, *unjust, un-
righteous*, 1 T.1,9 ; H.6,
10.

inlicio (ill-), 3, only P.P.
inlectus, *enticed, se-
duced*, Jas.1,14.*

inlicitus (ill-), a, um, *un-
lawful*, 1 P.4,3.*

inlido (ill-), lisus, 3, *dash
against*, L.6,48 f.*

inlucesco (ill-), luxi, 3, *grow
light, dawn, shine*, L.23,
54 ; 2 C.4,6.*

inludo (ill-), si, sus, 3, *mock*,
‖Mt.27,29 ff.; L.14,29.

inluminatio (ill-), onis, *f.*,
brightness, illumination,
2 C.4,4 ff.; 2 T.1,10.*

inlumino (ill-), 1, *enlighten ;
set in a clear light*, 2 T.
1,10.*

inlusor (ill-), oris, *m.*, *mocker*,
2 P.3,3 ; Jude 18.*

†**inlustratio (ill-), onis**, *f.*,
brightness, 2 Th.2,8.*

inmaculatus (imm-), a, um,
unstained, undefiled, E.
1,4 ; H.9,14.

inmarcescibilis (imm-), e,
unfading, 1 P.1,4 ; 5,4.*

inmensus (imm-), a, um,
*boundless, without mea-
sure* ; only in phrase
in inmensum, *beyond
measure*, 2 C.10,13 ff.

inmineo (imm-), 2, *be im-
minent, threaten*, A.27,
20 ; 28,2.*

inmitis (imm-), e, *rough,
cruel, 2 T.3,3.*
inmitto (imm-), 3, *put in,
insert,* ||Mt.9,16.*
inmobilis (imm-), e, *un-
movable,* A.27,41 ; *un-
changeable,* 1 C.15,58 ;
Co.1,23; H.6,18; 12,27 f.*
†inmobilitas (imm-), tatis, *f.,
immovableness,* H.6,17.*
inmortalis (imm-), e, *im-
mortal,* 1 T.1,17.*
inmortalitas (imm-), tatis, *f.,
immortality,* 1 C.15,53 f.;
1 T.6,16.*
inmunditia (imm-), ae, *f.,
uncleanness,* Mt.23,25 ;
Co.3,5 ; Ap.17,4.
inmundus (imm-), a, um,
unclean.
inmuto (imm-), 1, *change,*
R.1,26 ; 1 C.15,51 f.*
innocens, entis, *harmless,
innocent,* Mt.12,7 ; 27,
24 ; R.16,18 ; H.7,26.*
innotesco, 3, *become known,*
E.3,10 ; Ph.4,6.*
innumerabilis, e, *innumer-
able,* H.11,12.*
*innuo, ui, 3, *beckon,* L.1,22 ;
1,62 ; J.13,24.*
*innuptus, a, um, *unmarried,*
1 C.7,11 ; 7,34.*
inoboediens (-bed-), entis,
disobedient, Ti.1,10.*
inoboedientia (-bed-), ae, *f.,
disobedience,* R.5,19 ; 2
C.10,6 ; H.2,2.*

†§inoperor, 1, *work, be opera-
tive in* (Gk. ἐνεργῶ), Mk.
6,14.*
inopia, ae, *f., poverty, want,*
2 C.8,9 ; 8,14 (bis).*
†inordinate, *irregularly, disorderly,* 2 Th.3,6.*
†inpaenitens (impoe-), entis,
impenitent, R.2,5.*
†inparatus (imp-), a, um,
unprepared, 2 C.9,4.*
inpedio (imp-), 4, *hinder,* R.
15,22 ; G.5,7 ; 1 P.3,7.
inpendo (imp-), 3, *lay out, expend,* A.21,24; 2 C.12,15.*
inpertior (imp-), 4, *share
with, communicate, be-
stow,* R.1,11 ; 1 P.3,7.*
inpingo (imp-), pegi, 3, *thrust
or drive in,* A.27,41.*
*inplico (2 P.2,20) and im-
plico (2 T.2,4), 1, *entan-
gle.*
inpollutus (imp-), a, um,
undefiled, H.7,26.*
inpono (imp-), posui, positus,
3, *lay on,* Mt.21,7 ; *put
on,* Mt.27,48 ; L.10,34 ;
impose, H.9,10 ; *give*
(name), Mk.3,16 f.
†inportabilis (imp-), e, *un-
bearable, insupportable,*
Mt.23,4.*
inportune (imp-), *unseason-
ably,* 2 T.4,2.*
inportunus (imp-), a, um,
troublesome, unreasonable,
2 Th.3,2.*

*inpositio (imp-), onis, *f.,*
laying on (always with
manuum), A.8,18 ; 1 T.
4,14 ; 2 T.1,6 ; H.6,2.*
inpossibilis (imp-), e, *im-
possible.*

†inprobitas (imp-), tatis, *f.,*
audacity, boldness, L.11,
8.*

inproperium (imp-), ii, *n.,*
taunt, reproach, R.15,3 ;
H.11,26 ; 13,13.*

inpropero (imp-), 1, *reproach,
upbraid,* Mt.27,44 ; R.
15,3 ; Jas.1,5.*

inprudens (imp-), entis, *im-
prudent, foolish,* Mk.7,18;
E.5,17 ; 1 P.2,15.*

inpudicitia (imp-), ae, *f.,
want of chastity, lewdness,*
Mk.7,22; R.13,13; E.4,19.

†inpudicus (imp-), a, um,
lewd, unchaste, Ap.22,15.*

†inquiete, *restlessly,* 2 Th.
3,11.*

*inquietus, a, um, *restless,
unquiet,* 1 Th.5,14 ; 2 Th.
3,7 ; Jas.3,8.*

inquinamentum, i, *n., defilement,* 2 C.7,1.*

inquino, 1, *defile.* Ti.1,15 ;
H.9,13 ; 12,15 ; Ap.3,4.*

inquiro, quisii, quisitus, 3,
seek or *look for,* A.10,17 ;
enquire, A.23,20 ; *re-
quire,* L.11,50.

†inquisitio, onis, *f., enquiry,*
A.12,19.*

†§inquisitor, oris, *m., exam-
iner, investigator,* 1 C.
1,20.*

inquit (inquam not found),
defect. inquiens (Mk.
12,26), inquiunt (2 C.10,
10), *he says.*

†inrationabilis (irr-), e, *irra-
tional, without reason,* 2
P.2,12.*

inreprehensibilis (irr-), e, *ir-
reproachable, unblamable,*
Co. 1,22 ; 1 T.3,2 ; 5,7 ;
6,14 ; Ti.2,8.*

inrideo (irr-), 2, *laugh at,
mock,* Mk.5,40 ; A.2,13 ;
17,32 ; G.6,7.*

inruo (irr-), ui, 3, *rush on* or
upon, Mt.7,25 ff.; Mk.3,
10 ; L.1,12 ; 5,1.*

insania, ae, *f., madness,* A.
26,24.*

insanio, 4, *be mad,* J.10,20 ;
A.12,15 ; A.26,24 f.

*inscribo, scriptus, 3, *write
on, inscribe,* Mk.15,26 ;
§L.23,38 ; [Ap.21,12].*

inscriptio, onis, *f., inscription,* Mk.12,16.*

insensatus, a, um, *foolish,*
G.3,1.*

insero, serui, sertus, 3, (1)
ingraft, R.11,17 ff.; (2)
insert, intrude, 2 C.10,12;
1 T.6,10.*

†insero, situs, 3, *ingraft,*
Jas.1,21.*

insidiae, arum, *f., lying in*

wait, plot, A.9,24 ; 23,16;
snare, E.6,11.

insidior, 1, *lay wait for, plot
against,* Mk.6,19 ; L.11,
54 ; A.23,21.*

†**insigne, is,** *n.,* *sign* (of ship),
A.28,11.*

insignis, e, *notable,* Mt.27,16.*

insilio, 4, *leap upon,* A.19,
16.*

***insinuo,** 1, (1) *take into the
bosom,* 1 P.5,5 ; (2) *make
known, publish,* A.17,3.*

insipiens, entis, *foolish.*

insipientia, ae, *f.,* *foolishness,
folly.*

insisto, 3, *press upon,* L.11,
53.*

†**insolubilis, e,** *indissoluble,*
H.7,16.*

inspiratio, onis, *f.,* *breath,*
A.17,25.*

inspiro, 1, *inspire,* 2 T.3,16 ;
2 P.1,21.*

instabilis, e, *unstable,* 1 C.4,
11 ; 2 P.2,14 ; 3,16.*

instantia, ae, *f.,* *urgency,
constancy,* 2 C.11,28 ; E.
6,18.*

instauro, 1, *renew, restore,*
R.13,9; E.1,10.* (Gk.
ἀνακεφαλοῦμαι.)

†**instita, ae,** *f.,* *bandage,* J.11,
44.*

instituo, tutus, 3, (1) *make,
appoint,* H.11,7 ; (2)
educate, instruct, Ph.4,
12.*

institutio, onis, *f.,* *instruc-
tion, discipline,* 2 T.3,10;
(2) *foundation, making,*
H.4,3.*

insto, 1, *be urgent, insistent,*
L.23,23 ; A.18,5 ; *be
near, present,* 2 Th.2,2 ; 2
T.3,1.

instruo, uctus, 3, *instruct,*
1 C.2,16 ; 14,19 ; *furnish,*
2 T.3,17.

insuflo (-suff-), 1, *breathe
upon,* J.20,22.*

insula, ae, *f.,* *island.*

insulsus, a, um, *insipid,
tasteless,* Mk.9,50.*

†**insumo,** 3, *expend upon,*
Jas.4,3.*

insuper, *moreover, besides,*
A.2,26 ; 21,28 ; H.11,
36:*

insurgo, surrexi, 3, *rise up,*
Mt.10,21 ; A.18,12.*

integer, gra, grum, *whole,
entire,* A.3,16 ; 1 Th.5,
23 ; Jas.1,4.*

integritas, tatis, *f.,* *soundness,
integrity,* Ti.2,7.*

intellectus, us, *m.,* *understanding,* Mt.15,16 ; E.
4,18 ; *thought,* 2 C.10,5.

intellegentia (-lig-), **ae,** *f.,
mind, understanding,* Ph.
4,7.*

intellego (-ligo), **xi, ctus,** 3,
understand.

†**intemtator** (-ten-), **oris,** *m.,*
(Gk. ἀπείραστος), *one who*

does not tempt, Jas.1,
13.*

Intendo, 3, *pay attention to,*
give heed to, 1 T.1,4;
mark, L.14,7; *look at* or
upon, L.4,20; A.3,5;
2 C.3,7.

†**intentio, onis,** *f., intent,*
purpose, H.4,12.*

intercedo, 3, *occur, happen,*
intervene, H.9,15 f.*

interea, *meanwhile,* J.4,31.*

intereo, ii, 4, *perish,* Ap.8,
9.*

interficio, feci, fectus, 3, *kill.*

interimo, emi, 3, *slay,* A.2,23;
5,30.*

interior, oris, *inner,* A.16,24;
R.7,22; E.3,16; H.6,
19.*

interitus, us, *m., destruction,*
Ph.3,19; H.8,13.

†**interminatus, a, um,** *end-*
less, 1 T.1,4.*

intermissio, onis, *f., dis-*
continuance, ceasing (always with **sine**), A.12,
5; 1 Th.1,2; 2 T.1,3.

intermitto, 3, *leave off,*
neglect, H.6,1.*

interpello, 1, *address, pray,*
plead, A.25,24; R.8,34;
11,2; H.7,25.* (ἐντυγχάνω
always.)

interpono, posui, 3, *interpose,*
H.6,17; [A.18,4].*

interpres, etis, *c., interpreter,*
1 C.14,28.*

interpretatio, onis, *f., inter-*
pretation, 1 C.12,10; 14,
26.

interpretor, 1, (1) *expound,·*
interpret; (2) *be inter-*
preted, Mt.1,23; J.1,38 ff.

interrogatio, onis, *f., enquiry,*
A.25,26; 28,18; 1 P.
3,21.

interrogo, 1, *ask, make en-*
quiry, seek after.

intersum (only impers. **in-**
terest), *it concerns, makes*
a difference, G.2,6.*

interuallum, i, *n., interval,*
space, L.22,59.*

intingo and §**intinguo** (L.16,
24), **xi, ctus,** 3, *dip in,*
Mt.26,23‖; J.13,26 (bis).

intrinsecus, *inwardly,* Mt.7,
15.*

intro, *to the inside, in,* Mt.
26,58; [Mk.14,54]; A.12,
14.*

intro, 1, *enter.*

introduco, xi, 3, *bring in.*

†**introductio, onis,** *f., bring-*
ing in (Gr. ἐπεισαγωγή),
H.7,19.*

introeo, ii and **iui,** 4, *enter.*

introgredior, gressus, 3, *enter,*
A.16,29; 19,8.*

introitus, us, *m., entrance,* 1
Th.1,9; 2,1; H.10,19;
2 P.1,11.*

intueor, 2, *look on,* A.11,6;
behold, Mk.10,21; H.
7,4.

inundatio, onis, *f.*, *flood*, L.
6,48.*
inundo, 1, *overflow*, *inun-
date*, 2 P.3,6.*
inungo, 3, *anoint*, Ap.3,18.*
inutilis, e, *useless*, *unpro-
fitable*, L.17,10 ; R.3,12.
†inutilitas, tatis, *f.*, *unpro-
fitableness*, H.7,18.*
inuado, uasi, 3, *enter into*,
Mk.16,8 ; *lay hold of*, A.
28,3.*
inualesco, lui, 3, *be strong*,
urgent, L.23,5 ; *prevail*,
L.23,23 ; A.19,16.*
inuenio, ueni, uentus, 4, *find.*
inuentor, oris, *m.*, *inventor*,
R.1,30.*
inuestigabilis, e, *unsearch-
able*, R.11,33 ; E.3,8.*
inuicem, *one another, mutu-
ally.*
inuideo, 3, *envy*, G.5,26.*
inuidia, ae, *f.*, *envy.*
inuiolatus, a, um, *inviolate*,
unhurt, pure, 2 P.3,14.*
inuito, 1, *bid, invite*, Mt.22,
3 ff.; L.14,7 ff.*
inuitus, a, um, *unwilling*, 1
C.9,17.*
inuoco, 1, *call on*, R.10,12
ff.; *call*, Jas.2,7 ; 1 P.1,
17.
inuoluo, ui, utus, 3, *wrap*,
L.2,7 ; *roll up*, J.20,7 ;
Ap.6,14.
†°iota (indecl.), *n.*, *iota, jot*,
Mt.5,18.*

F

ira, ae, *f.*, *anger.*
iracundia, ae, *f.*, *wrath*, A.
14,2 ; E.4,26 ; 6,4 ; Ap.
15,7.*
iracundus, a, um, *wrathful*,
Ti.1,7.*
irascor, ratus, 3, *be angry.*
*°iris, is and idis, *f.*, *rainbow*,
Ap.4,3 ; 10,1.*
irr-, v. inr- in some cases.
irrito, 1, *irritate, provoke*, 1
C.13,5.*
irritus, a, um, *void, of no
effect*, ||Mt.15,6 ; G.3,17 ;
1 T.5,12 ; H.10,28.*
iter, itineris, *n.*, *journey.*
†iterato, *over again, once
more*, J.3,4.*
iterum, *again, a second time.*

I (consonantal)

iaceo, 2, *lie*, Mk.2,4 ; [Ap.11,
8] ; *lie sick*, Mk.5,40.
iacio, 3, (1) *cast*, Mk.4,26 ;
J.8,59 ; (2) *lay* (foundation), H.6,1.*
iacto, 1, *cast*, Mt.21,21 ;
Mk.12,41 ; *toss*, Mt.14,
24.
†iactura, ae, *f.*, *loss*, A.27,
21.*
iactus, us, *m.*, (1) *cast, throw*
(of a stone), L.22,41 ;
(2) *casting* (overboard),
A.27,18.*

[iampridem], iam pridem, *long since, long ago,* G.4, 13.*

ianitor, oris, *m., porter,* Mk. 13,34.*

ianua, ae, *f., door,* J.20,26 ; A.10,17.

ieiunatio, onis, *f., fasting, abstinence,* A.14,23 ; 27, 21.*

ieiunium, ii, *n., fast, fasting,* ‖Mt.17,21 ; 2 C.6,5.

ieiuno, 1, *fast,* Mt.4,2 ; A.13, 2 f.

ieiunus, a, um, *fasting, hungry, without food,* ‖Mt. 15,32 ; A.27,33.*

iubeo, iussi, iussus, 2, *order, command.*

iucunditas, tatis, *f., joy, enjoyment,* A.2,28 ; H.11, 25.*

incundor, 1, *be delighted,* Ap. 11,10.*

Iudaice, *in Jewish fashion,* G.2,14.*

Iudaicus, a, um, *Jewish,* Ti. 1,14.*

Iudaismus, i, *m., Jewish religion, Judaism,* G.1, 13 f.*

Iudaizo, 1, *act* or *live as a Jew,* G.2,14.*

iudex, icis, *c., judge.*

iudicium, ii, *n., judgment,* J.3,19 ; H.6,2 ; *trial,* 1 C.6,4 ff.

iudico, 1, *judge,* J.3,17 ;

adjudge, A.13,46 ; *decide, determine,* A.3,13.

iugum, i, *n., yoke,* Mt.11, 29 f.; 2 C.6,14 ; 1 T.6,1.

iumentum, i, *n., beast of burden,* L.10,34 ; A.23, 24 ; Ap.18,13.*

iunctura, ae, *f., fastening, band,* A.27,40 ; E.4,16.*

iungo, iunctus, 3, *join, unite,* A.9,26 ; 1 C.7,10 ; 7, 38.*

iuramentum, i, *n., oath,* Mt. 5,33 ; H.6,16 ; Jas.5, 12.

iuro, 1, *swear,* Mt.23,16 ff.; H.3,11 ; Ap.10,6.

iusiurandum, iurisiurandi, *n., oath,* L.1,73 ; H.6,17.

iussus, us, *m., command, voice of command,* 1 Th. 4,16.*

iuste, *justly,* L.23,41 ; §1 C. 15,34 ; 1 Th.2,10 ; Ti.2, 12.*

iustificatio, onis, *f., justification,* R.4,25 ; *righteousness,* R.8,4 ; *righteous act, ordinance,* L.1, 6.

iustifico, 1, *justify,* ‖Mt.11, 19 ; L.7,29 ; *account righteous,* R.2,13 ; *make righteous,* L.16,15.

iustitia, ae, *f., righteousness,* Mt.3,15 ; J.16,8.

iustus, a, um, *just, right, righteous.*

iuuencula, ae, *f.,* *young woman,* 1 T.5,2.*
†**iuuenilis, e,** *pertaining to youth, youthful,* 2 T.2, 22.*
iuuenis, e (compar. **iunior,** J.21,18, §**iuuenior,** 1 T.5, 14), *young ;* (as subst.) *young man.*
iuuentus, tutis, *f., youth, time of youth,* ||Mk.10,20 ; A.26,4.*

L

labium, ii, *n., lip,* ||Mt.15,8 ; R.3,13 ; 1 P.3,10.
labor, oris, *m., labour, toil.*
laboro, 1, *labour, toil,* Co.1, 29 ; 2 T.2,3 ff.
lac, lactis, *n., milk,* 1 C.3,2 ; 9,7 ; H.5,12 f.; 1 P.2, 2.*
lacrima (-ryma), ae, *f., tear.*
[**lacteo**], 2, *be a suckling,* Mt. 21,16.*
lacto, 1, (1) *give suck,* L.23, 29 ; (2) *be a suckling,* §Mt.21,16.*
lacus, us, *m., vat, wine vat,* Mk.12,1 ; Ap.14,19 f. ; [Ap.18,17].*
laedo, si, 3, *hurt, injure,* 2 C.7,2 ; G.4,12 ; Ap.2, 11 ; 6,6 ; 9,4 ; 11,5.*
laetifico, 1, *make glad,* 2 C. 2,2.*

laetitia, ae, *f., gladness,* A. 14,17 ; 1 P.1,8.*
laetor, 1, *rejoice, be glad,* A. 16,34 ; Ap.12,12.
°**laguena (-gena), ae,** *f., vessel, bottle,* Mk.14,13.*
lama (lamma), (Hebr.), *why?* Mk.15,34.*
lamento, 1, *lament, wail,* ||Mt. 11,17.*
lamentor, 1, *lament* or *wail over,* L.23,27.*
°**lampas, adis,** *f., torch, lamp,* Mt.25,1 ff.; A.20,8 ; Ap. 4,5.*
lana, ae, *f., wool,* H.9,19 ; Ap.1,14.*
lancea, ae, *f., spear,* J.19,34.*
†**lancearius, ii,** *m., spearman,* A.23,23.*
langueo, 2, *be faint, sick,* L.7,10 ; J.5,3 ; 11,1 ; 1 T.6,4.* **languerat** in L.7,10 is perhaps from **languesco.**
languidus, a, um, *sick, infirm,* Mt.14,14 ; J.5,7 ; A.19,12.*
languor, oris, *m., sickness, infirmity,* ||Mt.4,23 f.; A. 19,12.
†**lanterna (lat-), ae,** *f., lantern,* J.18,3.*
lapideus, a, um, *made of stone, stone,* J.2,6 ; 2 C. 3,3 ; Ap.9,20.*
lapido, 1, *stone,* A.5,26 ; 2 C. 11,25 ; H.11,37.

lapis, idis, *m.*, *stone.*

laqueus, i, *m.*, *noose*, Mt.27, 5 ; *snare*, R.11,9 ; 2 T. 2,26.

lateo, 2, *be hid, escape notice*, A.26,26 ; H.13,2.

laterna, v. lant-.

*latine, *in Latin*, J.19,20 ; Ap.9,11.*

†latinus, a, um, *Latin*, L.23, 38.*

latitudo, dinis, *f.*, *breadth*, E. 3,18 ; Ap.20,9 ; 21,16.*

latro, onis, *m.*, *robber*, J.10,1; 2 C.11,26.

latus, eris, *n.*, *side*, J.19,34 ; 20,20 ff.; A.12,7.*

latus, a, um, *broad, wide.*

laudo, 1, *praise.*

laus, laudis, *f.*, *praise.*

lauacrum, i, *n.*, *laver*, E.5, 26 ; Ti.3,5.*

lauo, laui, lotus, 1, *wash*, Mk. 7,2 f.; L.5,2 ; J.13,5 ff.

laxo, 1, *loose, let down*, L.5, 4 f.; A.27,40.*

lectio, onis, *f.*, *reading*, A.13, 15 ; 2 C.3,14 ; 1 T.4,13.

lectulus, i, *m.*, *bed*, A.5,15.*

lectus, i, *m.*, *bed, couch*, ‖Mt. 9,2 ; Ap.2,22.

legatio, onis, *f.*, *embassy*, L. 14,32 ; 19,14 ; 2 C.5,20 ; E.6,20.*

legio, onis, *f.*, *legion*, Mt.26, 53 ; ‖Mk.5,9.*

†legislatio, onis, *f.*, *giving of law*, R.9,4.*

legislator, oris, *m.*, *law-giver*, Jas.4,12.*

*legitime, *lawfully*, 1 T.1,8 ; 2 T.2,5.*

legitimus, a, um, *lawful*, A. 19,39.*

lego, gi, ctus, 3, (1) *read ;* (2) *coast along*, A.27,13.

lema (lamma) (Aram.), *why ?* Mt.27,46.*

lenitas, tatis, *f.*, *meekness, gentleness*, G.6,1.*

leo, onis, *m.*, *lion.*

lepra, ae, *f.*, *leprosy*, ‖Mt.8, 3.*

leprosus, a, um, *leprous ;* (as subst.) *leper.*

lĕuis, e, *light*, Mt.11,30 ; 2 C.4,17.*

leuita, also levites (A.4,36), ae, *m.*, *Levite*, L.10,32 ; J.1,19.*

leuitas, tatis, *f.*, *lightness, fickleness*, 2 C.1,17.*

leuiticus, a, um, *levitical*, H. 7,11.*

leuo, 1, *lift up*, L.17,13 ; 1 T.2,8.

lex, legis, *f.*, *law.*

libellus, i, *m.*, *writing*, Mt.5, 31 ; ‖19,7 ; *little book*, Ap.10,2.*

libenter, *gladly*, Mk.6,20 ; 12,37 ; A.21,17.

liber, bri, *m.*, *book.*

liber, era, erum, *free.*

[liberi], orum, *c.*, *children*, L. 20,28.*

libero, 1, *free, deliver.*

†**libertinus**, **i**, *m.*, *freed man*, A.6,9.*

†**libertus**, **i**, *m.*, *freed man* (in reference to his manumitter), 1 C.7,22.*

libido, **dinis**, *f.*, *lust*, Co.3, 5.*

***libra**, **ae**, *f.*, *pound*, J.12,3 ; 19,39.*

licentia, **ae**, *f.*, *freedom, liberty*, 1 C.8,9.*

licet (impers.), 2, *is lawful, permitted* ; **licent** (pers.) ; *be lawful*, 1 C.6,12 (bis) ; 10,23.

licet, *though*, Mk.6,23 ; 2 C. 4,16 ; 12,15 ; G.1,8.*

lictor, oris, *m.* (Gk.ῥαβδοῦχος), *lictor*, A.16,35 ff.*

ligneus, **a**, **um**, *made of wood, wooden*, 2 T.2,20 ; Ap. 9,20.*

lignum, **i**, *n.*, *wood*, Ap.18,12; *tree*, L.23,31 ; G.3,13 ; *staff*, Mk.14,43 ; *stocks*, A.16,24.

ligo, 1, *bind*, J.18,12 ; Ap. 20,2.

lilium, **ii**, *n.*, *lily*, ||Mt.6, 28.*

lingo, 3, *lick*, L.16,21.*

lingua, **ae**, *f.*, *tongue*, L.16, 24 ; *language*, 1 C.12,10.

[**linio**], 4, *smear*, J.9,6.*

§**lino**, **leui**, 3, *smear*, J.9,6.*

linteamen, **minis**, *n.*, *linen cloth;* L.24,12 ; J.20,5 ff.*

***linteum**, **i**, *n.*, *linen cloth, towel, sheet*, J.13,4 ; 19, 40 ; A.10,11 ; 11,5.*

°**linum**, **i**, *n.*, (1) *flax*, Mt.12, 20 ; (2) *linen* [Ap.15,6].*

lis, **litis**, *f.*, *strife, quarrel*, 2 T.2,23 ; Jas.4,1.*

†°**lithostrotus** (-tos), **i**, *m.*, *pavement*, J.19,13.*

litigiosus, **a**, **um**, *contentious, quarrelsome*, 1 T.3,3 ; Ti. 3,2.*

litigo, 1, *strive*, J.6,52 ; A. 7,26 ; 2 T.2,24 ; Jas.4, 2.*

littera, **ae**, *f.*, *letter* (of alphabet), L.23,38 ; G.6,11 ; *the letter* (opp. to the spirit), R.2,27 ff.; 7,6 ; 2 C.3,6 f. (In pl.) (1) *learning*, J.7,15 ; A.4,13; 26,24 ; (2) *writings*, J.5, 47 ; 2 T.3,15 ; (3) *bond*, L.16,7 ; (4) *epistle*, A. 28,21.*

litus (litt-), **oris**, *n.*, *shore*, J.21,4 ; A.21,5.

liuor, **oris**, *m.*, *bruise, stripe*, 1 P.2,24.*

loco, 1, *let* (on hire), *lease*, ||Mt.21,33.*

loculus, **i**, *m.*, (1) *bier*, L.7, 14 ; (2) *purse, bag*, J. 12,6 ; 13,29.*

locuples, **pletis**, *rich*, 1 P.3, 4 ; Ap.3,18.*

locupleto, 1, *enrich*, 2 C.6, 10 ; 9,11 ; Ap.3,17.*

locus, i, *m.*, (pl. loca), *place, position, room.*

locusta, v. luc-.

*longanimitas, tatis, *f.*, *long-suffering*, R.2,4 ; 2 T.3, 10.

†longanimiter, *patiently*, H. 6,15.*

longe, *far, far off ;* a longe, *afar off, from afar.*

longeuus (-aeuus), a, um, *long-lived*, E.6,3.*

longinquus, a, um, *distant*, L.15,13 ; 19,12.*

longitudo, dinis, *f.*, *length*, E.3,18 ; Ap.21,16.*

longus, a, um, *long* [Mt.23, 14] ; L.20,47.*

loquella (-ela), ae, *f.*, *speech, language*, J.4,42 ; 8,43 ; *manner of speech*, Mt. 26,73.*

loquor, locutus, 3, *speak.*

lorica, ae, *f.*, *breastplate*, E. 6,14 ; 1 Th.5,8 ; Ap.9, 9 ; 9,17.*

lorum, i, *n.*, *thong, scourge*, A.22,25.*

luceo, 2, *be light, shine*, Mt. 5,15 ; Ap.1,16.

lucerno, ae, *f.*, *lamp*, ‖Mt.5, 15 ; J.5,35.

†lucesco, 3, *begin to shine, dawn*, Mt.28,1.*

lucidus, a, um, *full of light, bright*, ‖Mt.6,22 ; 17,5.*

lucifer, feri, *m.*, *morning-star*, 2 P.1,19.*

[lucrifacio], lucri facio.

†lucrifio, fieri, *be gained, won*, 1 P.3,1.*

lucror, 1, *gain*, ‖Mt.16,26 ; 1 C.9,20.

lucrum, i, *n.*, *gain*, Ph.1,21 ; Ti.1,7 ff.

luctus, ūs, *m.*, *grief, mourning*, Jas.4,9 ; Ap.18,7.

lucusta (loc-), ae, *f.*, *locust*, ‖Mt.3,4 ; Ap.9,3 ff.*

ludibrium, ii, *n.*, *mockery*, H.11,36.*

ludo, 3, *play*, 1 C.10,7.*

lugeo, 2, *mourn*, Mt.5,5 ; Jas. 4,9 ; *mourn for* or *over*, 2 C.12,21.

lumbus, i, *m.*, *loin* (only in pl.). ‖Mt.3,4 ; 1 P.1,13.

lumen, inis, *n.*, *light, a light.*

luminare, is, *n.*, *light-giver, luminary*, Ph.2,15.*

luna, ae, *f.*, *moon.*

*lunaticus, a, um, *epileptic, lunatic*, Mt.4,24 ; 17, 15.*

lupus, i, *m.*, *wolf*, Mt.7,15 ; ‖10,16 ; J.10,12 ; A.20, 29.*

luscus, a, um, *one-eyed, with one eye*, Mk.9,47.*

lutum, i, *n.*, *mud, clay*, J.9, 6 ff.; R.9,21 ; 2 P.2,22.*

lux, lucis, *f.*, *light.*

luxurior, 1, *be wanton, revel*, 1 T.5,11 ; 2 P.2,13.*

†luxuriose, *riotously, prodigally*, L.15,13.*

[luxuriosus], a, um, *wanton*, 2 P.2,7.*

†lycaonice, *in the speech of Lycaonia*, A.14,11.*

M

†macellum, i, *n.*, *meat-market*, 1 C.10,25.*

maceria, ae, *f.*, *enclosure, wall*, E.2,14.*

macto, 1, *kill, slaughter*, J. 10,10.*

macula, ae, *f.*, *spot*, E.5,27 ; 2 P.2,13.

maculo, 1, *defile, stain*, Jas. 3,6 ; Jude 8, Jude 23.*

maereo (moe-), 2, *sorrow, grieve*, Mk.10,22.*

maeror (moe-), oris, *m.*, *grief, mourning*, H.12,11; Jas.4,9.*

maestus (moe-), a, um, *sad*, Mt.26,37 ; Ph.2,26.*

[†°magia], ae, *f.*, *magic, sorcery*, A.8,11.*

§°magicus, a, um, *pertaining to magic, magical*, A.8, 11.*

magis, *more, the more, rather.*

magnalia, ium, *n.*, *great things, mighty works*, A. 2,11.*

magnificentia, ae, *f.*, *greatness, magnificence*, Jude 25.*

magnifico, 1, *make great*, Mt.23,5; *magnify*, L.1,46; A.5,13.

magnificus, a, um, *great, eminent*, 2 P.1,17.*

magnitudo, dinis, *f.*, *greatness.*

magnus, a, um, *great.*

magus, i, *m.*, (1) *magian, magus, wise-man*, Mt.2, 1 ff.; (2) *sorcerer*, A.8,9 ; 13,6 ff.*

male, *ill, badly, grievously, evilly* ; male habere, *be ill.*

maledico, xi, ctus, 3, *speak evil of*, A.19,9 ; *curse*, G.3,10 ff.; Jas.3,9.

maledictio, onis, *f.*, *cursing, curse*, R.3,14 ; Jas.3,10; 2 P.2,14.*

maledictum, i, *n.*, *curse*, G. 3,10 ff.; Ap.22,3.

maledicus, a, um, *evil-speaking, slanderous*, 1 C.5,11; 6,10 ; 1 P.4,15.*

[malefacio], male facio, 1 P. 3,17 ; 3 J.11.*

*malefactor, oris, *m.*, *malefactor, evil-doer*, J.18,30 ; 1 P.2,12 ff.*

malignitas, tatis, *f.*, *malice, spite*, R.1,29.*

malignus, a, um, *evil, malicious*, L.8,2 ; (as subst.) *the Evil One*, 1 J.2,13 f.; 3,12 ; 5,18 f.

malitia, ae, *f.*, *evil*, Mt.6,34 ;

wickedness, malice, 1 C.
  5,8 ; 1 P.2,1.
malum, i, *n., evil, evil deed.*
malus, a, um, *bad, evil.*
mamilla, ae, *f., breast,* Ap.
  1,13.*
*mamona (mammo-), ae, *f.*
  .(Syr.) *riches, wealth,* Mt.
  6,24 ; L.16,9 ff.*
mancipium, ii, *n., slave,* Ap.
  18,13.*
mandatum, i, *n., commandment.*
mando, 1, *command,* ||Mt.4,
  6 ; J.8,5.
manduco, 1, *eat.*
mane, *in the morning, early.*
maneo, mansi, 2, *abide, remain, continue.*
†manico, 1, *come in the morning,* L.21,38.*
*manifestatio, onis, *f., mani-
  festing, manifestation,* 1
  C.12,7 ; 2 C.4,2.*
manifeste, *manifestly, openly.*
manifesto, 1, *manifest, make
  known.*
manifestus, a, um, *manifest,
  clear, known.*
manna, (indecl.) *n., manna,*
  J.6,31 ff.; H.9,4 ; Ap.2,
  17.*
mansio, onis, *f., abode, abid-
  ing-place,* J.14,2 ; 14,23.*
mansuetudo, dinis, *f., meekness.*
mansuetus, a, um, *meek,*
  Mt.21,5 ; 2 T.2,24.*

manufactus, a, um, *made by
  hands,* A.7,48; 17,24 (elsewhere, four times, manu
  factus).
manus, us, *f., hand.*
†maranatha (maran atha)
  (Aram.), *Our Lord cometh,*
  1 C.16,22.*
marcesco, 3, *wither, fade
  away,* Jas.1,11.*
mare, is, *n., sea.*
*°margarita, ae, *f., pearl,*
  Mt.7,6 ; 13,45 f.; 1 T.
  2,9.
maritimus, a, um, *by the sea,*
  maritima, Mt.4,13 ; L.
  6,17.*
°marmor, oris, *n., marble,*
  Ap.18,12.*
†°martyr, yris, *c., witness,
  martyr,* Ap.17,6.*
masculinus, a, um, *male,* L.
  2,23.*
masculus, a, um, *male,* G.3,
  28 ; Ap.12,5.
massa, ae, *f., lump, mass,*
  R.9,21 ; 11,16 ; 1 C.5,6 ;
  G.5,9.*
mater, tris, *f., mother.*
[materfamilias], mater familias, 1 T.5,14.*
†matricida, ae, *c., mother's
  murderer, matricide,* 1 T.
  1,9.*
matrimonium, ii, *n., marriage,* 1 C.7,10 ; 7,38.*
mature (only compar. -rius),
  soon, A.25,4.*

†maturus, a, um, *ripe*, Ap. 14,18.*

matutinus, a, um, *belonging to the morning, morning*, Ap.2,28 ; 22,16.*

maxilla, ae, *f.*, *cheek*, ‖Mt. 5,39.*

maxime, *most of all, especially*.

maximus, a, um, *greatest*.

. mediator, oris, *m.*, *mediator*, G.3,19 f.; H.8,6.

medicus, i, *m.*, *physician*, L.4,23 ; Co.4,14.

†medio, 1, *be in the middle*, J.7,14.*

meditor, 1, *meditate, meditate on*, A.4,25 ; 1 T.4,15.*

medium, ii, *n.*, *middle*.

medius, a, um, *middle, midmost*.

medulla, ae, *f.*, *marrow*, H. 4,12.*

mel, mellis, *n.*, *honey*, ‖Mt. 3,4 ; L.24,42 ; Ap.10, 9 f.*

melior, ius, *better*.

†°melota, ae, *f.*, *sheepskin*, H.11,37.*

membrana, ae, *f.*, *parchment*, 2 T.4,13.*

membrum, i, *n.*, *limb*, Mt.5, 29 f.; *member*, Jas.3,5 f.*

memini, . isse (imperat. memento, L.23,42), *remember*, J.16,21 ; A.20, 35.

memor, oris, *mindful*.

memoria, ae, *f.*, (1) *memory*, A.20,31 ; (2) *remembrance*, Ph.1,3 ; 2 T.1,3 ; (3) *memorial*, ‖Mt.26,13.

memoror, 1, (1) *remember*, L.1,54 ; 1,72 ; H.8,12 ; (2) *make mention of*, H. 11,22.*

mendacium, ii, *n.*, *lie, lying*.

mendax, acis, *lying;* (as subst.) *a liar*, J.8,44.

mendico, 1, *beg*, Mk.10,46 ; L.16,3 ; 18,35 ; J.9,8.*

mendicus, i, *m.*, *beggar*, L.16, 20 ff.; J.9,8.*

mens, mentis, *f.*, *mind, understanding*.

mensa, ae, *f.*, *table*.

mensis, is, *m.*, *month*.

mensura, ae, *f.*, *measure*, J. 3,34 ; *a measure*, Ap.21, 15.

menta (-tha), ae, *f.*, *mint*, ‖Mt.23,23.*

mentior, 4, *lie, tell lies*.

mercator, oris, *m.*, *merchant*, Ap.18,3 ff.*

mercennarius (-enarius), ii, *m.*, *hired servant*, Mk.1, 20 ; L.15,17 ff.; *hireling*, J.10,12 f.*

merces, edis, *f.*, *reward*, Mt. 5,12 ; *hire, pay*, Jas.5, 4.

*mercor, 1, *buy*, Mk.15,46 ; *trade*, Jas.4,13.*

mereor, 2, *deserve*, H.10, 29.*

meretrix, icis, *f., harlot,* L. 15,30.

*****mergo,** 3, *plunge into, submerge,* 1 T.6,9 ; (in pass.) *sink, be submerged, plunged,* Mt.14,30 ; L. 5,7 ; A.20,9.*

meridianum, i, *n., South,* A. 8,26.*

merum, i, *n., pure, unmixed wine,* Ap.14,10.*

merx, cis, *f.,* (in pl.) *merchandise, wares,* Ap.18, 11 f.*

messis, is, *f., harvest,* ‖Mt. 9,37 f.; J.4,35.

messor, oris, *m., reaper,* Mt. 13,30 ff.*

metior, mensus, 4, (1) *measure;* (2) *be measured,* §Mt.7, 2.

meto, messui, 3, *reap.*

°metreta, ae, *f., metretes* (a liquid measure), *firkin,* J.2,6.*

metuo, 3, *fear,* Mk.6,20 ; A. 10,7 ; H.11,7 ; 2 P.2, 20.

metus, us, *m., fear,* J.7,13 ; Ph.2,12.

mica, ae, *f., crumb,* ‖Mt.15, 27 ; L.16,21.*

migro, 1, *remove, depart,* Mt. 19,1 ; A.18,7.*

miles, litis, *m., soldier.*

milies (mill-), *a thousand times,* Ap.9,16.*

militia, ae, *f.,* (1) *host,* L.2,

13 ; A.7,42 ; (2) *warfare,* 2 C.10,4 ; 1 T.1,18.*

milito, 1, *serve as a soldier,* 2 T.2,4 ; *carry on war, strive,* Jas.4,1 ; 1 P.2, 11.

minae, arum, *f., threats, threatenings,* A.4,29 ; 9, 1 ; E.6,9.*

minime, *a very little,* A.20, 12.*

minister, tri, *m., attendant,* L.4,20 ; *minister,* 1 C.3,5 ; E.6,21 ; *servant,* J.2,5 ; *official,* A.5,22 ff.

ministerium, ii, *n., serving,* L.10,40 ; *ministering,* A. 6,1 ; *ministry, office, service,* A.1,17 ; 1 T.1,12.

*****ministratio, onis,** *f., administration, ministry, service,* 1 C.12,5 ; 2 C.3, 7 ff.*

†**ministrator, oris,** *m., servant,* L.22,26.*

ministro, 1, *do service, minister, serve,* Mt.8,15, J.12,2 ; *furnish, give,* 1 P.1,12 ; 2 P.1,5.

mino, 1, *drive,* A.18,16 ; Jas.3,4.*

minor, us (superl. **minimus, a, um**), *less.*

minoro, 1, (1) *be in want, lack,* 2 C.8,15 ; (2) in pass. (H.2,9), *be made less.**

minuo, ui, 3, *diminish, make less,* J.3,30 ; H.2,7.*

minus, *less.*
minutum, i, *n., smallest piece of money, mite,* ||Mk.12, 42 ; L.12,59.*
mirabilis, e, *marvellous, strange,* L.5,26 ; Ap.15, 1 ff.
miror, 1, *wonder, marvel.*
mirus, a, um, *strange, wonderful,* 2 C.11,14.*
misceo, cui, mixtus, 2, *mix, mingle,* Mt.27,34 ; L.13, 1 ; Ap.8,7.
miser, era, erum, *miserable, wretched, afflicted,* Jas.4, 9 ; Ap.3,17.*
miseratio, onis, *f., pity,* Ph. 2,1 ; H.10,28.*
miserator, oris, *m., pitiful, one who pities,* Jas.5, 11.*
misereor, sertus, 2, *pity, have mercy on.*
miseria, ae, *f., calamity, misfortune, trouble,* Jas. 5,1.*
misericordia, ae, *f., mercy, pity, compassion.*
misericors, cordis, *merciful.*
mitis, e, *gentle, meek,* Mt.5, 4 ; 11,29.*
mitto, misi, missus, 3, (1) *send;* (2) *cast; put,* Mk. 7,33 ; J.13,2 ; 20,25 ff. ; *lay,* J.7,44 ; Ap.2,24 ; *cast off,* §Ap.6,13.
†mixtura, ae, *f., mixture,* J. 19,39.*

°mna, ae, *f., mina, pound,* L.19,13 ff.*
mobilis, e, *movable, changeable,* H.12,27.*
modestia, ae, *f., moderation,* 2 T.2,25 ; 1 P.3,15 ; *gentleness,* 2 C.10,1 ; G.5,23.
modestus, a, um, *moderate, gentle, mild,* 1 T.3,3 ; Ti. 3,2 ; Jas.3,17.
modicum, i, *n., a little,* J. 6,7 ; *a little while,* H.10, 37.
modicus, a, um, *small,* Jas. 3,4 f.; *little,* A.28,2 ; *slender* [Mt.6,30] ; *scanty,* Ap.3,8.
modius, ii, *m., a measure for corn, peck, bushel,* ||Mt. 5,15.*
modo, *now, just now, lately, presently.*
modus, i, *m.,* (1) *measure, limit,* 2 C.1,8 ; 4,17 ; (2) *way, manner, method,* R. 3,2 ; Ph.1,18 ; H.1,1.
moechor, 1, *commit adultery.*
moer-, v. maer-.
moestus, v. maes-.
mola, ae, *f., millstone,* ||Mt. 18,6 ; 24,41 ; Ap.18,22.*
molaris, e, *belonging to a millstone, mill-;* L.17,2 ; (as subst.) *millstone,* Ap. 18,21.*
molestus, a, um, *troublesome,* ||Mt.26,10 ; L.11,7 ; 18,5 ; G.6,17.*

mollis, e, *soft,* L.7,25;
effeminate, 1 C.6,9.*.

molo, 3, *grind,* ||Mt.24,41.*

†**momentaneus, a, um,** *short,*
momentary, 2 C.4,17.*

momentum, i, n., (1) *moment,*
L.4,5; 1 C.15,52; (2)
season, A.1,7; 1 Th.5,1.*

moneo, 2, *warn, admonish,*
A.20,31; R.15,14; 1
C.4,14; 1 Th.5,12.*

mons, ntis, m., *mountain.*

monstro, 1, *show, point out,*
A.7,3.*

montanus, a, um, *belong to
a mountain, mountain-,
hill-,* L.1,39; 1,65.*

monumentum, i, n., *tomb,
grave.*

mora, ae, f., *delay* (only with
facere), Mt.24,49; 25,5;
L.12,45; A.20,16.*

mordeo, 2, *bite,* G.5,15.*

morior, mortuus, 3, *die.*

moror, 1, *abide, dwell,* J.11,
54; A.7,2; *tarry, delay,*
A.22,16.

mors, rtis, f., *death.*

mortifer, era, erum, *deadly,
fatal,* Mk.16,18; Jas.3,
8.*

†**mortificatio, onis, f.,** *putting
to death,* 2 C.4,10.*

mortifico, 1, *kill, destroy,* 2
C.6,9; 1 P.3,18; *mortify,
make weak,* R.7,4; 8,13.

°**morus, i, f.,** *mulberry tree,*
L.17,6.*

mos, oris, m., *custom, manner;* (in pl.) *manners,
conduct.*

[†**motio**], **onis, f.,** *moving,
movement, disturbance,* J.
5,4.*

motus, us, m., (1) *moving,
movement,* J.5,3; (2)
storm, Mt.8,24.*

moueo, moui, motus, 2, *move,
stir, influence.*

mox (with **ut**), *as soon as,*
Ph.2,23.*

muliebris, e, *female, feminine,*
1 P.3,7.*

mulier, eris, f., *woman, wife.*

†**muliercula, ae, f.,** *little
woman,* 2 T.3,6.*

multifariam, *in many places*
(Gk. πολυμερῶς), H.1,1.*

*****multiformis, e,** *manifold,*
E.3,10; 1 P.4,10.*

multiloquium, ii, n., *much
speaking,* Mt.6,7.*

multiplico, 1, *multiply.*

multo, *much, far.*

multum, *much.*

multus, a, um, *much, many.*

mundo, 1, *make* or *account
clean,* Mk.1,40; A.11,9;
cleanse, H.9,22.

mundus, a, um, *pure,* Ti.
1,15; Jas.1,27; *clean,*
J.13,10 f.; §1 J.1,7.

mundus, i, m., *world, universe, the world.*

†**municeps, cipis, c.,** *citizen,*
A.21,39.*

munio, 4, *make strong, secure*,
Mt.27,66.*

munitio, onis, *f., stronghold*,
2 C.10,4.*

munus, eris, *n., gift*, Mt.2,
11 ; L.21,1.

murmur, uris, *n., murmuring*,
J.7,12 ; A.6,1.*

murmuratio, onis, *f., murmuring*, Ph.2,14 ; 1 P.4,
9.*

†murmurator, oris, *m., murmurer*, Jude 16.*

murmuro, 1, *murmur*.

°murra (myrrha), ae, *f.,
myrrh*, Mt.2,11 ; J.19,
39.*

murro (myrrho), 1, *mix with
myrrh*, Mk.15,23.*

murus, i, *m., wall*.

°musicus, i, *m., musician*,
Ap.18,22.*

mustum, i, *n., must, new
wine*, A.2,13.*

muto, 1, *change*, A.6,14 ; R.
1,23 ; G.4,20 ; H.1,12.*

mutuor, 1, *borrow*, Mt.5,
42.*

mutus, a, um, *dumb*, 1 C.12,
2 ; 2 P.2,16.

mutuum, i, *n., loan ;* (only
with dare = *lend*), L.6,
34 f.*

mutuus, a, um, *mutual,
reciprocal*, 1 T.5,4 ; 1 P.
4,8.*

myrr-, v. murr-.

°mysterium, ii, *n., mystery*.

N

namque, *for*, H.3,4 ;   5,1 ;
6,13.*

°nardus, i, *f., nard*, Mk.14,3 ;
J.12,3.*

narratio, onis, *f., narration,
narrative*, L.1,1.*

narro, 1, *narrate, tell*, Mt.18,
31 ; L.8,39.

nascor, natus, 3, *be born*.

natalis, is, *m.* (sc. dies) *birthday*, ‖Mt.14,6.*

*natatoria, ae, *f., swimming-
place ; bath*, J.9,7 ff.*

natio, onis, *f., nation, people,*
A.2,5 ; Ph.2,15 ; (in pl.)
Gentiles, L.21,24.

natiuitas, tatis, *f., birth*, L.
1,14 ;   J.9,1 ;   Jas.1,23 ;
3,6.*

nato, 1, *swim*, A.27,43.*

naturalis, e, *natural*, R.1,
26 f. ; 11,21 ff.*

*naturaliter, *naturally, by
nature*, R.2,14 ;   2 P.2,
12 ; Jude 10.*

natus, us, *m., birth* (only in
abl. with maior = *elder*),
A.20,17 ; 22,5.*

natus, i, *m., son,* 1 J.5,2 ;
2 J.1.*

†°nauclerius (-rus), i, *m.,
ship-owner, ship-master*,
A.27,11.*

†naufragium, ii, *n., ship-
wreck*, 2 C.11,25.*

†naufrago, 1, *make ship-*
  wreck, 1 T.1,19.*
nauta, ae, *m.*, *sailor*, A.27,
  27 ff.; Ap.18,17.*
*naulcula, ae, *f.*, *little ship*,
  boat.
.*nauigatio, onis, *f.*, *sailing*,
  voyage, A.21,7 ; 27,9 f.*
*nauigium, ii, *n.*, *boat*, J.21,
  6 ff.*
nauigo, 1, *sail*, L.8,23 ff.;
  Ap.18,17.
nauis, is,*f.*, *ship, boat.*
nebula, ae, *f.*, *cloud*, 2 P.2,
  17.*
necdum, `not yet`, Mk.4,40 ;
  J.8,20 ; H.2,8.*
necesse, *necessary, needful ;*
  (with habeo) *need*, Mt.
  14,16 ; Mk.2,17 ; 1 Th.
  4,9 ; §1 J.3,17.
nefandus, a, um, *wicked*, 2
  P.2,7.*
neglego (-ligo), xi, 3, *neglect*,
  1 T.4,14 ; H.2,3, *despise*,
  H.12,5 ; *make light of,
  disregard*, Mt.22,5 ; H.
  8,9.*
nego, 1, *deny.*
negotiatio, onis, *f.*, *merchandise*, Mt.22,5 ; J.2,16.*
negotiator, oris, *m.*, *merchant*,
  Mt.13,45 ; Ap.18,11.*
negotior, 1, *trade, make
  profit, make merchandise*,
  L.19,13 ff.; 2 P.2,3.*
negotium, ii, *n.*, *business*,
  R.16,2 ; 1 Th.4,11 ; *af-*

fair, matter, 1 C.6,1 ; 2
  C.7,11 ; 1 Th.4,6 ; 2 T.
  2,4.*
neo, 2, *spin*, ||Mt.6,28.*
°neomenia, ae, *f.*, *new moon*,
  Co.2,16.*
†°neophytus, i, *m.*, *recent
  convert, neophyte*, 1 T.
  3,6.*
nepos, otis, *c.*, (in pl.) *grand-
  children*, 1 T.5,4.*
nequam, (indecl.) (compar.
  nequior, L.11,26, superl.
  nequissimus, E.6,16), *evil,
  wicked, worthless.*
[nequando], ne quando, *lest
  at any time*, Mt.13,15 ;
  Mk.4,12 ; 2 T.2,25.*
nequaquam, *by no means*,
  Mt.2,6 ; L.1,60 ; J.9,
  9 ; A.11,8 ; R.3,9.*
nequitia, ae, *f.*, *wickedness*,
  1 C.5,8 ; E.6,12.
nescio, 4, *not to know, be
  ignorant.*
nex, ecis, *f.*, *death*, A.7,60.*
nexus, us, *m.*, *fastening,
  joining*, Co.2,19.*
nidus, i, *m.*, (1) *nest* [Mt.
  8,20] ; L.9,58 ; (2) *nest-
  lings, brood*, L.13,34.*
niger, gra, grum, *black*, Mt.
  5,36 ; Ap.6,5 ff.*
nihilominus, *none the less*,
  H.6,5.*
nihilum, i, *n.*, *nothing* (always with ad or in), Mt.
  5,13 ; A.5,36 ; 19,27.*

†nimbus, i, *n., rain-storm,*
   L.12,54.*

nimis, *exceedingly, very,* Mt.
   8,28 ; Mk.9,3.*

nimius, a, um, *exceeding,*
   very great, E.2,4.*

nix, niuis, *f., snow,* ‖Mt.17,2 ;
   28,3 ; Ap.1,14.*

nobilis, e, *noble, honourable,*
   Mk.15,43 ; *notable,* R.
   16,7.

noceo, 2, *hurt, injure.*

†nociuus, a, um, *hurtful,*
   1 T.6,9.*

nolo, nolui, nolle, *be unwil-*
   ling, refuse.

nomen, inis, *n., name.*

nominatim, *by name,* J.10,
   3 ; [3 J.15].*

nomino, 1, *name, call.*

°nomisma (num-), atis, *n.,*
   piece of money, coin, Mt.
   22,19.*

nonaginta, *ninety,* ‖Mt.18,
   12 f.*

nondum, *not yet.*

nosco, noui, notus, 3, *know*
   (pres. stem not found in
   N.T.).

notitia, ae, f., knowledge,
   R.1,28 ; 2 C.2,14 ; H.
   10,26.*

noto, 1 (Gk. σημειῶ), *mark,*
   note, observe ; censure ?
   2 Th.3,14.*

notus, i, *m.,* (in pl,) *friends,*
   acquaintances, L.2,44 ;
   23,49.*

§nouellus, a, um, *new,* Mk.
   2,22.*

nouem, *nine,* ‖Mt.18,12 ; L.
   17,17.*

nouissime, *at last, latest.*

nouissimus, a, um, *last.*

nouitas, tatis, f., newness,
   novelty, R.6,4 ; 7,6 ; 12,
   2 ; 1 T.6,20.*

nouus, a, um, *new.*

nox, ctis, *f., night.*

nubes, is, *f., cloud.*

nubo, nupsi, nuptus, 3, *marry.*

nuditas, tatis, *f., nakedness,*
   R.8,35; 2 C.11,27; *shame,*
   Ap.3,18.*

§nudius, *it is now the . . . day*
   since (with quartana, sc.
   die), A.10,30.*

[nudiusquartus], a, um, *four*
   days ago, A.10,30.*

nudo, 1, *uncover,* Mk.2,4.*

nudus, a, um, *naked,* Ap.16,
   15 ; *bare,* 1 C.15,37 ;
   without outer garment,
   Mk.14,51 f.; J.21,7.

nullus, a, um, *no, none.*

numero, 1, *number,* ‖Mt.10,
   30.*

numerus, i, *m., number.*

numisma, v. nom-.

nummularius (numu-), ii,
   m., ‖Mt.21,12 ; 25,27 ;
   J.2,14 f.*

numquid (particle of interro-
   gation).

nuntio, 1, *announce, tell,*
   proclaim.

nuntius, ii, *m., messenger,*
　L.7,24 ; 9,52 ; Jas.2,
　25.*
nuper, *lately,* A.18,2.*
nuptiae, arum, *f., marriage,*
　wedding-feast.
*nuptialis, e, *pertaining to a*
　wedding, wedding-, Mt.
　22,11 f.*
†nuptus, us, *m., marriage,*
　Mt.24,38.*
nurus, us, *f., daughter-in-
　law,* ‖Mt.10,35.*
nusquam, *nowhere,* H.2,16.*
nutrio, 1, *give suck,* ‖Mk.13,
　17 ; *nurse, rear,* L.4,16 ;
　A.22,3 ; *nourish,* E.5,29.
nutrix, icis, *f., nurse,* 1 Th.
　2,7.*

O

obcaeco, 1, *blind, make blind,*
　Mk.6,52 ; 1 J.2,11.*
obdormio, 4, *fall asleep,* L.8,
　23 ; A.7,60.*
obduro, 1, *harden,* H.3,8 ff.;
　4,7.*
obed-, v. oboed-.
obeo, ii, 4, *die,* Mk.15,44.*
obicio (obiic-), 3, *throw out,*
　allege against, Mk.14,60 ;
　A.23,28 ; 25,7.*
obitus, us, *m., death,* Mt.2,15;
　2 P.1,15.*
obiurgatio, onis, *f., reproof,*
　rebuke, 2 C.2,6.*

oblatio, onis, *f., offering.*
obligatio, onis, *f., ensnaring,*
　entangling, A.8,23.*
obliuio, onis, *f., forgetfulness,*
　L.12,6 ; 2 P.1,9.*
†obliuiosus, a, um, *forgetful,*
　Jas.1,25.*
obliuiscor, litus, 3, *forget.*
obmutesco, tui, 3, *be* or
　become speechless, silent.
obnoxius, a, um, *liable to*
　punishment, liable, guilty,
　A.19,40 ; H.2,15.*
oboedio (obed-), 4, *obey.*
*oboeditio (obed-), onis, *f.,*
　obedience.
obprobrium (oppr-), ii, *n.,*
　reproach, L.1,25 ; 1 T.3,
　7 ; H.10,33.*
obscuro, 1, *darken* (only used
　in pass.), R.1,21 ; 11,10 ;
　Ap.8,12 ; 9,2.
obsecratio, onis, *f., supplica-
　tion, prayer.*
obsecro, 1, *entreat, beseech.*
obsequium, ii, *n., obedience,*
　service.
obseruatio, onis, *f., observa-
　tion, display,* L.17,20 ;
　observance, 1 C.7,19.*
obseruo, 1, *watch,* Mk.3,2 ;
　keep, observe, R.2,25 ;
　1 J.2,3 ; · in 1 C.7,35 =
　? *entreat.*
obstipesco (-stup-), pui, 3,
　be astonished, amazed,
　Mk.5,42 ; 10,24 ; 16,5 ;
　A.10,45 ; 12,16.*

obstruo, 3, *stop* (mouth), R. 3,19.*

obtempero, 1, *obey*, H.5,9; 12,9.*

*obtentus, us, *m.*, *pretext, pretence*, Mk.12,40; A. 27,30.*

obtineo, 2, *secure, lay hold of*, A.27,16.*

obturo, 1, *stop up, close*, H. 11,33.*

†obtundo, tunsus (-tusus), 3, *make blunt, dull*, 2 C. 3,14.*

†obumbratio, onis, *f.*, *overshadowing, obscuring*, Jas. 1,17.*

obumbro, 1, *overshadow*, ‖Mt. 17,5; L.1,35; A.5,15; H.9,5.*

obuiam, *towards, to meet*, J.12,13 ff.; 1 Th.4,17.

obuio, 1, *meet*, A.16,16; H. 7,1; 7,10.*

obuius, a, um, *so as to meet, meeting*, A.10,25.*

occasus, us, *m.*, *West*, L.12, 54; Ap.21,13.*

occidens, entis, *m.*, *West*, ‖Mt. 8,11; 24,27.*

occido, di, 3, *set* (of sun), Mk.1,32; L.4,40; E.4,26.*

occido, cidi, cisus, 3, *kill*.

occisio, onis, *f.*, *killing, slaughter*, A.8,32; R.8, 36; H.11,37; Jas.5,5.*

occulte, *secretly, privily*, Mt. 1,19; A.16,37.*

occulto, 1, *hide*, L.1,24; H. 11,23.*

occultus, a, um, *hidden, secret.*

occupo, 1, *occupy, fill up, cumber* (ground), L.13, 7; P.P. occupatus, *busy, engaged*, Ph.4,10.*

occurro, curri, 3, (1) *meet*, ‖Mt.8,28; J.4,51; (2) *attain to*, E.4,13; Ph. 3,11.

oculus, i, *m.*, *eye.*

odi, isse (fut. odiet, odient, L.16,13; Ap.17,16; partic. odiens), *hate.*

odibilis, e, *hateful*, R.1,30; Ti.3,3; [Ap.18,2].*

odium, ii, *n.*, *hatred, hate* (only in phrases odio esse, *be hateful*, and odio habere, *hate*).

odor, oris, *m.*, *odour.*

odoramentum, i, *n.*, *perfume, odour*, Ap.5,8; 18,13.*

†odoratus, us, *m.*, *sense of smell*, 1 C.12,17.*

offendiculum, i, *n.*, *offence*, A.24,16; *stumbling-block, hindrance*, R.14,13; 1 C. 8,9.

offendo, di, 3, *stumble, offend.*

†offensa, ae, *f.*, *offence*, Ph. 1,10.*

offensio, onis, *f.*, *stumbling, offence*, R.9,32 f.; *stumbling-block*, 2 C.6,3.

offero, obtuli and §optuli,

G

oblatus, ferre, *present, offer, bring.*

officium, ii, *n., office, duty, service,* L.1,23 ; 2 C.9, 12 ; H.9,6.*

*oleaster, tri, *m., wild olive tree,* R.11,17 ff.*

oleum, i, *n., oil,* Mk.6,13 ; H.1,9 ; Jas.5,14.

olim, *long ago, for a long while past.*

oliua, ae, *f.,* (1) *olive tree,* R.11,17 ff.; Ap.11,4 ; (2) *olive,* §Jas.3,12.

*oliuetum, i, *n., olive grove* (only in name mons Oliueti), J.8,1 ; A.1,12.

olus, v. holus.

omitto, 3, *leave undone, omit,* ||Mt.23,23.*

omnino, (1) *altogether,* 1 C. 5,1 ; 6,7; (2) (with negative), *at all,* Mt.5,34 ; L. 13,11 ; A.4,18.

omnipotens, entis; *almighty, omnipotent,* 2 C.6,18 and Ap. (six times).

onero, 1, *load, lade, burden,* Mt.11,28 ; L.11,46 ; 2 C.2,5 ; 2 T.3,6.*

onerosus, a, um, *burdensome,* 2 C.11,9.*

onus, eris, *n., burden, cargo,* A.21,3 ; 27,10.*

opera, ae, *f., service, work,* L.19,31 ; 1 C.12,21 ; *diligence,* L.12,58 ; 1 Th.4, 11 ; 2 P.1,15.*

operarius, ii, *m., worker, workman.*

operatio, onis, *f., operation, working, work.*

operio, opertus, 4, *cover, clothe.*

operor, 1, *work, do.*

†opifex, ficis, *c., worker, workman,* A.19,25.*

*opinio, onis, *f., fame, rumour,* Mt.4,24 ; ||24,6.*

†opitulatio, onis, *f., help, assistance,* 1 C.12,28.*

oportet, 2, (impers.) *it is necessary, needful, fit ; it behoves.*

*oportune (opp-), *conveniently, in due season,* Mk. 14,11 ; 2 T.4,2.*

oportunitas (opp-), tatis, *f.,* (1) *opportunity,* ||Mt.26, 16; (2) (Gr. χρεία), *need,* E.4,29.*

oportunus (opp-), a, um, *convenient, suitable, timely,* Mk.6,21 ; A.24,26 ; H. 4,16 ; 6,7.*

†oppositio, onis, *f., opposition,* 1 T.6,20.*

opprimo, pressus, 3, *oppress, trouble, vex,* L.11,53 ; A. 10,38 ; Jas.2,6 ; 2 P.2, 7.*

opprobrium, v. obp-.

optimus, a, um, *best.*

opto, 1, *wish, desire,* A.26, 29 ; 27,29 ; R.9,3.*

opus, eris, *n., work.*

opus (indecl.), *n.*, *need, necessity.*

ora, ae, *f., shore,* H.11,12.*

oratio, onis, *f., prayer.*

†**orator, oris,** *m., speaker, orator,* Λ.24,1.*

orbis, is, *m., world,* §A.17, 6.

ordeacus, v. **hordiaceus.**

ordinatio, onis, *f., ordinance,* R.13,2.*

ordino, 1, (1) *arrange, draw up in order,* L.1,1 ; (2) *ordain, order, appoint,* 1 C.16,1 ; 2 C.8,19 ; G. 3,19.

ordo, inis, *m., order.*

°**orichalcum (aur-), i,** *n., brass,* Ap.1,15 ; 2,18.*

°**orfanus (orpha-), i,** *m., orphan,* J.14,18.*

oriens, entis, *m., East.*

†**originalis, e,** *original, first,* 2 P.2,5.*

origo, inis, *f., origin, beginning,* H.9,26 ; Ap. 13,8.*

orior, ortus, 4, *spring up, rise, spring from.*

orno, 1, *adorn,* Ti.2,10 ; Ap. 21,2 ; *trim,* Mt.25,7.

oro, 1, *pray.*

ortus, us, *m., rising* (of sun), Ap.7,2 ; 16,12.

os, oris, *n., mouth.*

os, ossis, *n., bone.*

osanna (hos-), (Aram.), *save us,* ‖Mt.21,9 ff.*

osculor, 1, *kiss,* Mk.14,44 f.; A.20,37.

osculum, i, *n., kiss,* L.7,45 ; R.16,16.

ostendo, tendi, tensus, 3, *show, display, tell* ; (in pass.) *appear.*

ostensio, onis, *f., showing,* L.1,80 ; *display,* R.3, 25 f.

ostento, 1, *show, display,* H. 6,11.*

†**ostentus, us,** *m., display, spectacle,* H.6,6.*

ostiaria, ae, *f., doorkeeper,* J.18,16.*

ostiarius, ii, *m., doorkeeper, porter,* J.10,3.

ostiarius, a, um, *of* or *concerned with a door,* J.18, 17.*

ostium, ii, *n., door,* J.10,1 ff.

otiosus, a, um, *idle,* Mt.12, 36 ; 20,3 ff.; 1 T.5,13 ; §Jas.2,20.*

ouile, is, *n., sheepfold,* J.10, 1 ; 10,16.*

ouis, is, *f., sheep.*

ouum, i, *n., egg,* L.11,12.*

P

pacatus, a, um (only in superl.), *peaceful,* H.12, 11.*

pacifico, 1, *make peace,* Co. 1,20.*

pacificus, a, um, *peaceful, peaceable,* Mt.5,9; Jas.3, 17.*

paciscor, pactus, 3, *agree, stipulate,* L.22,5.*

*°**paedagogus** or **pedagogus,** (G.3,24 f.), **i,** *m., slave in charge of children, preceptor,* 1 C.4,15; G.3, 24 f.*

paene (pene), *almost* [L.5,7]; A.13,44; 19,26; H.9, 22.*

paeniteo (poe-), 2, (1) (pers. in passive) *repent,* Mk.1, 15; §Ap.2,21; (2) (impers.), *it repents,* L.17,4; 2 C.7,8.

†**paenula (pen-), ae,** *f., cloak, mantle,* 2 T.4,13.*

palam, *openly;* **in palam,** *in similar sense,* ‖Mk.4,22; J.7,4; 11,54.

palea, ae, *f., chaff,* ‖Mt.3,12.*

†**pallidus, a, um,** *pale,* Ap. .6,8.*

pallium, ii, *n., cloak,* Mt.5, 40.*

palma, ae, *f.,* (1) *hand, blow with the hand,* Mt.26,67; (2) *palm-tree,* J.12,13; *palm-branch,* Ap.7,9.*

palmes, mitis, *m., vine-branch,* J.15,2 ff.*

palpo, 1, *feel, handle,* L.24, 39.*

panis, is, *m., loaf, bread.*

pannus, i, *m., cloth,* ‖Mt.9,

16; (in pl.) *swaddling-clothes,* L.2,7 ff.*

par, paris, *equal,* Mt.20,12; (as subst.) *n., pair,* L.2, 24.*

°**parabola, ae,** *f., parable,* L.8,9; *figure,* H.9,9; 11, 19.

*°**Paracletus, i,** *m., advocate. Paraclete,* J.14,16; 14, 26; 15,26; 16,7.*

°**paradisus, i,** *m., paradise,* L.23,43; 2 C.12,4; Ap. 2,7.*

*°**paralyticus, a, um,** *palsied, paralytic,* Mt.8,6; (as subst.) *a paralytic,* ‖Mt. 9,2 ff.

*°**parapsis (-opsis), idis,** *f., dish,* Mt.23,25 f.; 26, 23.*

*°**parasceue, es** (acc. **-en**), *f., preparation, day of preparation,* ‖Mt.27,62.

parce, *sparingly,* 2 C.9,6 (bis).*

parco, peperci, 3, *spare.*

°**pardus, i,** *m., panther* or *leopard,* Ap.13,2.*

parens, entis, *c.* (in pl.) *parents,* E.6,1; Co.3,20.

pareo, 2, (1) *appear,* Jas.4, 14; (2) *obey,* A.10,7.

paries, etis, *m., wall, partition-wall,* A.23,3; E. 2,14.*

pario, peperi, 3, *bear, bring forth.*

pariter, *together*, Mt.14,9 ; A.2,1 ; 2,44.*

paro, 1, *prepare, make ready ;* in P.P., **paratus**, *ready.*

paropsis, v. **parap-.**

parr-, v. **patr-.**

particeps, cipis, *sharing, participant ;* (as subst.) *sharer, partaker, partner*, H.1,9 ; 3,1.

participatio, onis, *f., partaking, communion, fellowship*, 1 C.10,16 ; 2 C.6,14.*

participo, 1, *share in, be a partaker*, 1 C.10,30 ; H. 2,14. (The depon. form **participor** is found in 1 C.§9,13 ; §10,17.)*

partior, 4, *part, divide*, J. 19,24.*

parturio, 4, *travail, be in labour*, R.8,22.*

paruulus, a, um, *small ;* (as subst.) *child*, ||Mt. 19,13 f.

paruus, a, um, *small*, A.12, 18.*

pascha, ae, *f.* (Aram.), *Passover.*

pasco, 3, *feed, tend* (sheep, etc.).

pascuum, i, *n., pasture ;* (in pl.) J.10,9.*

passer, eris, *m., sparrow*, ||Mt.10,29 ff.

*****passibilis, e**, *capable of suffering* or *passions*, A.26,23 ; Jas.5,17.*

passio, onis, *f., suffering*, A.1,3 ; *passion*, R.1,26 ; 1 Th.4,5.

passus, us, *m., step, pace*, A. 7,5 ; as measure, Mt.5, 41 ; A.27,28 (bis).*

†**pastino**, 1, *prepare ground* (for vines), Mk.12,1.*

pastor, oris, *m., shepherd*, L.2,8 ff.; *pastor*, E.4,11.

*****patefacio, factus**, 3, *make* or *lay open*, Mk.2,4 ; R.16, 26.*

pateo, 2, *be open*, R.3,13 ; 2 C.6,11.*

pater, tris, *m., father.*

[**paterfamilias**] **pater familias.**

†**paternitas, tatis**, *f., ? fatherhood*, or *family*, i.e. *descendants of one father*, E.3,15.*

paternus, a, um, *ancestral, belonging to fathers*, A. 22,3 ; 28,17 ; G.1,14 ; 1 P.1,18.*

patienter, *patiently*, A.26,3 ; Jas.5,7 ; [1 P.2,20] ; 2 P. 3,9.*

patior, passus, 3, *suffer*, A. 3,18 ; 2 C.1,6 ; *bear with*, ||Mt.17,17.

patria, ae, *f., fatherland, country.*

°**patriarcha, ae**, *m., patriarch*, A.2,29 ; 7,8 f.; H.7,4.*

†**patricida** (parr-), **ae**, *c., murderer of a father, parricide*, 1 T.1,9.*

paucus, a, um (only in pl.),
   few.
§paulo, a little, somewhat,
   H.2,7.*
[paulominus], paulo minus,
   H.2,7.*
paululum, a little, a little way,
   Mk.14,35 ; 2 P.2,18.*
pauper, eris, poor.
pauperculus, a, um, poor,
   L.21,2.*
paupertas, tatis, f., poverty,
   2 C.8,2 ; Ap.2,9.*
paueo, 2, be afraid, Mk.14,
   33.*
pauor, oris, m., fear, Mk.16,
   8 ; L.4,36.*
pax, pacis, f., peace.
peccator, oris, m., sinner.
peccatrix, icis, f., sinner,
   L.7,37 ff.; (as adj.) sin-
   ful, Mk.8,38.*
peccatum, i, n., sin.
pecco, 1, sin.
pectus, oris, n., breast.
pecunia, ae, f., money.
pecus, oris, n. (only in pl.),
   cattle, J.4,12 ; 1 C.15,
   39 ; 2 P.2,12.*
pedagogus, v. paed-.
*pedester, tris, tre, on foot,
   ||Mt.14,13.*
peiero, (periuro), 1, forswear
   one's self, Mt.5,33.*
pelor, oris; worse.
°pelagus, i, n., sea, A.27,5.*
§pelliceo (pellicio, 3), 2, allure,
   entice, 2 P.2,14 ff.*

pellicius (-ceus), a, um, made
   of skins, ||Mt.3,4.*
pellis, is, f., skin, hide, H.
   11,37.*
peluis, is (acc. [-im]), f.,
   basin, J.13,5.*
pendeo, 2, hang, be hanged,
   Mt.22,40 ; L.23,39 ; A.
   28,4 ; G.3,13.*
pene, v. paene.
penes, in the power of, R.14,
   22.*
†penetrabilis, e (only compar.), penetrating, able
   to pierce, H.4,12.*
penetralia, ium, n., inner
   chamber, Mt.24,26.*
penetro, 1, enter, penetrate
   into, 2 T.3,6 ; H.4,14.*
penna, v. pinna.
°pentecoste, es (acc. -en), f.,
   Pentecost, A.2,1 ; 20,16 ;
   1 C.16,8.*
penula, v. paen-.
penuria, ae, f., want, poverty,
   Mk.12,44 ; Ph.4,11 f.*
°pera, ae, f., bag, wallet,
   ||Mt.10,10.
†perago, actus, 3, complete,
   end, A.27,9.*
peragro, 1, pass through, A.
   19,1.*
perambulo, 1, pass through,
   go about, L.5,15 ; 19,1 ;
   A.11,19.
percipio, 3, receive, obtain,
   Mk.10,17 ; perceive, A.
   2,14 ; 1 C.2,14.

percurro, 3, *pass through,
traverse*, Mk.6,55.*

percussor, oris, *m., striker*,
1 T.3,3 ; Ti.1,7.*

percutio, cussi, cussus, 3,
smite, strike, wound.

perdo, didi, 3, *lose*, J.6,39 ;
destroy, R.14,15 ; 1 C.1,
19.

perduco, xi, ctus, 3, *bring,
bring to.*

†perduro, 1, *continue, abide*,
A.2,46.*

[†pereffluo], 3, ? *drift away*
(L. & S. take = *forget*), H.
2,1.*

peregre, *abroad, to foreign
parts*, ‖Mt.21,33 ; ‖25, 14 ;
L.15,13 ; 20,9.*

peregrinatio, onis, *f., so-
journing, travel*, 2 C.8,
19.*

peregrinor, 1, *sojourn abroad,
be absent from*, 2 C.5,6 ff.;
1 P.4,12.*

peregrinus, a, um, *strange,
foreign*,(as subst.)*stranger*,
H.11,13 ; 1 P.2,11.

pereo, ii, 4, *perish, be lost.*

perfecte, *completely, perfect-
ly*, 1 P.1,13.*

perfectio, onis, *f., perfection,
completeness*, Co.3,14.*

perfectus, a, um, *perfect.*

perfero, tuli, latus, ferre,
bring, bear, announce,
A.23,30 ; 1 C.16,3 ; *bear
penalty of*, 1 P.2,24.

perficio, feci, fectus, 3,
finish, J.4,34 ; *accomplish*, L.12,50 ; R.7,18 ;
perfect, 1 P.5,10 ; *fulfil*,
Jas.2,8.

perfodio, 3, *dig through*,
‖Mt.24,44.*

pergo, perrexi, 3, *go*, J.8,1 ;
A.22,5.*

*perhibeo, 2 (only with testi-
monium), *bear* (witness).

periclitor, 1, *be in danger*,
L.8,23 ; A.19,27 ; 19, 40 ;
1 C.15,30.*

periculosus, a, um, *danger-
ous*, 2 T.3,1.*

periculum, i, *n., danger*, R.
8,35 ; 2 C.1,10 ; 11,26.*

†°peripsima (-sema), atis, *n.,
refuse, off-scouring*, 1 C.
4,13.*

periuro, v. peiero.

periurus, a, um, *oath-break-
ing, perjured*, 1 T.1,10.*

†perlucidus, a, um, *trans-
parent*, Ap.21,21.*

permaneo, mansi, 2, *remain,
abide, continue.*

†permissus, us, *m., permis-
sion*, A.26,12.*

permitto, misi, missus, 3,
allow, permit, give leave.

†permundo, 1, *thoroughly
cleanse*, Mt.3,12.*

pernicies, ei, *f., destruction*,
2 P.2,12.*

pernocto, 1, *spend the night*,
L.6,12.*

perpauci, ae, a, *very few,* H.13,22.*

†**perperam,** *wrongly, falsely,* 1 C.13,4.*

perpetior, pessus, 3, *suffer,* Mk.5,26.*

perpetuus, a, um, *perpetual.* Only in perpetuum (-tuo) =*for ever,* H.7,3 ; 7,25.*

persecutor, oris, *m., persecutor,* 1 T.1,13.*

persequor, secutus, 3, *follow after,* Ph.3,14 ; *persecute* (passim).

perseuero, 1, *endure,* Mt.10, 22 ; *continue,* J.8,7 ; 2 P. 3,4.

persona, ae, *f., person.*

perspicio, spexi, 3, *see clearly,* L.6,42 ; *see, perceive,* A. 28,26 ; *look at* or *into,* Jas.1,25 ; 1 J.1,1.*

persuadeo, suasi, suasus, 2, *persuade,* Mt.27,20 ; A. 12,20 ; 14,19 ; 18,13.*

†**persuadibilis, e,** *persuasive,* 1 C.2,4.*

persuasio, onis, *f., persuasion,* G.5,8.*

[**pertimeo**], 2, *fear greatly,* 1 P.3,6.*

pertineo, 2, *pertain to,* E.5,4 ; Philem.8 ; *concern,* Mk. 4,38.

pertingo, 3, *reach, extend to,* 2 C.10,13 f.; H.4,12.*

pertranseo, ii, 4, *pass through* or *by.*

perturbatio, onis, *f., disturbance, disquiet,* 1 P.3,6.*

peruenio, ueni, 4, *come,* A. 11,23 ; *come to, arrive at,* A.11,22 ; 16,1 ; *attain to,* Ph.3,16.

peruerto, uersus, 3 (only in P.P.), **peruersus,** *perverse, wrong,* ||Mt.17,17 ; A.20, 30 ; Ph.2,15.*

†**peruigilo,** 1, *keep watch,* H.13,17.*

pes, pedis, *m., foot.*

pessimus, a, um, *very wicked, evil, grievous.*

pestifer, era, erum, *pestilent, noxious, harmful,* A.24,5.*

pestilentia, ae, *f., pestilence,* ||Mt.24,7.*

petitio, onis, *f., request, prayer,* L.23,24 ; Ph.4,6 ; 1 J.5,15.*

peto, tii, titus, 3, *seek, ask, ask for.*

°**petra, ae,** *f., stone, rock,* Mt.16,18 ; R.9,33 ; 1 C. 10,4.

petrosus, a, um, *stony, rocky,* ||Mt.13,5 ; ||13,20.*

*°**phantasma, atis,** *n., appearance, apparition,* ||Mt. 14,26.*

Pharisaeus, i, *m., Pharisee.*

phiala, v. **fiala.**

†°**philosophia, ae,** *f., philosophy,* Co.2,8.*

†°**philosophus, i,** *m., philosopher,* A.17,18.*

†°**phylacterium, ii,** *n., phylactery,* Mt.23,5.*

pie, *piously,* 2 T.3,12 ; Ti. 2,12.*

pietas, tatis, *f., godliness, piety.*

piger, gra, grum, *idle, slothful,* Mt.25,26 ; R.12,11 ; Ph.3,1 ; Ti.1,12.*

pignus, oris, *n., pledge,* 2 C. 1,22 ; 5,5 ; E.1,14.*

†**pigritor,** 1, *be slow, tardy,* A.9,38.*

pilus, i, *m., hair,* ‖Mt.3,4.*

pinguido (-guedo), dinis, *f., fatness,* R.11,17.*

pinguis, e, *fat, rich,* Ap.18, 14.*

pinna (penna in L.13,34), **ae,** *f.,* (1) *wing,* L.13,34 ; (2) *pinnacle,* L.4,9.*

†**pinnaculum, i,** *n., pinnacle,* Mt.4,5.*

piscator, oris, *m., fisher,* ‖Mt.4,18 f.; L.5,2.*

pisciculus, i, *m., little fish,* ‖Mt.15,34.*

piscina, ae, *f., pool,* J.5,2 ; [5,4] ; 5,7.*

piscis, is, *m., fish.*

piscor, 1, *fish,* J.21,3.*.

†°**pisticus, a, um,** *pure, genuine,* J.12,3.*

pius, a, um, *godly, pious, righteous, holy,* 2 P.2,9 ; Ap.15,4.*

placeo, 2, *please.*

§**placitum, i,** *n., pleasure,* E. 1,9.*

plaga, ae, *f., stripe, wound,* A.16,23 ; 2 C.6,5, *plague* ; L.7,21 ; Ap.9,18 ff.

†**plagiarius, ii,** *m., manstealer,* 1 T.1,10.*

planctus, us, *m., mourning, lamentation,* A.8,2.*

plango, nxi, 3, *lament, bewail,* Mt.24,30 ; Ap.1,7.

planta, ae, *f., sole* (of the foot), A.3,7.*

plantatio, onis, *f., planting,* Mt.15,13.*

planto, 1, *plant.*

planus, a, um, *smooth,* L. 3,5.*

°**platea, ae,** *f., street.*

plebs, bis, *f., people, common people.*

plecto, 3, *weave, plait,* ‖Mt. 27,29.*

plenitudo, dinis, *f., fullness.*

plene (only in superl.), *fully,* R.4,21.*

plenus, a, um, *full,* R.1,29 ; Jas.3,8 ; *complete,* Co.4, 12.

plico, cui, 1, *fold,* L.4,20.*

ploratus, us, *m., wailing, weeping,* Mt.2,18.*

ploro, 1, *wail, weep.*

pluo, ui, 3, *rain.*

plurimum, *very greatly,* R. 15,22.*

plurimus, a, um, *very great, very much.*

plus, pluris, *more,* (in pl.) *many, the majority.* (In sing. used also as subst. and adv.)

pluuia, ae, *f.*, *rain*, Mt.7, 25 ff.; A.14,17; Jas. 5,18.*

poculum, i, *n.*, *cup*, Ap.17,4; 18,6.*

°poderis, is, *m.*, *garment reaching to the ankle*, Ap.1,13.*

poena, ae, *f.*, *punishment*, *penalty*, 2 Th.1,9; 1 J. 4,18; Jude 7.

poen-, v. **paen-.**

†**°poeta, ae,** *m.*, *poet*, A.17, 28.*

polliceor, 2, *promise*, Mt.14, 7; 1 J.2,25.*

pollicitatio, onis, *f.*, *promise*, G.3,14; H.4,1; 6,17.*

polluo, pollutus, 3, *defile*, *pollute*, 1 C.8,7; H.10, 29.*

pomum, i, *n.*, *fruit*, Ap.18, 14.*

pondus, eris, *n.*, *weight*, *burden*, Mt.20,12; 2 C.4, 17; H.12,1; Ap.2,24.*

pono, posui, positus, 3, *place*, *set*, *put*, *lay*, *lay down*, *lay up*, *set on* (table); *appoint*, Ph.1,16; 1 T. 1,9; *take* (account), Mt. 18,23 f.; *offer* (incense), L.1,9.

pontifex, icis, *m.*, *high-priest*, *chief-priest*, Mk.15,11; J. and H. (passim).

populus, i, *m.*, *people.*

*****porcus, i,** *m.*, *swine*, *pig.*

porrigo, rexi, 3, *reach out*, *give*, ||Mt.7,9 f.; L.24, 30; J.13,26.*

porro, *then*, *but*, Mt.8,27; L.10,42; 11,20; 1 C.7, 35.*

porta, ae, *f.*, *gate.*

portentum, i, *n.*, *marvel*, *wonder*, Mk.13,22; H. 2,4.*

porticus, us, *f.*, *porch*, J.5,2; 10,23; A.3,11; 5,12.*

portio, onis, *f.*, *portion*, L.15,12.*

porto, 1, *bear*, *carry*, G.6,2 ff.; *endure*, Mt.20,12.

portus, us, *m.*, *harbour*, A. 27,12 (bis).*

posco, poposci, 3, *ask*, J.4, 9; 11,22; 1 P.3,15.*

possessor, oris, *m.*, *possessor*, A.4,34.*

possideo, sedi, 2, *possess*, L. 11,21; 2 C.6,10; *get*, *acquire*, L.10,25; A.1,18.

possum, potui, posse, *be able.*

postea, *afterwards.*

[posteaquam], postea quam, L.14,29; A.27,27.*

posterus, a, um, *next* (only with **die** 5 times in A.); in compar. *later*, *latter*, 1 P.1,11; 2 P.2,20.*

†**posthac,** *afterwards,* H.4,8.*

postulatio, onis, *f.*, *supplication*, 1 T.2,1.*

postulo, 1, *ask*, Mt.14,7 ;
Jas.1,5 f.; *plead*, R.8,26 f.
potatio, onis, *f.*, *drinking,
drinking-bout,* 1 P.4,3.*
potator, oris, *m.*, *drinker,*
Mt.11,19.*
potens, entis, *able, powerful,
mighty, strong.*
potentia, ae, *f.*, *strength,
power.*
potestas, tatis, *f.*, *power,
authority; power* (angelic),
E.3,10 ; Co.1,16.
†§potiono, 1, *give to drink,*
Ap.14,8.*
potior, oris (compar.), *better,
preferable,* Ph.1,10.*
potius, *rather,* Mt.10,6 ; 1 C.
9,12.
poto, 1, *give,* or *make to
drink,* 1 C.12,13 ; [Ap.
14,8].*
potus, us, *m.*, *drinking,* R.
14,17 ; Co.2,16 ; *drink,*
J.6,55 ; 1 C.10,4 ; *draught,*
Mt.10,42 ; R.12,20.
praebeo, 2, *offer, present,
give,* ‖Mt.5,39 ; A.17,31 ;
1 C.7,35 ; *show, display,*
A.1,3 ; Ti.2,7.
praecedo, cessi, 3, *go before,
precede,* 1 T.1,18 ; H.7,18;
advance, R.13,12.
praecello, 3, *surpass, excel,*
R.3,9 ; 1 P.2,13.*
praeceps, cipitis, *n.*, *steep
place,* ‖Mt.8,32.*
praeceptor, oris, *m.*, *master,*

teacher (only in L. 7
times, as equivalent of
ἐπιστάτης and (once)
διδάσκαλος).
praeceptum, i, *n.*, *precept,
commandment.*
†praecessor, oris, *m.*, *a superior,* L.22,26.*
praecingo, nxi, nctus, 3, *gird,*
L.12,35 ff.; A.12,8 ; Ap.
1,13.
praecipio, cepi, ceptus, 3,
command, charge.
praecipito, 1, *cast headlong,*
Mk.5,13 ; L.4,29.*
praecipuus, a, um, *chief,
special,* H.7,4.*
praeclarus, a, um, *splendid,
glorious, bright,* Jas.2,3 ;
Ap.18,14.*
praeco, onis, *m.*, *herald,
preacher,* 2 P.2,5.*
†praecogito, 1, *think* or *meditate beforehand,* Mk.13
11.*
†praecognosco, nitus, 3, *foreknow, foresee,* 1 P.1,20.*
praecurro, cucurri, 3, *run
before, outrun,* L.19,4 ;
J.20,4.*
praecursor, oris, *m.*, *fore-
runner, precursor,* H.6,
20.*
*praedestino, 1, *fore-ordain,*
R.1,4 ; 1 C.2,7 ; E.1,
5 ff.
praedicatio, onis, *f.*, *preach-
ing.*

*praedicator, oris, *m., preacher,* 1 T.2,7 ; 2 T.1,11.*
praedico, 1, *preach, proclaim.*
praedico, dixi, dictus, 3, *foretell, say beforehand.*
*praedium, ii, *n., ground, estate,* Mk.14,32 ; J.4, 5 ; A.28,7.*
praeeo, 4, *go before,* Mk.11, 9 ; L.1,76 ; 18,39.*
praefinio, 4, *appoint beforehand,* G.4,2.*
praefinitio, onis, *f., appointment* or *fixing beforehand,* E.3,11.*
praegnas (nans), natis (nantis), *pregnant, with child,* ||Mt.24,19 ; L.2, 5.*
†§**praegredior,** 3, *go before, advance,* Mk.2,23.*
†**praeiudicium, ii,** *n., prejudging, prejudice,* 1 T. 5,21.* [L. & S. take as *damage, disadvantage.*]
prael-, v. **proel-.**
†**praemeditor,** 1, *meditate beforehand,* L.21,14.*
praemitto, 3, *send forward,* Ti.3,13.*
praemoneo, 2, *advise* or *instruct beforehand,* Mt.14, 8.*
*praenuntio. 1, *announce beforehand,* A.3,18 ; 7,52 ; G.3,8 ; 1 P.1,11.*
praeoccupo, 1, *detect, seize* (in an act), G.6,1.*

*praeordino, 1, *preordain, appoint beforehand,* A.10, 41 ; 13,48 ; 22,14.*
praeparatio, onis, *f., preparation,* E.6,15.*
praeparo, 1, *prepare, make ready.*
praepono, positus, 3, *set over,* 1 T.3,4.*
praepositus, i, *m:, chief, governor, overseer, director,* A.7,10 ; 2 C.11,32 ; H.13, 7 ff.*
praeputium, ii, *n., foreskin ;* (state of) *uncircumcision.*
praescientia, ae, *f., foreknowledge,* A.2,23 ; 1 P. 1,2.*
praescio, 4, *know beforehand, foreknow,* A.26,5 ; R.8,29 ; 11,2 ; 2 P.3, 17.*
praescribo, scriptus, 3, *write in front of,* G.3,1 ; *write* or *appoint beforehand,* Jude 4.*
praesens, entis, *present.*
praesentia, ae, *f., presence,* 1 C.16,17 ; 2 C.10,10 ; Ph.2,12 ; 2 P.1,16.*
praesepium, ii, *n., stall,* L.2, 7 ff.; 13,15.*
praeses, idis, *c., ruler, governor.*
praesto, stiti, 1, (1) *show, exhibit,* A.24,28 ; *maintain* (silence), A.22,2 ; (2) *give, furnish,* Mt.15,

14 ; L.7,4 ; *pay* (tribute) R.13,6.

praesto, *at hand, present* (always with **esse**), A.24, 19 ; H.7,13 ; 10,11 ; 2 P.1,9.*

praesum, esse, (1) *be over, rule,* 1 T.3,5 ff.; 5,17 ; (2) *carry on, show diligence in,* Ti.3,8 ; 3,14.*

praesumo, 3, *take first,* 1 C. 11,21.*

praetereo, iui or **ii, itus,** 4, *pass by* or *away ;* P.P. **praeteritus,** *past.*

praetergredior, 3, *pass through,* Mk.9,30.*

praeterquam, *except,* A.27, 22 ; G.1,8.*

***praetorium, ii,** *n., praetorium* (in various senses), (1) *governor's residence, palace,* ‖Mt.27,27 ; A. 23,35 ; (2) *camp of praetorian guards,* Ph.1, 13.

praeualeo, 2, *prevail,* Mt.16, 18.*

praeuaricatio, onis, *f., transgression, disobedience;* R. 2,23 ; 1 T.2,14.

praeuaricator, oris, *m., transgressor,* R.2,25 ff.; G.2, 18.*

praeuaricor, 1, *transgress,* A.1,25.*

praeuenio, ueni, 4, *come before,* or *beforehand,* 2

C.9,5 ; *anticipate,* Mt. 17,25 ; 1 Th.4,15.

prandeo, 2, *breakfast,* L.11, 37 ; J.21,12 ff.*

prandium, ii, *n., breakfast, luncheon,* Mt.22,4 ; L. 11,38 ; 14,12.*

prauus, a, um, *wicked, evil.*

preces, cum, *f., prayers,* H. 5,7 ; 1 P.3,12.*

precor, 1, *pray,* A.8,24.*

prendo, didi, 3, *take, catch,* J.21,3 ; 21,10.*

°presbyter, eri, *m., elder, presbyter.*

†°presbyterium, ii, *n., college of presbyters, presbytery,* 1 T.4,14.*

pressura, ae, *f., affliction, tribulation, anguish,* L. 21,23 ff.; J.16,21 ; 2 C. 1,4.

pretiosus, a, um, *precious, costly.*

pretium, ii, *n., price.*

†§pridem, *long ago, long since,* G.4,13.*

primatus, us, *m., first place, pre-eminence, primacy,* Co.1,18 ; 3 J.9.*

primitiae, arum, *f., first-fruits.*

primitiuus, a, um, *first of its kind, first-born, first-fruits,* R.16,5 ; H.11,28 ; 12,23 ; (as subst. in n. pl.), *birthright,* H.12, 16.*

primo, *first, first of all*, Mk.
9,12 ; 16,9.*
primogenitus, a, um, *first-
born*, or *first-begotten*, L.
2,7 ; Co.1,15 ff.
primum, *first, in the first
place, firstly*.
princeps, ipis, *m., chief, head,
prince*.
principalis, e, *principal*, A.
25,23.*
principatus, us, *m.*, (1)
sovereignty, dominion,
L.20,20 ; (2) *origin,
original state*, Jude 6 ; (3)
principality (rank of
angels), R.8,38 ; Co.1,
16.
principium, ii, *n., beginning.*
†principor, 1, *rule*, Mk.10,
42.*
prior, ius, *former, previous,
first.*
pristinus, a, um, *former,
ancient*, E.4,22 ; H.10,
32.*
prius, *before, first.*
[priusquam], prius quam.
priuo, 1, *deprive*, 1 T.6,5.*
probabilis, e, *approved, ac-
ceptable*, 2 T.2,15.*
†°probaticus, a, um, *belonging
to sheep, sheep-*, J.5,2.*
probatio, onis, *f., proving,
trial, probation*, R.5,4 ;
2 C.9,13 ; Jas.1,3 ; 1 P.
1,7.*
probo, 1, (1) *try, prove*, L.

12,56 ; 1 C.3,13 ; (2)
approve, approve of, R.
1,28 ; (3) *enlist, enroll*
(a soldier), 2 T.2,4.
†probus, a, um, *upright,
excellent, approved*, R.
16,10.*
procedo, cessi, 3, *proceed,
come* or *go forth, advance.*
procella, ae, *f., storm*, ‖Mk,
4,37 ; H.12,18 ; Jude
13.*
procido, di, 3, *fall forward* or
down, fall flat.
*proconsul, is, *m.* (Gk. ἀνθύ-
πατος), *proconsul*, A.13,
7 ff.; 18,12 ; [19,38].*
procreo, 1, *bring forth*, 1 T.
5,14.*
*procumbo, 3, *fall* or *lean
forward* or *down, fall on*,
Mk.1,7 ; L.24,12 ; A.
20,37.*
procurator, oris, *m., steward,
agent, manager*, Mt.20,8 ;
L.8,3.*
†procuro, 1, *be procurator*,
L.3,1.*
procurro, 3, *run forward*,
Mk.10,17.*
prodeo, ii, 4, *go forth*, J.11,
44 ; 1 J.2,19.*
prodigium, ii, *n., wonder.*
proditor, oris, *m., betrayer ;
traitor*, L.6,16 ; A.7,52 ;
2 T.3,4.*
prodo, 3, *betray*, Mk.14,10.*
produco, xi, ductus, 3, *bring*

or *lead forth;* A.12,4;
produce, Mk.4,29.
proelior (prae-), 1, *join battle,*
wage war, Ap.12,7.*
proelium (prae-), ii, *n., war,*
battle.
profanus, a, um, *profane,*
unholy, 1 T.6,20; 2.T.
2,16; H.12,16.*
profectio, onis, *f., setting out,*
departure, H.11,22.*
profecto, *assuredly, doubt-*
less, L.11,20; 11,48.*
profectus, us, *m., progress,*
increase, profit, Ph.1,12;
1,25; 1 T.4,15.*
profero, tuli, ferre, *bring*
forth.
†professio, onis, *f., register,*
census, A.5,37.*
proficio, feci, 3, *avail,* J.12,
19; *profit,* Mk.5,26; L.
9,25; *advance,* L.2,52;
G.1,14.
proficiscor, fectus, 3, *set out,*
depart, go forth.
profiteor, 2, *give in one's*
name (in a census), L.
2,3 ff.*
profluuium, ii, *n., flux, issue,*
Mk.5,25.*
profugio, gi, 3, *flee away,*
Mk.14,52.*
profundus, a, um, *deep;* (as
subst.) profundum, i, *n.,*
depth.
progenies, ei, *f., generation,*
Mt.3,7; 12,34; L.1,50.*

†progenitor, oris, *m., fore-*
father, ancestor, 2 T.1,3.*
progredior, gressus, 3, *go*
forward, advance, Mt.26,
39; Mk.1,19; [2,23].*
prohibeo, 2, *prevent, hinder.*
†prohibitio, onis, *f., hin-*
drance, A.28,31.*
proicio, ieci, iectus, 3, *cast,*
cast away, cast forth.
†prolabor, lapsus, 3, *fall*
away, H.6,6.*
†proles, is, *f., offspring,* A.
19,35.*
prolixe (only in compar.),
abundantly or ? *earnestly,*
L.22,43.*
prolixus, a, um, *long, great,*
Mk.12,40 (bis).*
†promereor, 2, *be propitiated,*
made favourable, H.13,
16.*
promissio, onis, *f., promise.*
promissum, i, *n., promise.*
promitto, misi, 3, (1) *promise,*
Mk.14,11; H.6,13; (2)
profess, make profession
of, 1 T.2,10; 6,21.
†promtus (-mpt-), us, *m.,*
readiness, 2 C.10,6.*
promtus (-mptus), a, um,
ready.
pronuntio, 1, *proclaim,* 1 C.
14,25.*
†propalo, 1, *make manifest,*
H.9,8.* [L. & S. *throw*
open].
prope (adv.and prep.), *near.*

propello, 3, *push forward*, A.
19,33.*

propero, 1, *hasten*, L.8,4 ; 2
P.3,12.*

°propheta, ae, *m.*, *prophet.*

°propheten, *f.*, accusative,
prophetess, Ap.2,20.* Gk.
προφῆτιν.

°prophetia, ae, *f.*, *prophecy.*

†°propheticus, a, um, *pro-
phetic*, 2 P.1,19.*

prophetissa, ae, *f.*, *prophetess*,
L.2,36.*

*prophetizo, 1, *prophesy*,
‖Mt.26,68.*

propheto, 1, *prophesy.*

propior, ius, *nearer*, R.13,
11.*

propitiatio, onis, *f.*, *propitia-
tion*, R.3,25 ; 1 J.2,2 ;
4,10.*

propitiatorium, ii, *n.*, *mercy-
seat* (of ark), H.9,5.*

propitius, a, um, *merciful,
propitious*, L.18,13 ; H.
8,12.*

propono, posui, positus, 3,
(1) *set* or *place before*, H.
6,18 ; 12,1 ; (2) *resolve,
determine*, A.19,21; 20,16.

propositum, i, *n.*, *purpose.*

proprius, a, um, *one's own.*

propterea, *therefore.*

prora, ae, *f.*, *forepart* (of
ship), *prow*, A.27,30 ; 27,
41.*

°proselytus, i, *m.*, *proselyte*,
Mt.23,15 ; A.2,11.*

[prosequor], secutus, 3, *follow
after*, Mk.1,36.*

prosper or prosperus, a, um,
prosperous, favourable,
R.1,10.*

prospere, *prosperously*, 3 J.
2 (bis).*

prospicio, spexi, 3, *look forward into*, J.20,11 ; 1 P.
1,12.*

prosterno, stratus, 3, *lay low,
overthrow*, L.19,44 ; 1 C.
10,5 ; H.3,17.*

prostitutio, onis, *f.*, *fornication*, Ap.17,2 ; 19,2.*

prosum, fui, prodesse, *be
advantageous, profitable,
profit.*

proteruus, a, um, *forward,
bold, wanton*, 2 T.3,4.*

protinus, *forthwith.*

protraho, traxi, 3, (1) *lengthen,
prolong*, A.20,7 ; (2) *de-
tain*, A.24,4.*

prout, *according as.*

prouenio, 4, *turn out, event-
uate*, Ph.1,19.*

†prouentus, us, *m.*, *issue, way
of escape*, 1 C.10,13.*

prouerbium, ii, *n.*, *proverb,
parable.*

prouideo, 2, (1) *provide*, R.
12,17 ; H.11,40; (2) *foresee*, A.2,25 ff.

prouidentia, ae, *f.*, *providence,
foresight*, A.24,2.*

prouincia, ae, *f.*, *province*,
A.23,34 ; 25,1.*

†prouocatio, onis, *f.*, *stimu-lus, encouragement,* H. 10,24.*

prouoco, 1, *provoke, stir up.*

prouoluo, uolutus, 3 (only pass.), *fall down, prostrate one's self,* Mt.17,14.*

proximo, 1, *draw nigh,* H. 7,19.*

proximus, a, um, *next, nearest,* (as subst.) *neigh-bour.*

prudens, entis, *wise, prudent.*

prudenter, *prudently,* L.16, 8.*

pruna, ae, *f., live coal,* J.18, 18; 21,9.*

†prurio, 4, *itch,* 2 T.4,3.*

°psallo, 3, *sing, sing hymns,* 1 C.14,15; E.5,19; Jas. 5,13.*

°psalmus, i, *m., psalm.*

†°pseudoapostolus, i, *m., false apostle,* 2 C.11,13.*

*°pseudochristus, i, *m., false Christ,* ‖Mt.24,24.*

°pseudopropheta, ae, *m., false prophet.*

*publicanus, i, *m., tax-gatherer.*

publice, *publicly,* A.16,37; 18,28; 20,20.*

publicus, a, um, *public,* A. 5,18.*

*pudicus, a, um, *chaste, pure.*

puella, ae, *f., girl.*

puer, eri, *m., boy, slave, servant.*

†pugillaris, e, (as subst.) *writing-table,* L.1,63.*

pugna, ae, *f., fighting, strug-gle,* 2 C.7,5; 1 T.6,4; Ti.3,9.*

pugno, 1, *fight.*

pullus, i, *m., young one,* Mt. 23,37; L.2,24; *colt,* ‖Mt. 21,2 ff.

†pulmentarium, ii, *n. relish; food,* J.21,5.*

pulso, 1, *knock* (at door), ‖Mt. 7,7 f.; A.12,13 ff.

puluis, ueris, *m., dust.*

pungo, pupugi, 3, *prick, pierce,* Ap.1,7.*

punio, 4, *punish,* A.4,21; 22,5; 26,11.*

pupillus, i, *m., orphan,* Jas. 1,27.*

*puppis, is, *f., stern* (of a boat or ship), Mk.4,38; A.27, 29; 27,41.*

†purgamentum, i, *n., off-scouring,* 1 C.4,13.*

purgatio, onis, *f., purifica-tion, purifying,* L.2,22; H.1,3; 2 P.1,9.*

purgo, 1, *cleanse, purify,* Mk.7,19; L.3,17; J.15, 2.*

purificatio, onis, *f., purifying, purification,* J.2,6; 3,25; A.21,26.*

purifico, 1, *cleanse, purify.*

purpura, ae, *f., purple.*

†purpuraria, ae, *f., dyer* or *seller of purple,* A.16,14.*

H

purpureus, a, um, *purple,* J.19,2 ff.*

purus, a, um, *pure* (1 T. and 2 T. only).

pusillanimis, e, *faint-hearted,* 1 Th.5,14.*

pusillus, a, um, *small, little, petty, weak,* (as subst.) **pusillum,** *a little,* Mt.26, 39.

puteus, i, *m., well,* L.14,5; J.4,12 f.; *pit,* Ap.9,1 ff.*

puto, 1, *think.*

putrefio (pass. of **putrefacio), factus, fieri,** *become rotten, putrefy,* Jas.5,2.*

°**pyra, ae,** *f., fire,* A.28,2.*

°**pytho, onis,** *m., familiar spirit,* A.16,16.*

Q

†**quadrageni, ae, a,** *forty each,* 2 C.11,24.*

****quadrans, antis,** *m., farthing,* Mt.5,26; Mk.12, 42.*

quadriduanus (quatr-), a, um, *of four days,* J.11,39.*

quadrupes, edis, *four-footed,* A.10,12; 11,6; R.1,23.* [n. pl. **quadrupedia** is perhaps from **quadrupedius, a, um.**]

quadruplus, a, um, *fourfold,* L.19,8.*

quadrus, a, um, *square,* Ap. 21,16.*

quaero, quaesiui, 3, *seek, seek for,* Mt.2,13; L.2, 48; *question, enquire,* L.22,23.

quaestus, us, *m., gain,* A. 16,16 ff.; 19,24; 1 T.6, 5 f.; Jude 16.*

qualiter, *in what way, how,* Mk.5,16; L.12,11; Ap. 3,3.

quamdiu, *as long as.*

quamobrem, *wherefore.*

****quamquam,** *although,* J.4,2; Ph.3,4; H.7,5; 12,17.*

quamuis, *although,* A.17,27.*

quando, v. **nequando.**

quanto, *by how much, the more.*

†§**quantulus, a, um,** *how little, how small,* H.10, 37.*

quapropter, *wherefore.*

†§**quartanus, a, um,** *belonging to the fourth* (day), A.10,30.*

quasi, *as if.*

quasso, 1, *shake,* Mt.12,20.*

quaternio, onis, *m., body of four soldiers, quaternion,* A.12,4.*

quatrid-, v. **quadrid-.**

quemadmodum, *as.*

querella (-ela), ae, *f.,* (1) *matter for complaint, blame,* Co.3,13; (2) *sine* **querella** (6 times) = *blame-*

less, blamelessly, L.1,6 ;
Ph.2,15 ; 3,6.
†**querellosus (querul-), a, um,**
full of complaints, Jude
16.*
queror, 3, *blame, find fault,*
R.9,19.*
quiesco, eui, 3, *rest, cease,*
A.21,14.*
quietus, a, um, *quiet,* 1 Th.
4,11 ; 1 T.2,2 ; 1 P.3,4.*
quilibet, quaelibet, quodlibet,
*no matter who, the first
that comes ;* (with neg.)
especial, extraordinary,
A.19,11.*
†§**quippini,** *by all means, certainly,* L.11,28.* (Gk.
μενοῦν.)
quippe, *for* (5 times = γάρ).
quisnam, quaenam, quidnam,
who, which, what (only
once, J.13,11, in masc.,
elsewhere neuter).*
**quispiam, quaepiam, quod-
piam,** *someone,* Mk.15,
21.*
quisque, quaeque, quodque,
each, L.19,15 ; A.2,45 ;
4,35.*
quoad, only with **usque** =
until.
[**quoadusque**], quoad usque.
quocumque, *whithersoever.*
quot, *how many.*
quotid-, v. cotid-.
quotiens (-ies), *how many
times,* Mt.18,21.*

quotienscumque (-ies-), *as
often as,* 1 C.11,25 f.; Ap.
11,6.*
quotquot, *as many as,* J.1,12 ;
how many soever, 2 C.1,
20.
[**quousque**], quo usque, *how
long.*

R

*rabbi (Hebr.), *my master,
master.*
*rabboni (Aram.), *my master,*
Mk.10,51 ; J.20,16.*
†**racha (-ca)** (Aram.), *vain,
silly* (as term of abuse),
Mt.5,22.*
radico, 1, only in P.P.
radicatus, *rooted,* E.3,17 ;
Co.2,7.*
radix, icis, *f., root.*
rado, 3, *shave,* A.21,24.*
ramus, i, *m., branch.*
rana, ae, *f., frog,* Ap.16,13.*
rapax, acis, *ravenous, greedy,*
Mt.7,15 ; [A.20,29] ; *avar-
icious,* 1 C.5,10 f.; 6,10.*
rapina, ae, *f., rapine, robbery,*
‖Mt.23,25 ; Ph.2,6 ; H.
10,34.*
rapio, pui, raptus, 3, *seize,*
A.6,12 ; 19,29 ; *snatch
away,* A.8,39 ; 1 Th.4,
17.
†**raptor, oris,** *m., robber,*
L.18,11.*

ratio, onis, *f.*, (1) *account,*
L.16,2 ; R.14,12 ; (2)
method, manner, 1 C.15,
2 ; (3) *reason, ground,*
A.25,27 ; 1 P.3,15 ; (4)
rule, proportion, R.12,6.

rationabilis, e, *reasonable,
pertaining to the reason,
rational,* R.12,1 ; 1 P.
2,2.*

reaedifico, 1, *rebuild,* Mt.[26,
61] ; 27,40 ; [Mk.15,29] ;
A.15,16.*

recedo, cessi, 3, *depart, fall
away.*

recipio, cepi, ceptus, 3, *receive.*

reclino, 1, *lay, lay down,*
||Mt.8,20 ; L.2,7.*

recogito, 1, *consider,* H.12,
3.*

reconciliatio, onis, *f.*, *recon-
ciliation,* R.5,11 ; 11,15 ;
2 C.5,18 f.*

reconcilio, 1, *reconcile.*

recondo, 3, *lay up,* 1 C.16,2.*

recordatio, onis, *f.*, *remembrance,* 2 T.1,5.*

recordor, 1, *remember.*

recte, *rightly,* L.7,43 ; *cor-
rectly,* Mk.7,35 ; *justly,*
A.18,14.

rector, oris, *m.*, *ruler,* E.
6,12.*

rectus, a, um, *right, upright,
erect, straight.*

†recubitus, us, *m.*, *place,* or
seat at table, Mt.23,6.*

recumbo, bui, 3, *recline, sit
at meat.*

recuso, 1, *refuse,* A.25,11 ;
H.12,25 (bis).*

reda (rhe-), ae, *f.*, *carriage,*
Ap.18,13.*

*redarguo, 3, *reprove, con-
vict,* E.5,11 ; Ti.1,11 ;
Jas.2,9.*

redargutio, onis, *f.*, *reproof,
contempt,* A.19,27.*

reddo, didi, ditus, 3, *pay, pay
back,* ||Mt.22,21 ; *reward,
render,* H.13,17 ; Ap.18,
6.

redemptor, oris, *m.*, *saviour,
redeemer,* A.7,35.*

redeo, ii, 4, *return.*

redigo, actus, 3, *bring down,
reduce,* A.5,36 ; 1 C.6,12.

redimo, emi, emptus, 3,
redeem.

reduco, 3, (1) *bring back,* R.
15,15 ; (2) *draw off, put
out* (from shore), L.5,3.*

refectio, onis, *f.*, *guest chamber,* Mk.14,14.*

refero, rettuli, referre, (1)
bring back, bear away,
Mt.27,3 ; 2 C.5,10 ; (2)
relate, tell, A.14,26 ; 15,
27 ; (3) *bear* (fruit), L.
8,14.*

reficio, feci, fectus, 3, (1)
refresh, Mt.11,28 ; A.28,2 ;
(2) *repair,* Mt.4,21.

refloresco, rui, 3, *bloom again,*
Ph.4,10.*

*reformo, 1, *re-form, change*, R.12,2 ; Ph.3,21.*

refreno, 1, *bridle, check*, Jas. 1,26.*

refrigerium, ii, *n., refreshment*, A.3,20.*

refrigero, 1, *cool, refresh*, L. 16,24 ; R.15,32 ; 2 T. 1,16.*

†refrigesco, 3, *grow cold*, Mt.24,12.*

refugio, 3, *escape from*, 2 P. 2,20.*

refulgeo, fulsi, 2, *shine*, L. 9,29 ; A.12,7.*

regalis, e, *royal*, Jas.2,8 ; 1 P.2,9.*

*regeneratio, onis, *f., regeneration*, Mt.19,28 ; Ti.3, 5.*

†regenero, 1, *regenerate, beget again*, 1 P.1,3.*

regina, ae, *f., queen*, ‖Mt.12, 42 ; A.8,27 ; Ap.18,7.*

regio, onis, *f., region, district, country*.

regius, a, um, *royal*, A.12, 21.*

regno, 1, *reign*.

regnum, i, *n., kingdom*.

rego, rectus, 3, *rule, govern*.

regredior, gressus, 3, *return*.

regula, ae, *f., rule*, 2 C.10, 13 ff. ; G.6,16 ; Ph.3,16.*

regulus, i, *m., petty king, prince*, J.4,46 ff.* (Gk. βασιλικός.)

*reicio, iectus, 3, *cast away*,

reject, Mk.14,52 ; 1 T.4, 4.*

†reinuito, 1, *invite in return*, L.14,12.*

religio, onis, *f., religion*, A. 26,5 ; Jas.1,26 f.; *worshipping*, Co.2,18.*

religiosus, a, um, *religious*, A.2,5 ; 10,2 ; 13,50 ; Jas.1,26.*

relinquo, iqui, ictus, 3, *leave, forsake*.

reliquiae, arum, *f., remnants, remainder*, ‖Mt.14,20 ; L.24,43 ; R.9,27 ; 11,5.*

reliquus, a, um, *remaining* (in pl.), *the rest, the others*.

remaneo, mansi, 2, *remain*.

rememoror, 1, *remember*, H. 10,32.*

remetior, 4, *measure back* (only in pass. sense, *be measured back*), [Mt.7,2] ; Mk.4,24 ; L.6,38.*

remigo, 1, *row*, Mk.6,48 ; J.6,19.*

reminiscor, 3, *remember*, J. 16,4 ; 2 C.7,15.*

remissio, onis, *f.*, (1) *deliverance, relief*, 2 C.8,13 ; (2) *forgiveness*, L.1,77 ; H. 9.22.

remissus, a, um (only in compar.), *tolerable*, Mt. 11,‖ 22 ff.*

remitto, misi, missus, 3, (1) *send back*, L.23,7 ff.; (2)

relax, remit, cease, E.6,9 ;
H.12,12 ; *forgive*, Mt.
9,2.
*remuneratio, onis, *f.*, reward*, 2 C.6,13 ; H.10,
35 ; 11,26.*
†remunerator, oris, *m.*, *re-
warder*, H.11,6.*
renascor, natus, 3, *be born
again* [J.3,3 f.] ; 3,5 ; 1
P.1,23.*
renes, renium, *m.*, *kidneys,
reins*, Ap.2,23.*
†renouatio, onis, *f.*, *renewal,*
Ti.3,5.*
renouo, 1, *renew*, 2 C.4,16 ;
E.4,23 ; Co.3,10 ; H.6,6.*
renuntio, 1, (1) *bring back
word*, Mt.2,8 ; Mk.6,30 ;
(2) *renounce, say farewell
to*, L.9,61 ; 14,33.
repello, reppuli, 3, *thrust
away, reject*, A.7,27 ; R.
11,1 f.; 1 T.1,19.
repente, *suddenly*, Mk.13,36 ;
A.2,2.*
repentinus, a, um, *sudden*,
L.21,34 ; 1 Th.5,3.*
repeto, 3, *seek again*, L.6,30 ;
demand, ask back, L.
12,20.*
repleo, eui, etus, 2, *fill,
satisfy.*
repono, positus, 3, *lay up*,
L.19,20 ; Co.1,5 ; 2 T.
4,8 ; 2 P.3,7.*
reporto, 1, *obtain, gain*, H.
10,36 ; 1 P.1,9.*

reprehendo, di, 3, (1) *seize,
lay hold of*, L.20,26 ; (2)
blame, censure, 1 J.3,
20 f.*
†reprehensibilis, e, *blame-
worthy*, G.2,11.*
reprehensio, onis, *f.*, *blame*,
Ph.2,15.*
†reprobatio, onis, *f.*, *rejec-
tion*, H.7,18.*
reprobo, 1, *reject.*
reprobus, a, um, *rejected,
reprobate*, 1 C.9,27 ; 2
C.13,5 ff.
repromissio, onis, *f.*, *promise.*
repromitto, misi, 3, *promise.*
repropitio, 1, *make propitia-
tion for*, H.2,17.*
reptilis, e, *creeping, reptile*,
A.11,6.*
repudium, ii, *n.*, *divorce*,
Mt.5,31 ; ‖19,7.*
repugno, 1, *fight against*, A.
5,39 ; R.7,23 ; H.12,4.*
reputo, 1, (1) *ponder*, L.11,
38 ; (2) *account, impute,
reckon*, A.19,27 ; R.2,26.
requies, ei (only in acc. -em),
f., *rest.*
requiesco, eui, 3, *rest.*
requietio, onis, *f.*, *rest*, A.7,
49.*
requiro, quisii, 3, (1) *seek for*,
L.2,44 f.; A.12,19 ; (2)
require, L.11,51.
res, rei, *f.*, *thing, matter.*
†rescindo, 3, *abrogate, annul*,
Mk.7,13.*

rescisco, iui, 3, *find out*, A.
22,29.*

reseruo, 1, *keep, reserve*, 2 P.
2,4 ff.; [3,7]; Jude 6.*

resideo, sedi, 2, *sit down, sit
up*, Mk.9,35; L.7,15;
A.9,40.*

residuus, a, um, *remaining*,
1 Th.4,15.*

†resipisco, 3, *recover one's
self, escape*, 2 T.2,26.*

resisto, stiti, 3, *resist*.

†resolutio, onis, f., *unloosen-
ing, departure*, 2 T.4,6.*
[L. & S. take as *es-
cape*.]

respicio, spexi, 3, *behold*,
Mt.6,26; *regard, look,
look upon*, A.3,4; *have
regard to*, Mt.22,16.

resplendeo, 2, *shine brightly*,
Mt.17,2.*

respondeo, di, sus, 2, *answer*.

responsum, i, n., *answer*.

respuo, ui, 3, *reject*, G.4,14.*

restituo, utus, 3, *restore*.

restitutio, onis, f., *restora-
tion*, A.3,21.*

resurgo, surrexi, 3, *rise, rise
from the dead*.

resurrectio, onis, f., *resur-
rection*.

resuscito, 1, *raise up; stir
up*.

rete, is, n., *net*.

retineo, nui, tentus, 2, *keep,
retain*, L.8,15; J.20,23
keep in memory, A.20,31.

retribuo, 3, *render, recompense*.

retributio, onis, f., *reward,
recompense*.

retro, (1) *behind*, Mt.9,20;
Ap.4,6; *back*, ‖Mk.13,16;
L.9,62; (2) as a prep. =
after, 1 T.5,15.

retrorsum, *back, backwards*,
J.18,6; 20,14; 2 P.2,21.*

reus, i, m., *an accused* or
guilty person; (as adj.)
guilty, Mt.5,21 f.; Mk.
3,29.

reuelo, 1, *uncover, disclose,
reveal*.

reuerentia, ae, f., *fear, awe,
reverence*, H.5,7; 12,28;
shame, 1 C.15,34.*

reuereor, 2, *fear, reverence*,
Mk.12,6; L.18,2 ff.; H.
12,9.*

reuertor, uersus, 3, *return*.

†reuinco, 3, *convict, refute*,
A.18,28.*

reuiuisco, uixi, 3, *become
alive again*, L.15,24 ff.;
R.7,9.*

reuoco, 1, *recall*, R.10,7.*

*reuoluo, uolui, uolutus, 3,
roll back, Mt.28,2; ‖Mk.
16,3; *unroll*, L.4,17.*

rex, regis, m., *king*.

rheda, v. re-.

rhomphaea, v. rom-.

rideo, 2, *laugh*, L.6,21 ff.*

rigo, 1, *water, wet*, L.7,38 ff.;
1 C.3,6 ff.*

risus, us, *m., laughter*, Jas.
4,9.*

rixa, ae, *f., quarrel, conten-
tion*, G.5,20.*

rogo, 1, *entreat, ask, pray.*

°romphea (rhomphaea), ae,
f., sword, Ap.2,12.*

rota, ae, *f., wheel*, Jas.3,6.*

ruber, bra, brum, *red* (only
with mare), A.7,36 ; H.
11,29.*

rubicundus, a, um, *red, ruddy*,
Mt.16,2.*

rubor, oris, *m., shame*, L.
14,9.*

rubus, i, *m., bramble-bush,
bush.*

†rudens, entis, *m., rope, cord*,
2 P.2,4.*

rudis, e, *rough, unused, un-
dressed* (of cloth), ||Mt.
9,16.*

rufus, a, um, *red*, Ap.6,4 ;
12,3.*

ruga, ae, *f., wrinkle*, E.5,
27.*

rugio, 4, *roar*, 1 P.5,8 ; Ap.
10,3.*

ruina, ae, *f., fall*, ||Mt.7,27 ;
L.2,34.*

rumor, oris, *m., rumour,
report*, Mk.1,28.*

rumpo, ruptus, 3, *burst,
break*, ||Mt.9,17 ; L.5,6 ;
8,29.*

§ruo, rui 3, *fall*, H.11,30.*

rursus or rursum, *again*

†ruta, ae, *f., rue*, L.11,42.*

rutilo, 1, *be reddish, glow*,
Mt.16,3.*

S

sabaoth (sabba-) (Hebr.),
hosts, R.9,29 ; Jas.5,4.*

†°sabbatismus, i, *m., keeping
of a sabbath*, H.4,9.*

sabbatum, i, *n.* (also in pl.
sabbata, orum), (1) *sab-
bath* ; (2) *week*, 1 C.16,2.

sabacthani (Aram.), *thou hast
forsaken me*, ||Mt.27,46.*

sacculus, i, *m., purse*, L.10,
4 ; 12,33 ; 22,35 f.*

saccus, i, *m., sackcloth*, Ap.
6,12 ; 11,3.*

sacer, cra, crum, *sacred*, 2
T.3,15.*

sacerdos, dotis, *m., priest.*

sacerdotalis, e, *priestly*, A.
4,6.*

sacramentum, i, *n., mystery.*

†sacrarium, ii, *n., sanctuary*,
1 C.9,13 (bis).

sacrificium, ii, *n., sacrifice.*

sacrifico, 1, *sacrifice*, A.14,13 ;
1 C.8,1.*

sacrilegium, ii, *n., sacrilege*,
R.2,22.*

sacrilegus, i, *m., robber of
temples*, A.19,37.*

Sadducaeus, i, *m., Sadducee.*

*saecularis, e, (1) *belonging
to the world, worldly* ; (2)
eternal, 2 T.1,9 ; Ti.1,2.

saeculum, i, *n.,* (1) *age, generation ;* (2) *world,* 2 T.4,9 ; Ti.2,12.

saepes (sep-), is, *f., hedge, fence,* ∥Mt.21,33 ; L.14, 23.*

saeuus, a, um, *fierce,* Mt.8, 28 ; *grievous, sore* (of a wound), Ap.16,2.*

°**sagena, ae,** *f., drag-net, seine,* Mt.13,47.*

sagino, 1, *fatten,* L.15,23 ff.*

sal, salis, *n., salt.*

salio, 4, *leap, spring up,* J. 4,14.*

sallio (salio), 4, *season, salt,* Mt.5,13 ; Mk.9,49 (bis).*

salsus, a, um, *salted, salt,* Jas. 3,12.*

saltim (-tem), *at least,* A.5, 15.*

salto, 1, *dance,* ∥Mt.11,17 ; ∥14,6.*

salus, utis, *f. safety, salvation.*

salutaris, e, (as subst.) **salutaris,** *m., Saviour,* L.1, 47 ; . **salutare,** *n., salvation,* L.2,30 ; 3,6 ; A. 28,28.*

saluto, 1, *greet, salute.*

saluator, oris, *m., saviour.*

***saluifico, 1,** *save,* J.12,27 ; 12,47.*

saluo, 1, *save, make whole.*

saluus, a, um, *safe, whole.*

sancio, sanctus (sancitus), 4, *enact, ratify,* H.8,6.*

†**sancte,** *holily,* 1 Th.2,10.*

sanctificatio, onis, *f.,* (1) *sanctification,* 1 Th.4,3 ff.; (2) *holiness,* R.1,4 ; 2 C.7,1.

sanctifico, 1, *sanctify, make holy.*

sanctimonia, ae, *f., holiness,* H.12,14.*

sanctitas, tatis, *f., holiness,* L.1,75 ; E.4,24 ; 1 Th. 3,13.*

sanctum, i, *n.* (and pl., **sancta, orum**), *sanctuary,* H.8,2 ; 9,1 ff.

sanctus, a, um, *holy.*

°**sandalium, ii,** *n., slipper, sandal,* Mk.6,9.*

sanguis, uinis, *m., blood.*

sano, 1, *heal, cure.*

sanus, a, um, *whole, sound.*

°**saphirus (sapph-), i,** *f., sapphire,* Ap.21,19.*

sapiens, entis, *wise.*

sapienter, *wisely,* Mk.12, 34.*

sapientia, ae, *f., wisdom.*

sapio, 3, (1) *taste, savour of,* ∥Mt.16,23 ; (2) *think, consider, regard,* R.11,20 ; 14,6 ; 1 C.13,11.

sapphirus, v. saph-.

sarcina, ae, *f., burden,* L. 11,46.*

*°**sardinus, a, um,** *sardian, carnelian,* Ap.4,3 ; (as subst.) *the carnelian,* Ap. 21,20.*

[°sardius], ii, *m.*, *the carnelian*, Ap.21,20.*

†°sardonix (-yx), ichis (ychis), *m.* and *f.*, *sardonyx*, Ap. 21,20.*

sarmentum, i, *n.*, *faggot, brushwood*, A.28,3.*

satago, 3, *be busy, have enough to do*, L.10,40 ; 2 P.1,10 ; [3,14].*

*Satanas, ae, *m.*, *adversary, Satan.*

satio, 1, *satiate, satisfy*, A. 27,38 ; Ph.4,12.*

satis, *enough*, L.22,38 ; A. §17,9 ; 20,11.*

satisfacio, 3, *satisfy*, Mk.15, 15 ; A.24,10.*

satisfactio, onis, *f.*, *apology, explanation*, 1 P.3,15 ; *security, bail* [A.17,9].*

satum, i, *n.*, (in pl.) *crops, standing corn*, ||Mt.12,1.*

satum, i, *n.*, *a measure* (of corn), ||Mt.13,33.*

saturitas, tatis, *f.*, *fulness, repletion*, Co.2,23.*

saturo, 1, *satisfy.*

saxum, i, *n.*, *stone*, Mt.27, 60.*

scabellum (also scabillum, Mt.22,44), i, *n.*, *footstool.*

°scandalizo, 1, *cause to stumble.*

°scandalum, i, *n.*, *stumbling-block, cause of offence*, L.17,1 ; Ap.2,14.

°scapha, ae, *f.*, *small boat, skiff*, A.27,16 ff.*

sceleratus, a, um, *impious, unholy*, 1 T.1,9.*

scelestus, a, um, *impious, unholy*, 2 T.3,2.*

†scenofactorius, a, um, *belonging to tent-making*, A.18,3.*

°scenopegia, ae, *f.*, *feast of Tabernacles*, J.7,2.*

°schisma, atis, *n.*, *division*, J.9,16 ; 1 C.1,10 ; 12, 25.*

†°schola, ae, *f.*, *school*, A.19, 9.*

scientia, ae, *f.*, *knowledge.*

scindo, idi, issus, 3, *rend.*

scio, 4, *know.*

sciscitor, 1, *enquire*, Mt.2,4.*

scissura, ae, *f.*, *rent*, ||Mt. 9,16 ; *division*, 1 C.11, 18.*

scopa, ae, *f.*, (in pl.) *broom, besom*, ||Mt. 12,44.*

scorpio, onis, also scorpius, ii (Ap.9,5), *m.*, *scorpion.*

scriba, ae, *m.*, *scribe.*

scribo, psi, ptus, 3, *write.*

scriptura, ae, *f.*, *writing, scripture.*

scrutor, 1, *search.*

sculptura, ae, *f.*, *carving*, A.17,29.*

†scurrilitas, tatis, *f.*, *buffoonery*, E.5,4.*

scutum, i, *n.*, *shield*, E.6, 16.*

secedo, cessi, 3, *go aside,*
retire, depart.

secessus, us, *m., place of*
retirement, privy, ||Mt.
15,17.*

seco, sectus, 1, *cut asunder,*
H.11,37.*

secreto, *privately,* ||Mt.17,
19 ; 20,17 ; 24,3.*

secta, ae, *f., sect,* A.24,5 ;
division, G.5,20.

†**sectator, oris,** *m., follower,*
Ti.2,14.*

sector, 1, *follow.*

secundo, *secondly, in second*
place.

§**secundoprimus,** a, um,
second-first, L.6,1.*

secundus, a, um, *second.*

securis, is, *f., axe,* ||Mt.3,10.*

securitas, tatis, *f., safety,* 1
Th.5,3.*

securus, a, um, *free from*
care, Mt.28,14.*

secus, *near, by, at.*

sedeo, sedi, 2, *sit.*

sedes, is, *f., seat, throne.*

sedile, is, *n., seat,* Ap.4,4.*

†**seditiosus, a, um,** *turbulent,*
seditious, Mk.15,7.*

sedo, 1, *quiet, allay,* A.14,
18 ; 19,35 f.*

seduco, xi, ctus, 3, *lead astray,*
seduce.

seductio, onis, *f., misleading,*
deceit, 2 Th.2,10.*

seductor, oris, *m., deceiver,*
Mt.27,63 ; Ti.1,10 ; 2 J.7.

†**segnis, e,** *dilatory, lazy,* H.
6,12.*

segrego, 1, *separate.*

semen, inis, *n., seed.*

sementis, is, *f., seed,* Mk.4,
26.*

semicinctium, ii, *n., girdle,*
apron, A.19,12.*

†**seminiuerbius,** a, um, *scat-*
tering words, babbling, A.
17,18.* (Gk. σπερμολόγος.)

semino, 1, *sow.*

semita, ae, *f., path,* ||Mt.
3,3.*

semiuiuus, a, um, *half-dead,*
L.10,30.*

semper, *always.*

sempiternus, a, um, *ever-*
lasting, eternal.

§**senecta, ae,** *f., old age,* L.
1,36.*

[**senectus**], **tutis,** *f., old age*
[L.1,36].*

senesco, nui, 3, *become old,*
J.21,18 ; H.8,13.*

senex, nis, *old, aged ;* (as
subst.) *old man.*

senior, oris, *older, old ;* (as
subst. in pl.), *elders.*

sensus, us, *m., mind, under-*
standing, L.24,45 ; R.
11,34 ; Ap.17,9 ; *sense,*
H.5,14.

sententia, ae, *f., opinion,*
judgment [1 C.1,10] ; *vote,*
A.26,10.*

sentio, sensi, 4, *feel, think,*
judge, perceive.

seorsum, *apart.*

separatim, *privately, apart,* Mk.13,3 ; J.20,7.*

separatio, onis, *f., division,* L.12,51.*

separo, 1, *separate, sunder.*

sepelio, ii, pultus, 4, *bury.*

sepis, v. **sae-.**

[**†sepono**], 3, *lay aside,* 1 C. 16,2.*

septies, *seven times,* Mt.18, 21 f. ; L.17,4.*

sepulchrum, i, *n., sepulchre.*

sepultura, ae, *f., burial,* Mt. 27,7 ; Mk.14,8 ; J.12,7.*

sequor, secutus, 3, *follow.*

serenus, a, um (as subst. **serenum**), *fair weather,* Mt.16,2.*

sericum, i, *n., silk,* Ap.18, 12.*

sermo, onis, *m., word, saying, report.*

sero, 3, *sow,* Mt.6,26.*

sero, *late, in the evening,* Mt.20,8 ; Mk.4,35 ; J. 6,16.

serotinus, a, um, *latter, late* (of rain), Jas.5,7.*

serpens, entis, *m.,* and *f., serpent.*

seruio, 4, *serve, worship, do service to.*

seruitus, tutis, *f., servitude, bondage,* R.8,15 ff.; G. 2,4 ; *worshipping* (of idols), E.5,5 ; Co.3,5.

seruo, 1, *keep,* A.12,5 ; *ob-* *serve,* 1 T.6,14 ; Jas.2,10 ; *save,* A.27,43 ; *reserve,* §2 P.3,7.

seruus, i, *m., slave, servant.*

†seueritas, tatis, *f., severity* R.11,22 (bis).*

†sicarius, ii, *m., assassin,* A.21,38.*

sicco, 1, *dry up,* Mk.5,29 ; Ap.16,12.*

sicera (indecl.) [acc. **siceram**], *strong drink,* L.1,15.*

sicuti, *as,* E.3,5 ; 1 J.3,2.*

sidus, eris, *n., star,* A.7,43 ; 27,20 ; H.11,12 ; Jude 13.*

sigillum, i, *n., seal,* Ap.5,1 ; 6,3 ff.; 8,1.*

signaculum, i, *n., seal,* R.4, 11 ; 1 C.9,2 ; 2 T.2,19 ; Ap.5,2 ff.; §6,1.*

significo, 1, *signify, make known, point out.*

signo, 1, *seal, seal up.*

signum, i, *n., sign,* J.2,11 ; 2 C.12,12 ; *seal,* Ap.7,2 ; 9,4.

silentium, ii, *n., silence.*

sileo, 2, *keep silent, quiet,* L. 23,56.*

†siliqua, ae, *f., pod, husk* (esp. of carob tree), L.15, 16.*

silva, ae, *f., wood,* Jas.3,5.*

silvestris, e, *belonging to the woods, wild,* ‖Mt.3,4.*

simila, ae, *f., finest flour,* Ap.18,13.*

similis, e, *like*.

similiter, *likewise, in like manner*.

similitudo, dinis, *f.*, (1) *likeness*, R.1,23 ; H.7,15 ; (2) *parable* (in Luke).

†similo, 1, *make like*, H.2, 17.*

simplex, plicis, (1) *simple, single*, ‖Mt.6,22 ; (2) *honest, frank, straightforward, guileless*, Mt.10, 16 ; R.16,19.

simplicitas, tatis, *f.*, *simplicity, frankness, openness.*

simul, *together, at the same time.*

simulacrum, i, *n.*, *image, idol.*

simulatio, onis, *f.*, *dissimulation, hypocrisy.*

simulo, 1, *feign, make pretence of*, L.20,20 ; 20, 47.*

sin, *if not*, L.10,6 ; 13,9 ; Ap.2,5.*

*°sinapi, is, *n.*, *mustard*, ‖Mt.13,31 ; ‖17,20.*

†sincere, *sincerely*, Ph.1,17.*

*sinceritas, tatis, *f.*, *sincerity*, 1 C.5,8 ; 2 C.1,12 ; 2,17.*

sincerus, a, um, irregular plur. sinceres, Ph.1,10 ; *sincere*, 2,20 ; 2 P.3,1.*

°sindon, onis, *f.*, *fine cotton, muslin*, ‖Mt.27,59 ; Mk. 14,51 f.*

singillatim (singula-), *one by one*, Mk.14,19.*

singularis, e, *solitary, alone*, Mk.4,10.*

sinister, tra, trum, *on the left, the left* ;(as subst.) sinistra, *left hand.*

sino, 3, *allow, permit, let alone, let be.*

sinus, us, *m.*, *bosom.*

[siquidem], si quidem.

†sisto, 3, *set*, L.2,22.*

sitio, 4, *thirst.*

sitis, is, *f.*, *thirst*, 2 C.11, 27.*

siue, *if, whether, or.*

sm-, v. zm-.

sobrie, *soberly*, Ti.2,12.*

sobrietas, tatis, *f.*, *soberness, sobriety.*

sobrius, a, um, *sober, temperate, prudent.*

socer, cri, *m.*, *father-in-law*, J.18,13. *

societas, tatis, *f.*, *fellowship.*

socius, a, um (as subst. socius *m.*), *fellow, partner, comrade, partaker.*

socrus, us, *f.*, *mother-in-law*, ‖Mt.8,14 ; ‖10,35.*

sol, solis, *m.*, *sun.*

solacium, and solatium, H. 13,22, ii, *n.*, *consolation*, R.15,5 ; Ph.2,1 ; Co.4, 11 ; H.6,18.*

solemnis, v. soll-.

soleo, 2, *be accustomed*, Mk. 15,6.*

solido, 1, *make firm, establish,* 1 P.5,10.*

solidus, a, um, *solid* (of food), H.5,12 ff.*

solitudo, dinis, *f., wilderness.*

sollemnis (solem-), e, *solemn, festive* (with **dies** = *feast*), Mt.27,15 ; L.2,41.*

sollicite, *earnestly, diligently,* L.7,4 ; 2 T.1,17 ; 2,15 ; Ti.3,13.*

sollicitudo, dinis, *f., care, anxiety.*

sollicitus, a, um, *anxious, careful.*

solum, *only.*

solummodo, *only,* A.24,21 ; H.9,9.*

solus, a, um, *alone.*

solutio, onis, *f., loosing, release,* 1 C.7,27.*

soluo, ui, utus, 3, (1) *loose, release,* ||Mk.1,7 ; *relax* ; (2) *break up, divide,* A. 23,7 ; (3) *destroy,* Mt.5, 17 ff.; (4) in 1 J.4,3 = λύω in sense of "*annul*"?

somnio, 1, *dream,* A.2,17.*

somnium, ii, *n., dream,* A.2,17.*

somnus, i, *m., sleep.*

sonitus, us, *m., sound,* L.21, 25 ; 1 C.14,7.*

sono, 1, *sound, resound,* 1 C. 13,1.*

sonus, i, *m., sound,* A.2,2 ; R.10,18 ; H.12,19.*

sordes, is, *f.,* (only pl.) *filth, filthiness,* 1 P.3,21 ; Ap. 22,11.*

sordesco, 3, *be filthy,* Ap. 22,11.*

sordidus, a, um, *filthy,* Jas. 2,2.*

soror, oris, *f., sister.*

sors, sortis, *f., lot, that which is assigned by lot, share, portion.*

sortior, 4, (1) *cast lots,* J. 19,24, (2) *obtain,* A.1,17 ; H.8,6 ; 2 P.1,1.*

spargo, arsi, 3, *scatter,* Mt. 12,30 ; 25,24 ff.*

†**§sparsio, onis,** *f., sprinkling,* H.12,24.*

spatiosus, a, um, *broad,* Mt.7,13.*

spatium, ii, *n., space, interval* (of time), A.5,7 ; *distance,* L.24,13 ; *leisure,* Mk.6,31.*

species, ei, *f., form, fashion, appearance.*

speciosus, a, um, *beautiful,* Mt.23,27 ; A.3,2 ; 3,10; R.10,15.*

spectaculum, i, *n., sight, spectacle,* L.23,48 ; 1 C.4, 9 ; H.10,33.*

specto, 1, *behold,* L.23.35.*

speculator, oris, *m.,* (1) *soldier of the guard,* Mk.6, 27 (where Clem. reads **spic-**) ; (2) *eye-witness, spectator,* 2 P.1,16.*

speculor, 1, *observe, examine,* 2 C.3,18.*

speculum, i, *n., mirror,* 1 C. 13,12 ; Jas.1,23.*

spelunca, ae, *f., cave.*

sperno, spreui, 3, *despise, reject.*

spero, 1, *hope.*

spes, ei, *f., hope.*

spica, ae, *f., ear of corn,* ‖Mt. 12,1 ; Mk.4,28 (bis).*

†**spicatus, a, um,** *furnished with spikes* or *ears* (spica), Mk.14,3.* (Gk. πιστικός).

spiculator, v. spec-.

spina, ae, *f., thorn,* ‖Mt.7,16 ; ‖13,7 ; H.6,8,

*****spineus, a, um,** *made of thorns,* Mk.15,17 ; J.19, 5.*

spiritalis (-tualis), e, *spiritual.*

*****spiritaliter (-tualiter),** *spiritually,* 1 C.2,14 ; Ap.11, 8.*

spiritus, us, *m., wind,* J.3,8 ; A.2,2 ; *breath,* 2 Th.2,2 ; (vital) *spirit,* L.8,55 ; *a* (good or evil) *spirit; the Spirit* (of God).

spiro, 1, *breathe, blow,* J.3, 8 ; [A.9,1].*

splendeo, 2, only in partic. **splendens,** *shining, bright,* Mk.9,3 ; Ap.19,8.*

*****splendesco,** 3, *shine,* 2 C. 4,6.*

†**splendide,** *splendidly, sumptuously,* L.16,19.*

splendidus, a, um, *clear, bright,* Ap.22,1 ; 22,16.*

splendor, oris, *m., brightness,* Mk.13,24 ; A.26,13 ; H., 1,3.*

spolium, ii, *n., spoil,* L.11, 22.*

spondeo, spopondi, 2, *promise,* L.22,6.*

*°**spongia, ae,** *f., sponge,* ‖Mt.27,48.*

sponsa, ae, *f., bride.*

sponsor, oris, *m., surety,* H.7,22.*

sponsus, i, *m., bridegroom.*

spontanee, *willingly,* 1 P. 5,2.*

*****sporta, ae,** *f., basket, hamper,* ‖Mt.15,37 ; ‖16,10 ; A.9,25 ; 2 C.11,33.*

spuma, ae, *f., foam,* L.9, 39.*

*****spumo,** 1, *foam,* Mk.9,17 ff.*

spurcitia, ae, *f., filthiness,* Mt.23,27.*

†**sputum, i,** *n., spittle,* J.9, 6.*

squama, ae, *f., scale,* A.9, 18.*

stabilio, 4, *establish, strengthen,* H.13,9.*

stabilis, e, *steadfast, steady, immutable,* 1 C.15,58 ; 2 C.7,10 ; Co.1,23.*

†**stabularius, ii,** *m., innkeeper,* L.10,35.*

stabulum, i, n., inn, L.10,34.*

°stadium, ii, n., (1) stade, furlong, L.24,13 ; J.6, 19 ; 11,18 ; (2) stadium, race-course, 1 C.9,24..

stagnum, i, n., lake (Gk. λίμνη.) (Luke and Apocalypse.)

°stater, eris, m., stater, shekel, Mt.17,27.*

statera, ae, f., balance, Ap. 6,5.*

statim, immediately, forthwith.

statuo, ui, utus, 3, (1) set, place, Mt.4,5 ; establish, R.3,31 ; H.10,9 ; (2) appoint, A.1,23 ; (3) resolve, determine, A.27,12 ; Ti.3,12.

statura, ae, f., stature, ||Mt. 6,27 ; L.19,3.*

status, us, m., place, position, standing, H.9,8.*

stella, ae, f., star.

stercus, oris, n., dung, L.13, 8 ; Ph.3,8.*

sterilis, e, barren.

sterno, straui, stratus, 3, strew.

sterquilinium, ii, n., dunghill, L.14,35.*

°stigma, atis, n., brand, mark, G.6,17.*

stimulus, i, m., (1) goad, A. [9,5] ; 26,14 ; (2) sting, 1 C.15,55 f.; (3) ? stake, 2 C.12,7.*

stipendium, ii, n., wages, pay (Gk. ὀψώνιον), L.3, 14 ; R.6,23 ; 1 C.9,7 ; 2 C.11,8.*

stipula, ae, f., stubble, 1 C. 3,12.*

sto, steti, 1, stand.

†°stoicus, a, um, Stoic, A.17, 18.*

°stola, ae, f., robe.

°stomachus, i, m., stomach.

strideo, 2, gnash, Mk.9,18 ; A.7,54.*

*stridor, oris, m., gnashing (of teeth).

stringo, nxi, 3, bind fast, A. 16,24.*

structura, ae, f., (1) construction, mode of building, Ap.21,18 ; (2) edifice, building, Mk.13,1.*

studeo, 2, strive, be diligent, A.24,16.*

†stultiloquium, ii, n., foolish talking, E.5,4.*

stultitia, ae, f., foolishness.

stultus, a, um, foolish ; (as subst.) fool.

stupefio, factus, fieri, be benumbed, amazed, Mk.9, 14 ; A.9,7.*

stupeo, 2, be astonished, amazed.

stupor, oris, m., wonder, astonishment.

suadeo, 2, persuade, advise.

†suadibilis, e, easy to persuade, Jas.3,17.*

suauis, e, *pleasant*, Mt.11, 30.*

suauitas, tatis, *f.*, (1) *sweetness*, E.5,2 ; Ph.4,18 ; (2) *gentleness*, 2 C.6,6.*

subdo, ditus, 3, only in P.P. subditus, *subject*.

†subdolus, a, um, *somewhat crafty, deceitful*, 2 C.11, 13.*

†subduco, ductus, 3, *draw up* (boats), L.5,11.*

subeo, ii, 4, *go up*, J.6,3.*

†subinfero, ferre, *add*, 2 P. 1,5.*

†subintro, 1, *enter stealthily*, R.5,20.*

†subintroduco, ductus, 3, *bring in secretly*, G.2,4.* (P.P. = Gk. παρείσακτος.)

subintroeo, ii, 4, *enter secretly*, G.2,4 ; Jude 4.*

subito, *suddenly*.

subiaceo, 2, *be subject*, H. 13,17.*

subicio (-iicio), ieci, iectus, 3, *subdue, subject*.

*subiectio, onis, *f.*, *subjection*, G.2,5 ; 1 T.2,11.*

*subiugalis, e, (as subst.) *beast of burden*, Mt.21,5 ; 2 P.2,16.* (Gk. ὑποζύγιον.)

subleuo, 1, *lift up*, J.6,5 ; 17, 1.*

sublimis, e, *lofty, high*, L.12, 29 ; R.13,1 ; 1 T.6,17.*

sublimitas, tatis, *f.*, (1) *height*, E.3,18 ; (2) *loftiness, ele-*

vation, excellence, 1 C.2,1 ; 1 T.2,2.

*subministratio, onis, *f.*, *furnishing, supplying*, E. 4,16 ; Ph.1,19.*

subministro, 1, *furnish, supply, give*, Co.2,19 ; 1 T. 5,10 ff.*

submitto, v. summ-.

subnauigo, 1, *sail under the lee of*, A.27,4.*

subsequor, secutus, 3, *follow after*.

substantia, ae, *f.*, (1) *substance, goods*, L.8,43 ; 15,12 f.; (2) *essence*, H. 1,3 ; (3) (as trans. of ὑπόστασις), *confidence*, 2 C.9,4 ; 11,17 ; H.3,14.

substerno, 3, *strew beneath*, L.19,36.*

†subterfugio, fugi, 3, *avoid, shun*, A.20,27.*

†§subtilitas, tatis, *f.*, *acuteness, subtlety* (Gk. πιθανολογία) Co.2,4.*

†subtractio, onis, *f.*, *drawing back*, (Gk. ὑποστολή), H.10,39.*

subtraho, traxi, 3, *withdraw, keep back*, A.20,20 ; G. 2,12 ; 2 Th.3,6 ; H.10, 38.*

subuersio, onis, *f.*, *overturning, ruin*, 2 T.2,14.*

subuerto, uerti, uersus, 3, *upset, overturn*, J.2,15 ; *ruin, pervert*, L.23,2 ; A.

I

13,10 ; 2 T.2,18 ; Ti.1,
11 ; 3,11.*
succendo, di, 3, *burn*, Mt.22,
7.*
successor, oris, *m.*, *successor*,
A.24,28.*
succido, 3, *cut down*, L.13,
7 ff.*
succingo, nxi, nctus, 3, *gird*,
J.21,7 ; E.6,14 ; 1 P.1,
13.*
succlamo, 1, *cry out*, L.23,
21.*
*sudarium, ii, *n.*, *napkin*,
L.19,20 ; J.11,44 ; 20,
7 ; A.19,12.*
sudor, oris, *m.*, *sweat*, L.22,
44.*
sufferentia, ae, *f.*, *sufferance*,
patience, Jas.5,11.*
*suffero, ferre, *suffer*, *endure*,
1 C.13,7 ; Jas.1,12 ; 1 P.2,
20.
*sufficientia, ae, *f.*, *sufficiency*,
2 C.3,5 ; 9,8 ; 1 T.6,6.*
sufficio, 3, *suffice*, *be sufficient*.
suffoco, 1, *strangle*, Mt.18,
28 ; A.15,20 ; *choke*,
‖Mt.13,7 ; ‖Mk.5,13.
suffodio, fodi, 3, *dig down*,
R.11,3.*
suggero, 3, *bring to mind*,
suggest, J.14,26.*
†suggillo (sugi-), 1, *beat
black and blue*, L.18,5.*
sugo, suxi, 3, *suck*, L.11,
27.*

sulphur, uris, *n.*, *brimstone*,
sulphur, L.17,29 ; and
six times in Ap.
†sulphureus, a, um, *of sulphur*, Ap.9,17.*
summa, ae, *f.*, *sum*, A.22,
28.*
summitto (subm- three
times), misi, missus, 3,
(1) *let down*, Mk.2,4 ; A.
9,25 ; (2) *suborn*, A.6,11.
summus, a, um, *highest*,
chief.
sumo, sumsi (-mpsi), 3, *take*.
sumptus, us, *m.*, *cost*, L.14,
28 ; 1 C.9,18.*
†superabundanter, *very abundantly*, E.3,20.*
superabundo, 1, *abound more*,
abound greatly, R.5,20 ;
2 C.7,4 ; E.1,8 ; 1 T.1,
14.*
†superadultus, a, um, *past
maturity*, 1 C.7,36.*
*superaedifico, 1, *build over*
or *upon*.
superbia, ae, *f.*, *pride*, Mk.
7,22 ; 1 T.3,6 ; Jas.4,
16 ; 1 J.2,16.*
superbus, a, um, *proud*.
†supercertor, 1, *fight for*,
Jude 3.*
supercilium, ii, *n.*, *brow* (of
hill), L.4,29.*
†supercresco, 3, *increase
above measure*, 2 Th.1,3.*
superduco, 3, *bring upon*,
2 P.2,1.*

†**supereffluo**, 3, *overflow*, L. 6,38.*

***superemineo**, 2 (only in partic. **supereminens**), *be excellent*, E.1,19 ; 3,19.*

†**supererogo**, 1, *spend in addition* (Gk. προσδαπανῶ), L.10,35.*

[**superexalto**], 1, *exalt above others*, Jas.2,13.*

†§**superexulto**, 1, *boast, glory over*, Jas.2,13.*

superextendo, 3, *stretch above measure*, 2 C.10,14.*

supergredior, 3, *step over, go beyond, transgress*, 1 Th. 4,6.*

†**superinpendo** (-imp-), 3, *spend*, 2 C.12,15.*

†**superinduo**, 3, *put on over* (other things), 2 C.5,2.*

superior, ius, *higher*, A.10, 9 ; 19,1 ; Ph.2,3.*

superius, *higher, above*, L. 14,10 ; H.10,8.*

†**superlucror**, 1, *gain besides*, Mt.25,20.*

*̂**supernus, a, um**, *high, celestial*, J.8,23 ; Ph.3, 14.*

supero, 1, (1) *overcome*, R.8, 37 ; 2 P.2,19 f.; (2) *exceed, abound*, 2 P.1,8 ; (3) *be left over, remain*, ‖Mk.8,8.*

†**superordino**, 1, *add something to* (Gk. ἐπιδιατάσσομαι), G.3,15.*

superpono, positus, 3, *lay on*, J.11,38 ; 21,9.*

superscribo, 3, *write on*, H. 8,10 ; 10,16.*

†**superscriptio, onis,** *f.*, *superscription*, [Mt.22,20] ; L. 23,38.*

†**supersemino**, 1 *sow above* (other seeds), Mt.13,25.*

superstitio, onis, *f.*, *superstition*, A.25,19 ; Co.2,23.*

†**superstitiosus, a, um**, *superstitious*, A.17,22.* (Gk. δεισιδαίμων.)

†**supersubstantialis, e**, *necessary to support life*, Mt. 6,11. (Gk. ἐπιούσιος.)

supersum, fui, esse, *be over, be left, remain*.

superuenio, ueni, 4, *come upon*.

†**superuestio**, 4, *clothe upon*, 2 C.5,4.*

***supplementum, i,** *n.*, *filling up, supply*, Mk.2,21 ; 2 C.8,14.*

suppleo, eui, etus, 2, *supply*, 1 C.16,17 ; 2 C.8,14 ; *fulfil*, Jas.2,23.

supplicatio, onis, *f.*, *supplication*, H.5,7.*

supplicium, ii, *n.*, *punishment*, Mt.25,46 ; H.10, 29.*

suppono, posui, 3, *lay down, place under*, R.16,4.*

supporto, 1, *bear with*, 2 C. 11,1 ; E.4,2 ; Co.3,13.*

†§**suprascriptio, onis,** *f.,* *superscription,* Mt.22, 20.*

surdus, a, um, *deaf.*

surgo, surrexi, 3, *rise, arise.*

sursum, (1) *above,* G.4,26 ; Co.3,1 f.; (2) *upwards, up,* H.12,15.

sus, suis, *c., pig, sow.*

suscipio, cepi, ceptus, 3, *take, receive, take up, support.*

suscito, 1, *raise* or *rouse up.*

suspendo, di, pensus, 3, *hang, suspend.*

suspicio, 3, *look up,* Mk.7, 34 ; L.19,5.*

suspicio, onis, *f., suspicion,* 1 T.6,4.*

suspicor, 1, *suspect, suppose,* A.25,18 ; 27,27.*

sustentatio, onis, *f., forbearance,* R.3,26.*

sustinentia, ae, *f., endurance, patience,* 1 Th.1,3.*

sustineo, nui, 2, (1) *bear, bear with, endure, sustain,* R.9,22 ; 1 C.4,12 ; (2) *wait, tarry,* ||Mt.26,38 ; *continue with,* Mk.8,2.

†**susurratio, onis,** *f., whispering,* 2 C.12,20.*

susurro, onis, *m., whisperer,* R.1,29.*

°**sycomorus, i,** *f., fig-mulberry tree,* L.19,4.* (Gk. συκομορέα.)

°**symphonia, ae,** *f., music,* L.15,25.*

°**synagoga, ae,** *f., synagogue.*

T

taberna, ae, *f., tavern,* A. 28,15.*

tabernaculum, i, *n., tent, tabernacle.*

tabesco, 3, *melt away,* 2 P. 3,12.*

tabula, ae, *f., tablet, table,* 2 C.3,3 ; H.9,4 ; *plank,* A.27,44.*

taceo, 2, (1) *be silent ;* (2) *pass over in silence* (so **tacitus,** R.16,25).

taedeo, 2, (1) (pers.), *be weary,* Mk.14,33 ; (2) (impers.), *it wearies, disgusts,* 2 C.1,8.*

talentum, i, *n., talent.*

taliter (Gk. οὕτως), *so, in such wise,* H.10,33.*

†**talitha**(Aram.), *maiden,* Mk. 5,41.*

*****tametsi,** *although,* 2 C.12, 11 ; H.6,9.*

tango, tetigi, 3, *touch.*

tantum, *only.*

tantummodo, *only,* Mk.5,36.*

†**tarde,** *slowly,* A.27,7.*

tardo, 1, *tarry, delay,* L.1, 21 ; 1 T.3,15 ; H.10,37 ; 2 P.3,9.*

tardus, a, um, *slow*, L.24, 25 ; Jas.1,19 (bis).*

†tartarus, i, *m.*, *hell*, *Tartarus*, 2 P.2,4.*

taurus, i, *m.*, *bull*, Mt.22,4 ; A.14,13 ; H.9,13 ; 10,4.*

tectum, i, *n.*, *roof, housetop*.

tego, tectus, 3, *cover*, R.4,7 ; 1 T.6,8.*

†tegula, ae, *f.*, *tile*, L.5,19.*

*°teloneum (-nium), i, *n.*, *custom-house*, *place of toll*, ‖Mt.9,9.*

telum, i, *n.*, *weapon*, E.6, 16.*

temere, *rashly*, A.19,36.* (Gk. προπετές.)

tempero, 1, *mingle duly*, *temper*, 1 C.12,24.*

tempestas, tatis, *f.*, *storm*, *tempest*, Mt.16,3 ; L.8, 24 ; A.27,18 ff.*

templum, i, *n.*, *temple*.

*temporalis, e, *temporary*, ‖Mt.13,21 ; 2 C.4,18 ; H. 11,25.*

temporaneus, a, um, *timely*, *early* (of rain), Jas.5,7.* (Gk. πρόϊμος.)

tempus, oris, *n.*, *time*.

temtatio (tent-), onis, *f.*, *temptation*.

†temtator (tent-), oris, *m.*, *tempter* (Gk. ὁ πειράζων), Mt.4,3.*

temto (tento), 1, (1) *handle*, *feel*, 2 P.1,9 ; (2) *tempt*, *try, prove*, 1 C.7,5 ; H.2,

18 ; (3) *endeavour*, A.9, 26 ; 16,7.

tendo, 3, (1) *lay* (ambush), A.25,3 ; (2) *direct one's course*, A.27,40.*

tenebrae, arum, *f.*, *darkness*.

tenebrosus, a, um, *dark*, ‖Mt. 6,23 ; Ap.16,10.*

teneo, nui, 2, *hold, take hold of, seize, take, obtain, hold fast*.

tener, era, erum, *tender*, ‖Mt.24,32.*

tent-, v. temt-.

†tepidus, a, um, *luke-warm*, Ap.3,16.*

tergeo, tersi, 2, *wipe*, L.7,38 ; 7,44.*

termino, 1, *define, limit*, H. 4,7.*

terminus, i, *m.*, *limit, bound*, Mt.24,31 ; A.17,26.*

terra, ae, *f.*, *land, earth*.

terrenus, a, um, *earthly*, J. 3,12 ; 1 C.15,47 ff.; Ph. 3,19 ; Jas.3,15.*

terreo, 2, *terrify*.

*terrestris, e, *belonging to the earth, terrestrial*, 1 C. 15,40 ; 2 C.5,1 ; Ph.2, 10.*

terribilis, e, *terrible*, H.10, 27 ; 12,21.*

terror, oris, *m.*, *object of terror* (Gk. φόβητρον), L.21,11.*

tertio, *for the third time, thirdly*.

testamentum, i, *n., covenant;* testament.

†**testator, oris,** *m., testator,* H.9,16.*

testificor, 1, *bear witness, testify.*

testimonium, ii, *n., witness, testimony.*

testis, is, *c., witness.*

testor, 1, (1) *testify,* L.16,28 ; 1 J.1,2 ; (2) *make testament* or *covenant,* H.9,17 ; 10,16.

*°**tetrarcha, ae,** *m., tetrarch.*

*°**theatrum, i,** *n., theatre,* A. 19,29 ff.*

°**thesaurizo,** 1, *lay* or *treasure up.*

°**thesaurus, i,** *m., treasure.*

thorus, v. torus.

°**thronus, i,** *m.,* (1) *seat, throne,* Mt.5,34 ; H.1,8 ; Ap.4,4 ff.; (2) *a dignity among angels,* Co.1,16.

thuribulum, v. tur-.

thus, v. tus.

°**thyinus, a, um,** *thyine, made of citrus-tree,* Ap.18,12.*

tibia, ae, *f., pipe, flute,* L.7, 32 ; 1 C.4,17 ; Ap.18,22.*

†**tibicen, inis,** *m., flute player,* Mt.9,23.*

†§**timefactus, a, um,** *frightened, alarmed,* A.24,26.*

timeo, 2, *fear, be afraid.*

timidus, a, um, *fearful, timid,* ‖Mt.8,26 ; Ap.21,8.*

timor, oris, *m., fear.*

***timoratus, a, um,** *devout, God-fearing,* L.2,25 ; A. 8,2.*

tinea, ae, *f., moth,* Mt.6,19 f.; L.12,33 ; Jas. 5,2.*

tinnio, 4, *clang, resound,* 1 C.13,1.*

titulus, i, *m., title, inscription,* Mk.15,26 ; J.19, 19 f.*

tolerabilis, e (only in compar.), *tolerable,* Mt.10, 15.*

†**tolerantia, ae,** *f., endurance,* 2 C.1,6.*

tollo, sustuli, sublatus, 3, (1) *take, take* or *raise up,* ‖Mt.4,6 ; *take away,* L. 8,12 ; (2) *weigh anchor, put out to sea,* A.27,2 ff.; 27,21.

tondeo, totondi, 2, *shave,* A. 18,18 ; 1 C.11,6 (bis) ; *shear,* A.8,32.

tonitruum, ui (gen. pl., Ap. 19,6, §**tonitruum,** as if from **tonitru** or **tonitrus**), *n., thunder, thundering.*

°**topazius, ii,** *f., topaz,* Ap. 21,20.*

torcular, aris, *n., winepress,* Mt.21,33 ; Ap.19,15.*

tormentum, i, *n., torment, torture.*

torqueo, tortus, 2, (1)·*twist,* 1 T.2,9 ; (2) *torture, torment,* Mt.8,6 ; ‖8,29 ; A. 22,24 ff.*

torrens, entis, *m., torrent,* J.18,1.*

†**tortor, oris,** *m., tormentor,* Mt.18,34.*

torus (tho-), i, *m., bed,* H. 13,4.*

trabs, trabis, *f.,* ‖Mt.7,3 ff.*

†**tractabilis, e,** *that may be touched* (Gk. ψηλαφώμενος), H.12,18.*

tracto, 1, (1) *treat,* A.7,6 ; 27,3 ; (2) *discuss, treat of,* Mk.9,33 ; 2 T.2,15.*

†**traditor, oris,** *m., traitor.*

trado, tradidi, traditus, 3, (1) *give up,* Mt.4,12 ; *hand over, deliver,* A.23,33 ; *give* (in marriage), L.20, 34 ; (2) *betray,* Mt.10,4 ; (3) *hand down, transmit,* L.1,2 ; A.6,14.

traduco and **transduco** (2 P. 3,17), **xi, ctus, 3,** (1) *lead* or *bring over,* 2 P.3,17 ; (2) *make a show of, disgrace,* Mt.1,19 ; Co. 2,15.*

traho, traxi, 3, *drag, draw.*

tranquillitas, tatis, *f., calm,* ‖Mt.8,26.*

tranquillus, a, um, *peaceful,* 1 T.2,2.*

transcendo, di, 3, *cross over,* Mk.5,21.*

transduco, v. trad-.

transeo, ii, 4, *cross, cross over,* L.16,26 ; H.11,29 ; *pass away,* 2 C.5,17.

transfigo, xi, 3, *pierce,* J. 19,37.*

transfiguro, 1, (1) *transform, transfigure,* ‖Mt.17,2 ; 2 C.11,13 ff.; (2) *express in figure,* 1 C.4,6.*

†**transformo, 1,** *transform, change,* 2 C.3,18.*

transfreto, 1, *cross over by sea,* ‖Mt.14,34 ; A.21, 2.

transgredior, 3, *transgress,* Mt.15,2 f.*

transgressio, onis, *f., transgression,* G.3,19.*

transgressor, oris, *m., transgressor,* Jas.2,9 ff.*

transigo, actus, 3, *end, finish,* A.25,13.*

transitus, us, *m., passing. passage,* 1 C.16,7.*

***translatio, onis,** *f., transference, removal,* H.7,12 ; 12,27 ; *translation* (to heaven), H.11,5.*

†**transmeo, 1,** *cross over,* L. 16,26.*

transmigratio, onis, *f., removal, deportation* (Gk. μετοικεσία), Mt.1,11 ff.*

†**transmutatio, onis,** *f., change,* Jas.1,17.*

†**transnauigo, 1,** *sail past,* A. 20,16.*

transplanto, 1, *transplant,* L.17,6.*

†**transpono, posui, 3,** *remove, transfer,* A.27,6.*

tremo, 3, *tremble,* Mk.5,33 ; [A.9,6].*
tremebundus, a, um, *trembling,* H.12,21.*
***tremefactus, a, um,** *quaking, trembling,* A.7,32 ; 16, 29 ; [24,26].*
tremor, oris, *m., trembling.*
tribulo, 1, *afflict,* 2 C.1,6 ; 2 Th.1,6 f.*
tribulus, i, *m., thistle,* Mt.7, 16 ; H.6,8.*
tribunal, alis, *n., judgment-seat.*
tribunus, i, *m., military tribune, chief captain, chief.*
tribuo, 3, *give, bestow.*
tribus, us (dat. and abl. pl. **tribubus**), *f., tribe.*
tributum, i, *n., tribute.*
triduum, ui, *n., space of three days.*
triennium, il, *n., space of three years,* A.20,31.*
tristis, e, *sad.*
tristitia, ae, *f., sadness.*
tristor, 1, *be sad,* Jas.5, 13.*
triticum, i, *n., wheat.*
trituro, 1, *tread* (corn), *thresh,* 1 C.9,9 f.; 1 T.5,18.*
triumpho, 1, *triumph over, lead in triumph,* 2 C.2, 14 ; Co.2,15.*
tuba, ao, *f., trumpet.*
†tumidus, a, um, *swollen, puffed up,* 2 T.3,4.*

tumor, oris, *m., swelling,* A.28,6.*
tumultuor, 1, *make a tumult* or *uproar,* Mt.9,23.*
tumultus, us, *m., tumult, uproar.*
tunica, ae, *f., tunic, coat.*
turba, ae, *f., crowd, multitude.*
turbatio, onis, *f., commotion, disturbance,* A.12,18 ; 19, 23.*
turbo, 1, *disturb, trouble,* L. 1,12 ; J.14,1.
turbo, inis, *m., whirlwind, storm,* H.12,18; 2 P.2, 17.*
turibulum (thu-), i, *n., censer,* H.9,4 ; Ap.8,3 ff.*
turpis, e, *disgraceful, shameful.*
turpitudo, dinis, *f., dishonour, shame,* R.1,27 ; E.5,4 ; Ap.16,15.*
turris, is (acc. **-em**), *f., tower,* ||Mt.21,33 ; L.13, 4 ; 14,28.*
turtur, uris, *m., turtle-dove,* L.2,24.*
tus (thus), turis, *n., frankincense, incense,* Mt.2,11 ; Ap.18,13.*
†tutor, oris, *m., guardian, tutor,* G.4,2.*
tutus, a, um, *safe, secure,* A.27,9 ; H.6,19.*
†°typhonicus, a, um, *like a typhoon, stormy,* A.27, 14.*

U

uber, eris, *n.*, *breast*, L.11,27 ;
　23,29.*
uber, eris, *rich, plentiful*,
　L.12,16.*
ubicumque, *wherever.*
ubique, *everywhere.*
ulcisor, 3, *avenge*, 2 C.10,6.*
ulcus, eris, *n.*, *sore, ulcer*, L.
　16,20 f.*
ulna, ae, *f.*, *arm*, L.2,28.*
†ulterius, *further, any longer*,
　R.15,23.*
ultimus, a, um, (as subst.)
　ultimum, *end*, A.1,8.*
ultio, onis, *f.*, *vengeance*, L.
　21,22 ; A.7,24 ; 28,4.*
ultro, *spontaneously, of one's
　own accord*, Mk.4,28 ; A.
　12,10.*
ululatus, us, *m.*, *wailing*, Mt.
　2,18.*
ululo, 1, *howl, wail*, Jas.
　5,1.*
umbra, ae, *f.*, *shadow.*
umerus (hum-), i, *m.*,
　shoulder, Mt.23,4 ; L.
　15,5.*
unanimis, e, *of one mind,
　harmonious.*
unanimiter, *with one accord*
　(six times in Acts).
unctio, onis, *f.*, *anointing,
　unction*, 1 J.2,20 ff.*
unde, *whence.*

undique, *from all sides*, Mk.
　1,45 ; L.19,43.*
ungentum (-guentum), i, *n.*,
　ointment.
ungo, xi, 3, *anoint.*
unicus, a, um, *only, sole*, L.
　7,12 ; 8,42 ; 9,38.*
unigenitus, a, um, *only-
　begotten.*
*unitas, tatis, *f.*, *unity*, E.
　4,3 ; 4,13.*
uniuersitas, tatis, *f.*, *universe,
　world* (Gk. κόσμος), Jas.
　3.6.*
uniuersus, a, um, *whole, all.*
†§unoculus, a, um, *one-eyed*
　(Gk. μονόφθαλμος), Mt.
　18,9.*
urbs, urbis, *f.*, *city*, A.16,12 ;
　16,39 ; [17,6].*
urceus, ei, *m.*, *pitcher, pot*,
　Mk.7,4 ff.*
urgeo, 2, *impel, urge*, 2 C.
　5,14.*
urna, ae, *f.*, *urn, jar*, H.9,
　4.*
uro, 3, *burn*, 1 C.7,9 ; 2 C.
　11,29.*
ursus, i, *m.*, *bear*, Ap.13,2.*
usque, *up to, as far as.*
[usquequo], usque quo, *how
　long?* ‖Mt.17,16 ; Ap.
　6,10.*
usura, ae, *f.*, *interest*, ‖Mt.
　25,27.*
usus, us, *m.*, *use*, R.1,26 f.;
　need, want, Ph.4,16 ; Ti.
　3,14.

uter, utris, *m., wine-skin,* ||Mt.9,17.*

uterus, i, *m., womb.**

†**utl,** *that,* Philem.14.*

utilis, e, *useful.*

utilitas, tatis, *f., profit,* R. 3,1 ; 1 C.7,35 ; 12,7.*

utinam, *would that,* 1 C. 4,8 ; 2 C.11,1 ; G.5,12 ; Ap.3,15.*

utique, *surely, certainly.*

utor, usus, 3, *use.*

ut puta, *as for example,* 1 C. 14,10 ; 15,37.*

utrum, *whether,* J.7,17.*

uua, ae, *f., grape, bunch of grapes,* ||Mt.7,16 ; Jas. 3,12 ; Ap.14,18.*

uxor, oris, *f., wife.*

V

ua (uah) (interj.) *Ah !* [Mt. 27,40] ; Mk.15,29.*

uaco, 1, (1) *be empty, be without,* Mt.12,44 ; H. 8,7 ; (2) *have leisure, be unoccupied,* A.17,21 ; 1 C.7,5.*

uacuus, a, um, (1) *empty,* 1 C.15,10 ; (2) *disengaged ;* 1 C.16,12 ; *idle,* 2 P.1,8 ; **uacuum est** (impers.), 1 C.16,12 ; **in uacuum,** *in vain,* 2 C.6,1 ; G.2,2 ; Ph.2,16.*

uado, 3, *go* (frequent in the imperative).

uae, (1) *woe !* (2) in Ap. as subst., *a woe.*

uaenundo, v. uen-.

uagina, ae, *f., sheath,* J.18, 11.*

uah, v. ua.

ualde, *greatly, very much, very.*

†**ualedico, xi,** 3, *bid farewell,* A.20,1.*

[***ualefacio],** feci, 3, *bid farewell,* A.18,18 ; 21,6 ; 2 C.2,13.*

ualeo, 2, (1) *be strong, able, efficacious,* L.16,3 ; J. 21,6 ; H.9,17 ; *prevail,* Ap.12,8 ; (2) *be well, healthy,* ||Mt.9,12 ; (in imperative) **uale, ualete,** *farewell,* A.15,29; [23,30].

§**ualide,** *strongly, mightily,* A.27,18.*

ualidus, a, um, *mighty, strong,* L.15,14 ; H.5,7 ; *boisterous* (of wind), Jas. 3,4.

uallis, is, *f., valley,* L.3,5.*

uallum, i, *n., rampart, wall,* L.19,43.*

†**uaniloquus, a, um,** *idly talking, prating,* Ti.1, 10.*

†**uaniloquium, ii,** *n., idle talking,* 1 T.1,6 ; [2 T. 2,16].*

uanitas, tatis, *f., vanity,*

emptiness, R.8,20 ; E.
4,17 ; 2 P.2,18.*
uanus, a, um, *vain, profit-
less.*
uapulo, 1, *be beaten*, Mk.13,
9 ; L.12,47 f.*
uarius, a, um, *various, di-
verse.*
uas, uasis, *n., vessel.*
[†**uasculum**], i, *n., vessel,*
1 P.3,7.*
uasto, 1, *lay waste, destroy*,
H.11,28.*
uectigal, alis, *n., tribute, tax,*
R.13,7.*
uehemens, entis, *mighty,
vehement*, A.2,2.*
uehementer, *greatly, mightily,
strictly.*
uelamen, inis, *n., veil.*
uelamentum, i, *n., veil.*
uello, 3, *pluck*, ‖Mt.12,1.*
uelo, 1, *veil, cover, hide.*
ueloclter, *quickly*, A.12,7 ;
22,18 ; R.16,20 ; Ap.
22,7.*
uelox, ocis, *swift, speedy,*
R.3,15 ; Jas.1,19 ; 2 P.
1,14.*
uelum, i, *n., veil*, ‖Mt.27,51.*
uendo, didi, 3, *sell.*
ueneflcium, ii, *n., magic,
witchcraft*, G.5,20 ; Ap.
9,21 ; 18,23.*
ueneficus, i, *m., sorcerer.*
Ap.21,8 ; 22,15.*
uenenum, i, *n., poison*, R.
3,13 ; Jas.3,8.*

ueneo, ii, 4, *be sold*, ‖Mt.10,
29 ; J.12,5 ; 1 C.10,25.*
uenio, ueni, 4, *come.*
uenter, tris, *m., belly.*
uentilabrum, i, *n., fan*, ‖Mt.
3,12.*
uentus, i, *m., wind.*
uenundo (uaen-), **datus,** 1,
sell, Mt.18,25 ; ‖26,9 ;
A.5,4.
uerax, acis, *true, truthful.*
uerber, eris, *n., lash, whip,*
H.11,36.*
uerbero, 1, *beat*, 1 C.9,26.*
uerbosus, a, um, *wordy,
talkative*, 1 T.5,13.*
uerbum, i, *n., word ; the
Word, Logos.*
uere, *truly, indeed.*
uerecundia, ae, *f., modesty,
shame*, 1 C.6,5 ; 1 T.2,9.*
uereor, 2, *fear, reverence.*
ueritas, talis, *f., truth.*
uermis, is, *m., worm*, Mk.
9,44 ff.; A.12,23.*
uersutia, ae, *f., craftiness,*
Mk.12,15.*
uerto, ti, uersus, 3, *turn*, Mk.
3,21 ; J.16,20 ; H.11,34.*
[**uerumtamen**],**uerum tamen.**
uerus, a, um, *true, real.*
uesper, eris, *m.* (only abl.),
evening.
uespera, ae, *f., evening*, Mk.
11,11 ; 11,19 ; A.4,3 ;
28,23.* [In Mk.11,11
uespera is perhaps an
adjective.]

uestigium, ii, *n., footstep,*
R.4,12 ;   2 C.12,18 ;   1
P.2,21.*

uestimentum, i, *n., garment,
raiment.*

uestio, 4, *clothe.*

uestis, is, *f., garment, raiment.*

uestitus, us, *m., raiment,* L.
9,29.*

ueteresco (-asco), 3, *grow old,*
L.12,33 ;   H.1,11.*

†**uetero,** 1, *make* or *count old*
(Gk. παλαιῶ), H.8,13.*

ueto, atus, 1, *forbid,* L.18,16 ;
A.16,6.*

uetus, eris, *old.*

uetustas, tatis, *f., oldness,*
R.7,6.*

uexo, 1, *harass, vex, afflict.*

uia, ae, *f., way.*

uicies, *twenty times,* Ap.9,
16.*

uicinus, a, um, *neighbouring,
near,* (as subst.) *neigh-
bour.*

uicis (genitive), *f.,* (1) *alter-
nation, return, recom-
pense,* 1 T.5,4 ; (2) *course
of duty* (of priests), L.
1,5 ff.*

uicissitudo, dinis, *f., change,*
Jas.1,17.*

uictima, ae, *f., victim,* Mk.
9,49 ;   A.7,42.*

uictus, us, *m., livelihood,
means of subsistence,* ||Mk.
12,44 ;   Jas.2,15.*

uicus, i, *m., village.*

uideo, di, uisus, 2, *see,* (in
pass. also) *seem.*

uidua, ae, *f., widow.*

uigilia, ae, *f.,* (1) *watch* (of
night), Mk.6,48 ;   L.12,
38 ;   (2) *watching, wake-
fulness,* 2 C.6,5 ;   11,27.

uigilo, 1, *watch, keep watch,
be wakeful.*

uillicatio (uilli-), onis f.,
stewardship, L.16,2 ff.*

†**uilico (uilli-),** 1, *be a steward,*
L.16,2.*

uillicus, (uilli-), i, m., *steward,* L.16,1 ff.*

uilla, ae, *f.,* (1) *town, village,*
Mt.26,36 ;   L.8,34 ;   (2)
farm, field, country, Mt.
22,5 ;   L.14,18.

uillicus, etc., v. uilli-.

uincio, nxi, nctus, 4, *bind.*

uinco, uici, 3, *conquer, overcome.*

uinculum, i, *n., chain, bond.*

uindemio, 1, *gather grapes,*
L.6,44 ;   Ap.14,18 f.*

uindex, icis, c., *avenger,* R.13,
4 ;   1 Th.4,6.*

uindico, 1, *avenge,* L.18,3 ff.;
A.7,24.

uindicta, ae, *f., vengeance,*
R.12,19 ;   2 Th.1,8.

uinea, ae, *f.,* (1) *vineyard* ;
(2) *vine,* Ap.14,18 f.

uinolentia, ae, *f., wine-bib-
bing, intoxication,* 1 P.4,
3.*

*uinolentus, a, um, *given to wine, drunken*, 1 T.3,3; Ti.1,7.*

uinum, i, *n.*, *wine*.

uiolentus, a, um, *violent*, Mt.11,12.*

uiolo, 1, *profane, violate*, Mt.12,5; A.21,28; 24,6; 1 C.3,17.*

uipera, ae, *f.*, *viper*.

uir, uiri, *m.*, *man*; *husband*.

uirga, ae, *f.*, *staff, rod, sceptre*.

uirginitas, tatis, *f.*, *virginity*, L.2,36.*

uirgo, ginis, *f.*, *virgin*.

uiridis, e, *green*, Mk.6,39; L.23,31; Ap.8,7; 9,4.*

uiriliter, *manfully, like a man*, 1 C.16,13.*

uirtus, utis, *f.*, (1) *power, strength, ability*, 1 C.1,18; 1 P.1,5; *mighty work*, Mt.7,22; (2) *virtue, excellence*, 1 P.2,9; 2 P. 1,5; (3) *power* (rank of angels), E.1,21; 1 P.3,22.

uis (acc. uim, abl. ui), *f.*, *violence*; (in pl.) (L.10,27), *strength*.

uiscera, um, *n.*, *bowels, tender mercy*.

*uisibilis, e, *visible*, Co.1,16; H.11,3.*

uisio, onis, *f.*, *vision*; *thing seen; appearance*, Ap.4,3.

uisitatio, onis, *f.*, *visitation*, L.19,44; 1 P.2,12; 5,6.*

uisito, 1, *visit*.

uisus, us, *m.*; (1) (*gift of*) *sight*, L.7,21; A.7,31; (2) *vision*, A.9,10; 10,3.

uita, ae, *f.*, *life*.

uitis, is, *f.*, *vine*, ||Mt.26,29; J.15,1 ff.; Jas.3,12.*

uitium, ii, *n.*, *fault, defect*.

*uitreus, a, um, *glassy, of glass*, Ap.4,6; 15,2 (bis).*

uitrum, i, *n.*, *glass*, Ap.21, 18 ff.*

uitula, ae, *f.*, *calf*, H.9,13.*

uitulus, i, *m.*, *calf*, L.15,23 ff.; A.7,41; H.9,12; 9,19; Ap.4,7.*

uitupero, 1, *blame, find fault*, Mk.7,2; 2 C.6,3; 8,20; H.8,8.*

uiuifico, 1, (1) *quicken, make alive;* (2) *preserve alive*, A.7,19.

uiuo, uixi, 3, *live*.

uiuus, a, um, *living, alive*.

uix, *scarcely, with difficulty*.

*uocatio, onis, *f.*, *calling*.

uociferor, 1, *cry out*, A.22, 23.*

uoco, 1, *call, name, invite*.

uolatilis, e, *flying, winged*, (in n. pl. as subst.) *birds*, Mt.6,26; A.10,12; 11, 6.*

uolo, 1, *fly* (only in Ap. six times).

uolo, uolui, uelle, *wish, be willing*.

uolucris, is, *f.*, *bird*.

uoluntarie, *willingly, voluntarily,* H.10,26 ; Jas.1, 18 ; 1 P.5,2.*

uoluntarius, a, um, *willing, voluntary,* 2 C.8,3 ; Philem.14.*

uoluntas, tatis, *f., will, good, pleasure.*

uoluptas, tatis, *f., pleasure,* L.8,14 ; 2 T.3,4 ; Ti.3, 3 ; 2 P.2,13.*

†uolutabrum, i, *n., wallowing-place,* 2 P.2,22.*

uoluto, 1, (in pass.) *wallow, roll about,* Mk.9,19.*

uomitus, us, *m., vomit,* 2 P. 2,22.*

uorax, acis, *gluttonous,* Mt. 11,19.*

uotum, i, *n., vow,* A.18,18 ; 21,23 ; 24,17.*

uox, uocis, *f., voice, sound, word.*

uulgus, i, *n., multitude, common people,* A.17,5.*

uulnero, 1, *wound,* ||Mk.12,4; A.19,16.*

uulnus, eris, *n., wound,* L. 10,34 ; Ap.16,2 ; 16,11.*

uulpes, is, *f., fox,* ||Mt.8,20 ; L.13,32.*

uultus, us, *m., face, countenance.*

uulua, ae, *f., womb,* L.2,23 ; R.4,19.*

Z

°zelo, 1, (1) *desire earnestly,* Jas.4,2 ; (2) *be envious,* A.17,5.*

°zelotes, ae, *m., a zealot,* L. 6,15 ; A.1,13.*

°zelus, i, *m.,* (1) *zeal,* J.2,17 ; (2) *envy, jealousy,* A.5, 17 ; 13,45.

°zizania, orum, *n., tares,* Mt. 13 (six times).

°zmaragdinus (sm-), a, um, *belonging to the emerald, emerald,* Ap.4,3.*

°zmaragdus (sm-), i, *f., emerald,* Ap.21,19.*

°zona, ae, *f., girdle,* ||Mt.3,4 ; ||10,9 ; A.21,11 ; Ap.1, 13 ; 15,6.*

The Mayflower Press, Plymouth, England. William Brendon & Son, Ltd.